THE
National ⚾ Pastime

FROM SWAMPOODLE TO SOUTH PHILLY

Baseball in Philadelphia & the Delaware Valley

Edited by Morris Levin

Published by
The Society for American Baseball Research

DEDICATION

"Time is an enormous, long river, and I'm standing in it, just as you're standing in it. My elders are the tributaries, and everything they thought and every struggle they went through and everything they gave their lives to, and every song they created, and every poem that they laid down flows down to me—and if I take the time to ask, and if I take the time to see, and if I take the time to reach out, I can build that bridge between my world and theirs. I can reach down into that river and take out what I need to get through this world."

– U. Utah Phillips

This book is dedicated to her majesty, the city of Philadelphia, and to her rivers, which flow with stories of Octavius Catto, Cap Anson, Ben Chapman, and Jackie Robinson. May we learn from those who came before us, and may we all merit to be judged on our abilities to bat, pitch, and field.

THE NATIONAL PASTIME

Editor: Morris Levin
Design and Production: Lisa Hochstein
Cover Design: Lisa Hochstein
Fact Checker: Clifford Blau

Front cover: Library of Congress

Published by:
The Society for American Baseball Research, Inc.
4455 E. Camelback Road, Ste. D-140
Phoenix, AZ 85018

Phone: (800) 969-7227 or (602) 343-6455
Web: www.sabr.org
Twitter: @sabr
Facebook: Society for American Baseball Research

Copyright © 2013
The Society for American Baseball Research
Printed in the United States of America

ISBN 978-1-933599-37-3

All rights reserved.
Reproduction in whole or part without permission is prohibited.

Contents

Foreword

NOTES ON EDITIONS

SABR is publishing two editions of The National Pastime in 2013. This is the print edition; there is also an electronic edition. The electronic edition is the complete journal; this print edition is an abridged presentation.

The electronic edition tells a comprehensive story of baseball in Philadelphia and the Delaware Valley. SABR's Philadelphia chapter received well over fifty submissions in response to the call for papers, in addition to suggestions for reprints. The electronic edition is over 160,000 words reflecting the strength and scope of articles.

THANK YOU

Thank you to the Philadelphia Connie Mack Chapter. Thank you Seamus Kearney, Dick Rosen, and Peter Mancuso for their support of this specific publication, and in leading a local chapter of which this editor is glad to be a member.

This publication happened because of the readers and editors who volunteered and assisted. Thank you to Bob Barsotti, Seamus Kearney, Mitchell Nathanson, Dick Rosen, Andrew Milner, Samantha Mogil, Douglas Skipper, and Stephen Workman.

Thank you Cecilia Tan, Clifford Blau, and Lisa Hochstein for their professional guidance and stewardship.

— Morris Levin
Philadelphia, July 2013

1915

PHILADELPHIA CLUBS AT HOME

NATIONAL LEAGUE.   AMERICAN LEAGUE.

BOSTON - April -22-23-24-26
BROOKLYN-'' - 27-28-29-30
NEW YORK-''- Mar - - -1-3-4-5
PITTSBURG - - -'' - - 11-12-13-14
ST.LOUIS - - - '' - - 15-17-18-19
CINCINNATI - - -'' - -20-21-22-24
CHICAGO - - - - - - -25-26-27
BROOKLYN - - - June - -25-26-28-29
BOSTON - - - - - - - - - - - - 30
BOSTON - - - - - -July - - - -1-2-3
EW YORK - - - - - - - - - 5-5-6-7
TSBURG - - - - '' - - - - 8-9-10-12
LOUIS - - - - - '' - - - 13-14-15-16
CHICAGO - - - - '' - - -17-19-20-21
CINCINNATI - - - - '' - - - -22-23-24
BOSTON - - - - August - -13-14-16
CINCINNATI - - - - '' - - - - 17
PITTSBURG - - - '' - - 18-19-20
CHICAGO - - - - '' - - 21-21-23-24
CINCINNATI - - '' - - -25-26-27
ST.LOUIS - - - '' - - 28-30-31
N.YORK- Sept.- - 8-9-10
BROOK'N-Oct - - - 4-5-7

BOSTON - April - - 14-15-16
NEW YORK - '' - 17-19-20-21
WASH'GT'N - May - - - 6-7-8
BOSTON - - - - 28-29-31-31
WASHINGTON - June - - -1-2-3
ST.LOUIS - - - '' - - - 4-5-7-8
CLEVELAND - - '' - - - 9-10-11
DETROIT - - - - - 12-14-15-
CHICAGO - - - - - - -17-1
NEW YORK - - - - - -21-21-22-
ST.LOUIS - - - July - - - - - -2
CLEVELAND - - - - - - - - -
CLEVELAND - - - August - - -
DETROIT - - - - - '' - - - -4-
CHICAGO - - - - - '' - - 9-10-1
BOSTON - - - - Sep't - - -1-2-3-
WASHINGTON - '' - - - 6-6-7
ST.LOUIS - - - - - - 11-13-14-15
CLEVELAND - - - - - -16-17-18-20
DETROIT - - - - - - 21-22-23
CHICAGO - '' - -24-25-27-28
WASH'GT'N-'' - - - 29-30
N.YORK-Oct - - - -1-2

:BASE BALL SCHEDULE:
THE NATIONAL & AMERICAN LEAGUE
CLUBS AT HOME

Prelude to the Formation of the American Association

Brock Helander

Six of the eight most populous cities in the United States were not represented in the National League for the baseball season of 1881. New York, Philadelphia, Brooklyn, St. Louis, Baltimore, and Cincinnati were not members of the League, which included only two charter members (Chicago and Boston) and teams from the smaller cities of Cleveland, Buffalo, Detroit, Providence, Worcester, and Troy. Nonetheless, independent teams throughout the United States enjoyed both popularity and financial success and the need for a second major league became obvious. The prelude to the formation of the American Association in November 1881 is herein examined in the context of the September Western tours of the interregnum Atlantics and Athletics and the principals supposedly involved in a preliminary meeting in October.

The Atlantics of Brooklyn was a venerated name in the early history of baseball. The club, organized on August 14, 1855,[1] was a member of the National Association of Base Ball Players (NABBP) from 1858 to 1870, playing professionally in 1869 and 1870.[2] An Atlantic club was also a member of the National Association of Professional Base Ball Players (NAPBBP) from 1872 through September 1875 when it disbanded. An entirely new Atlantic nine formed to play on the Capitoline Grounds in April 1878, but in less than two weeks, most of the team, including Candy Cummings and Bill Barnie, were spirited away to New Haven by Ben Douglas for his International Association team.[3] Another Atlantic team, initially attributed to Barnie, was organized in April 1879 by manager Jack Chapman, but by the end of May he had left to manage an International Association team in Holyoke.[4] Eventually, Barnie, in April 1881, organized yet another Atlantic team to play at the Union Grounds, joining the short-lived Eastern Championship Association.[5]

The Athletics of Philadelphia originally formed as a town ball club on May 31, 1859, and reorganized as a base ball club on April 7, 1860.[6] The Athletics were members of the NABBP from 1861 to 1870, playing professionally in 1869 and 1870, in the NAPBBP from 1871 to 1875, and in the National League of Profes-

sional Base Ball Clubs in 1876.[7] After being expelled from the NL for failing to complete their final Western trip, an independent Athletics team organized in 1877 as a stock company under new president Charles H. Downing and joined the League Alliance in order to protect the club from player raids by National League clubs.[8] The Athletics reorganized for 1878 under manager Alfred H. Wright, utilizing 40 players en route to a 45–16–1 record as an independent team.[9] Yet another Athletic club formed in 1879 under William W. Hincken and reorganized for 1880 with William Sharsig as president.[10] With Sharsig as nominal president through 1883, the 1881 Athletics joined the Eastern Championship Association under manager Horace Phillips.[11]

THE WESTERNERS

O.P. Caylor and Justus Thorner: Oliver Perry Caylor, born in Dayton, Ohio, on December 14, 1849, was admitted to the bar in Cincinnati in 1872, but opted for a journalistic career with the *Cincinnati Enquirer* in November 1874. Ascending to the position of sports editor, Caylor garnered a reputation for his clever, humorous, and often acerbic reporting.[12]

Justus Thorner, a manager for local breweries, was president of the semi-professional Star Club of Cincinnati in 1879.[13] After President J. Wayne Neff of the rival Cincinnati National League club announced that his players would be released on October 1, 1879, and forwarded the club's resignation from the League, Thorner met with National League president William Hulbert in Chicago, formally applying for membership in the League.[14] At the annual meeting of the National League, held in December in Buffalo, New York, rather than Cincinnati, as originally scheduled, the organization's Board of Directors admitted the Star Club to membership and Thorner was elected to the Board of Directors.[15] On December 22, the stockholders of the new Cincinnati club elected directors and officers, including Thorner as president.[16] Thorner and Caylor represented the club at a special meeting of the National League on February 26, 1880, in Rochester, New York.[17]

In early July, the directors of the club requested and received the resignation of Thorner as president, and W.C. Kennett represented Cincinnati at the special meeting of the League on October 4 at Rochester, New York. Henry Root, president of the Providence club, proposed an amendment to the League constitution that would prohibit the sale of alcoholic beverages on club grounds and the use of such grounds for Sunday baseball, both of which the Cincinnati club depended on. All except Kennett pledged to vote in favor of the amendment at the League's December meeting.[18] On October 6, the membership of Cincinnati in the League was declared vacant.[19]

By late April 1881, a new baseball club had been formed in Cincinnati. It began play in St. Louis May 28, with Caylor reporting on the games.[20] Only days earlier, the leasehold and grounds of the Cincinnati club had been sold to "four prominent Cincinnati gentlemen," later revealed to be Caylor, Thorner, Victor Long, and John Price.[21] Caylor resigned his position with the *Cincinnati Enquirer* in August, ostensibly to return to the practice of law. Nonetheless, Caylor soon joined the staff of the *Cincinnati Commercial Gazette*.[22]

Alfred Spink. Alfred Henry Spink was born on August 24, 1854, in Quebec, Canada. Moving with his family to Chicago after the Civil War, he moved in 1875 to St. Louis, Missouri, where his brother Billy was sports editor for the *St. Louis Globe-Democrat*. Soon thereafter, Alfred began covering baseball for the *Missouri Republican*, subsequently becoming sporting editor for a number of St. Louis newspapers, including the *St. Louis Post-Dispatch*. Becoming acquainted with saloon owner Chris Von der Ahe, vice president of the Grand Avenue Base Ball Club in 1877, Alfred and Billy began organizing semi-professional baseball teams in 1878. Their 1879 team, called the Browns or Brown Stockings, won 20 of 21 games.[23]

Because dates and sources conflict, the baseball situation in St. Louis becomes convoluted beginning in 1880. Most likely Al Spink, with veteran player Ned Cuthbert, organized the co-operative St. Louis Browns and, with a number of local men, organized the St. Louis Base Ball Association.[24] In May, another team using the Brown Stockings name was organized under the presidency of Chris Von der Ahe.[25] By the end of May, the *St. Louis Globe-Democrat* was referring to Cuthbert's club as the Reds or Red Stockings and Von der Ahe's club as the Browns or Brown Stockings.[26]

In October, Von der Ahe and others formed the Sportsman's Park and Club Association, with Spink as secretary, and secured the lease on Grand Avenue Park, which was to be enlarged and improved and would be known as Sportsman's Park.[27] In March 1881 the Sportsman's Park and Club Association incorporated.[28] The Brown Stockings were organized in April, formally opening Sportsman's Park on May 22 with a defeat of the rival St. Louis Red Stockings before at least 2,500 people.[29] Five of the Browns players had been members of the Reds in 1880, most significantly Bill and Jack Gleason.

THE EASTERNERS

Horace B. Phillips. Horace B. Phillips was born in Salem, Ohio, most likely on May 14, 1853, yet earlier reported as May 20, 1856.[30] Growing up in Philadelphia, he began his baseball playing career with local amateur teams in 1870. Securing his first professional engagement with the Philadelphia club in 1877, Phillips soon succeeded Fergy Malone as manager. A baseball vagabond in his early career, he subsequently played for and managed clubs in Hornellsville and Syracuse, New York, before managing clubs in Troy and Baltimore in 1879 and Baltimore and Rochester, New York in 1880. Returning to Philadelphia in 1881, Phillips was reported managing the independent professional Athletics team by the end of May.[31]

Billy Barnie. William Harrison Barnie, born in New York City on January 26, 1853, began playing for amateur baseball clubs in Brooklyn at an early age, manning the Nassau club for three years beginning in 1870 and the Atlantics of Brooklyn in 1873. He initiated his professional career with Hartford in 1874, playing with the Buckeye club of Columbus, Ohio, in 1876 and managing it in 1877. Barnie played for and managed the Buffalo club later in 1877 and was a member of the Atlantics team that moved to New Haven, then Hartford, in 1878. After playing for the Knickerbocker club of San Francisco in 1879 and 1880, he returned to Brooklyn and organized an independent professional Atlantics club in April 1881, becoming its secretary.[32]

THE PITTSBURGHERS

Al Pratt. Albert G. Pratt was born on November 19, 1848, in Allegheny, Pennsylvania, and joined the Union Army at the age of 15, serving in the infantry. He helped form the Enterprise Base Ball Club of Pittsburgh in 1866 and later joined the Allegheny Club. After a season with the Riverside Club of Portsmouth, Ohio, Pratt pitched for the famous Forest City Club of Cleveland from 1869 to 1872. He returned to Pittsburgh and pitched for the Enterprise club from 1873 to 1875 and played with the Xantha club from 1876 to 1879.[33] Pratt then served as a National League umpire in 1879 and substitute umpire in 1880.[34]

H.D. "Denny" McKnight. Harmar Denny McKnight was born in 1847 in Pittsburgh and graduated from Lafayette College in 1869. Pursuing a business career, he became director of an iron manufacturing company in 1876. That year he helped organize the independent Allegheny baseball club, serving as one of its directors. The following year McKnight was instrumental in the formation of the International Association of Professional Base Ball Players and served as its president after Candy Cummings resigned. However, the Allegheny club disbanded in June 1878.[35]

OUT WEST

As Alfred Spink stated in his book *The National Game*: "I wrote to O.P. Caylor, then the sporting editor of the *Cincinnati Enquirer* and I suggested to him the idea of picking up all that was left in Cincinnati of the old professional players, forming them into a nine, christening them the Cincinnati Reds and bringing them here to play three games on a Saturday, Sunday and Monday with my reconstructed St Louis Browns." Spink continued: "Mr. Caylor, accepting my suggestion, quickly got together a team of semi-professionals, called it the Cincinnati Reds and brought it here to help open the reconstructed St. Louis baseball grounds, which my brother William had named Sportsman's Park."[36] Their Sunday, May 29 game, won by the Browns 16–2, drew an estimated four thousand spectators, making it a substantial success.[37]

More Spink: "The Dubuques, the Cincinnati Reds and the Chicago prairie teams came to St. Louis and the games drew such crowds, especially on Sundays, that soon news of the prosperity wave reached the East."[38] Among the well-attended Sunday games in St. Louis were the July 3 game against the Eckfords of Chicago (4,000), the July 17 game against Dubuque (nearly 5,000), and the August 14 game against the Buckeyes of Cincinnati (over 5,000).[39]

Spink: "Later I wrote to Horace B. Phillips, then managing the Athletics of Philadelphia, and to William Barnie, then operating the Atlantics of Brooklyn. Both the Athletics and the Atlantics were free lances outside the pale of the National League and were willing to come all the way to St. Louis to meet the St. Louis Browns for a division of the gate receipts."[40] Barnie later reminisced: "Horace Phillips of the Athletics and myself then formed the idea of organizing a big league. We learned through the papers that large audiences were being attracted by base ball teams in Cincinnati, Louisville and St. Louis and began negotiating for a trip to those cities. The Western clubs guaranteed us more than enough to pay our expenses on the round trip. We accepted and both the Atlantics and Athletics took the journey."[41]

In late July, Cincinnati applied for admission to the National League for 1882.[42] In mid-August Phillips was reported to be in Chicago, meeting with National League President William Hulbert to request admission for the Athletics, who withdrew the application within two weeks and released Phillips only days before the October meeting.[43]

THE TOURS

The Athletics were the first to embark on a Western tour. On September 2 in Louisville the Athletics defeated the Eclipse of Louisville, with manager Phillips playing in center field. The next day in St. Louis, the St. Louis Browns beat the Athletics. On Sunday, September 4, before an astounding 7,000 fans, the Browns proved victorious. The final game in St. Louis September 5 was won by the Athletics. Returning to Louisville, the Athletics on September 8 lost to the Eclipse morning and

LIBRARY OF CONGRESS

The Atlantics of Brooklyn and the Athletics of Philadelphia formed one of the most intense rivalries during baseball's pioneer era. This graphic depicts a match between the clubs at Philadelphia from 1865.

LIBRARY OF CONGRESS BAIN COLLECTION

VON DER AHE—PRESIDENT ST. LOUIS

One of the most enigmatic figures of nineteenth-century baseball, president Chris Von der Ahe led the St. Louis Browns to four consecutive pennants during the ten-year existence of the American Association.

afternoon games. On September 9 the Athletics defeated an ad hoc team in Cincinnati.[44] According to one source, Thorner found out about the game and joined the crowd of 200 in the eighth inning.[45] Later, in a letter to the *Cincinnati Commercial Gazette*, Phillips stated that he did indeed consult Caylor on this occasion.[46] The next day on their way home, the Athletics lost to the Detroit National League club in Allegheny (near Pittsburgh) before 2,000 fans, with Al Pratt serving as umpire.[47]

After defeating the Athletics in Philadelphia on September 14 and 15, the Atlantics arrived in Louisville on September 17 and bested the Eclipse. The next day the Eclipse prevailed and again on September 19. On September 22 the Eclipse again won. Heading to St. Louis, the Atlantics prevailed over the Browns on September 24, scoring the winning run in the top of the ninth. On Sunday, September 25, the Browns were victorious. The game scheduled for September 26 was canceled due to the death of President Garfield. The third game, postponed due to rain, was played September 28, but was suspended due to darkness with the score Atlantics 13, Browns 12. The following day, the Atlantics beat the St. Louis Reds by the identical score. As the St. Louis Browns devolved into chaos at the beginning of October, the Atlantics defeated one of the clubs claiming the Browns' name on October 9. On their way home to Brooklyn, the Atlantics stopped over in Philadelphia and defeated the Athletics.[48]

Phillips, upon his return to Philadelphia, stated that "the movement [to form a new league] was meeting with great favor in St. Louis, Pittsburgh, Louisville, and Cincinnati...."[49] *The Cincinnati Enquirer*, probably Frank Wright, agreed: "The outlook is very promising. (A) scheme is on foot to organize a new association, to include St. Louis, Louisville, Philadelphia, Baltimore, Washington, Cincinnati, Pittsburgh, and New

York. Already the proposition has been entertained in St. Louis and Louisville, and a meeting will be held in Pittsburgh, October 10, to perfect arrangements."[50] *The Clipper* reported: "THE NEW ASSOCIATION will hold a meeting Oct. 10 in Pittsburgh. Clubs who intend sending representatives will please communicate with H.B. Phillips, Great Western Hotel, Philadelphia Pa."[51]

THE MEETINGS

Who was actually at the meeting is a matter of conjecture. Justus Thorner's 1889 account of the meeting erroneously stated that Phillips was there. Later, Caylor stated: "The Association was christened at the Pittsburgh meeting, and neither Mr. Phillips nor Mr. Von der Ahe was present."[52] Nonetheless Thorner recalled: "We called another meeting at the St. Clair Hotel, Pittsburgh and I brought on with me O.P. Caylor from Cincinnati and another reporter named Wright. These two, Mr. Phillips and myself were all the people who showed up.... Phillips and I took a stroll into Diamond Street and there learned that a baseball crank named Al Pratt was working in one of the mills and we found him. He told us of Denny McKnight and he was also secured. [W]e organized for all practical purposes, and I suggested that we have baseball representatives at Louisville, Washington, Philadelphia, New York, and St. Louis to send me their proxy as to where the next meeting should be held. We led everyone wired to believe that he was the only one absent from the meeting, and that caused an immediate reply."[53] In another account by Thorner from 1894, he stated: "It was during the latter part of 1881 that I read in some paper of a call for a meeting, at a Pittsburg hotel, of all those favoring a new baseball organization. In company with O.P. Caylor I took a run down to Pittsburg and...found the call to be on the order of a hoax, as no one showed up outside Caylor and myself. I inquired of the hotel keeper whether any one in town was fond of baseball, and was referred to Denny McKnight and Al Pratt. We called on these gentlemen.... We then declared the meeting adjourned to Cincinnati, November 2, and Caylor and I returned home."[54]

The day after the meeting, numerous newspapers published virtually identical accounts. Possibly authored by Frank Wright of the *Cincinnati Enquirer*, the report was replete with misspellings and name-dropping, perhaps in an effort to impress prospective league members. It stated, with the correct names in parentheses, that temporary officers chosen were M.F. Day (John B. Day), of the Metropolitan club, Christ Van Derahe (Von der Ahe), James J. Williams (James A. Williams), and H.D. McKnight. Justus

LIBRARY OF CONGRESS

CHAMPIONS OF AMERICA.

This 1865 photograph of the Atlantics of Brooklyn by Charles H. Williamson depicts the "Champion Nine" of 1864 and was given to opposing teams who played The Atlantic Club. In September and October of 1882 the club undertook a tour, making stops for multiple games in Philadelphia, Louisville, and St. Louis, with a second stop in Philadelphia on the way home. Such tours were part of the basis of formation of the league known as the American Association.

Thorner and Charles Fulmer were appointed to a committee to draft a constitution and by-laws.[55] John B. Day was owner of the highly-successful independent professional New York-based Metropolitan club and James A. Williams was a former pitcher and the secretary, treasurer, and main driving force behind the recently defunct (Inter)National Association.[56] Charles Fulmer was a prominent Philadelphia baseball player who accompanied the Athletics on their Western tour.[57] Despite the supposed selection of officers, none of the accounts specifically stated who was actually present at the meeting.

The *New York Clipper* was more circumspect: "An informal meeting was held Oct. 10 in Pittsburg in the place of the proposed convention of clubs to organize a new Association, at which there were but two or three of the representatives of the clubs present who were to have sent delegates. After some talk together it was resolved to hold a meeting for permanent organization at the Gibson House, Cincinnati, Nov. 2."[58]

Despite numerous unanswered questions, conventional wisdom holds to Harold Seymour's account. That is, that Phillips instigated the meeting but dropped out; that Justus Thorner, Caylor, and Frank Wright went to Pittsburgh and met with Al Pratt and Denny McKnight; and that they sent to prominent non-National League clubs telegrams worded so as to give the impression that each absentee was the only one not present at the meeting.[59]

The American Association of Professional Base Ball Clubs formed on November 2, 1881, at the Gibson House in Cincinnati, Ohio, with six charter members;

the Athletics of Philadelphia, the Atlantics of Brooklyn, St. Louis, Cincinnati, the Alleghenys of Pittsburgh, and the Eclipse of Louisville. Delegates to the convention included O.P. Caylor and Justus Thorner, Chris Von der Ahe, Billy Barnie, and Denny McKnight. Charles Fulmer represented the Athletics, and Horace Phillips represented the Philadelphia club of Al Reach. After some talk of consolidation, Fulmer was admitted as the representative of the Athletics, and Phillips was excluded. McKnight was made temporary chairman and Jimmy Williams was chosen temporary secretary.[60] At the March 1882 meeting of the American Association, the Atlantic Club of Brooklyn resigned, to be replaced by a club from Baltimore.[61]

AFTERWORD

Who should receive credit for the formation of the American Association? Alfred Spink and O.P. Caylor had been reporting baseball since 1875. Justus Thorner had been involved in Cincinnati baseball since 1879. Veterans Billy Barnie and Horace Phillips had faced each other on the field for years, including 1881, when their teams were members of the Eastern Championship Association. Spink helped form an independent team in St. Louis and encouraged Caylor to do the same in Cincinnati. Spink wrote to Philips and Barnie, inviting their teams west. Barnie and Phillips noted the success of teams in St. Louis, Cincinnati and Louisville. Caylor and Phillips met in September. Soon thereafter, Phillips issued the call for the first meeting. All these men deserve a measure of credit in this enterprise. ∎

Notes

1. Preston D. Orem, *Baseball (1845–1881) from the Newspaper Accounts.* (Altadena, California: Preston D. Orem, 1961), 14.
2. Marshall D. Wright, *The National Association of Base Ball Players, 1857–1870* (Jefferson, North Carolina; McFarland & Co., Inc., 2000).
3. *New York Clipper;* April 27, 1878; *New York Clipper,* May 4, 1878
4. *New York Clipper;* April 12, 1879, *Brooklyn Eagle;* April 13, 1879, 4; *New York Clipper.* May 31, 1879.
5. *Brooklyn Eagle,* March 25, 1881, 1; *New York Clipper,* April 2, 1881; *New York Times,* April 12, 1881 8.
6. *New York Clipper,* October 13, 1883.
7. Wright.
8. *New York Clipper,* January 6, 1877; Chicago Tribune, March 4, 1877, 7; *New York Clipper,* March 10, 1877.
9. *New York Clipper,* April 6, 1878; *New York Clipper,* November 23, 1878.
10. *New York Clipper,* May 10, 1879; *New York Clipper,* May 8, 1880; New York Clipper, March 24, 1883.
11. *New York Clipper,* March 19, 1881; *Brooklyn Eagle,* April 17, 1881, 6; (Philadelphia) *North American,* May 16, 1881.
12. David L. Porter, *Biographical Dictionary of American Sports: Baseball* (Westport, Connecticut: Greenwood Press, 2000), 235–236; Frank V. Phelps, "Oliver Perry Caylor (O.P.)," *Baseball's First Stars* (Cleveland: Society for American Baseball Research, 1996), 25; *Sporting Life,* October 23, 1897; *New York Clipper,* October 30, 1897.
13. *Cincinnati Commercial Tribune,* November 17, 1881, 4; *Harold Seymour, Baseball: The Early Years* (New York: Oxford University Press, 1960), 137.
14. *Chicago Tribune,* September 25, 1879, 5; *The New York Times,* October 25, 1879, 2; *Chicago Tribune,* October 28, 1879, 7; *Chicago Tribune,* November 16, 1879, 11.
15. *New York Clipper,* December 14, 1878; *Brooklyn Eagle,* November 17, 1879, 3; *New York Clipper,* December 13, 1879.
16. *New York Clipper,* January 3, 1880
17. *New York Clipper,* February 27, 1880.
18. *St. Louis Globe-Democrat,* October 5, 1880, 3; *Chicago Tribune,* October 5, 1880, 3.
19. *Chicago Tribune,* October 7, 1880, 5.
20. *New York Sun,* April 21, 1881; *St. Louis Globe-Democrat,* April 27, 1881, 6; *Chicago Tribune,* May 31, 1881, 6.
21. *New York Clipper,* July 2, 1881; *Rocky Mountain News,* October 2, 1882, 2; *Cincinnati Commercial Gazette,* December 31,
22. (Chicago) *Daily InterOcean,* August 28, 1881 3, citing the *Buffalo Courier; Brooklyn Eagle,* September 1, 1881, 3; *Cincinnati Commercial Tribune,* October 8, 1882, 7; Frank V. Phelps, "Oliver Perry Caylor (O.P.)," *Baseball's First Stars,* 25.
23. Ray Schmidt, "Alfred Henry Spink," *Baseball's First Stars,* 156; William A. Kelsoe, *St. Louis Reference Record: A Newspaper Man's Motion Picture of the City* (St. Louis: Von Hoffman Press, 1926), 14; Alfred H. Spink, *The National Game* (Carbondale and Edwardsville, Illinois: Southern Illinois University Press, 2000), 46; *St. Louis Globe-Democrat,* March 11, 1877, 6; *New York Clipper,* November 22, 1879.
24. *St. Louis Globe-Democrat,* April 12, 1880, 7; *Washington Post,* January 6, 1898, 8; *The Sporting News,* June 12, 1913, 4; *Sporting Life,* June 14, 1913, Vol. 61, Number 15, 9.
25. *St. Louis Globe-Democrat,* May 9, 1880, 12.
26. *St. Louis Globe-Democrat,* May 30, 1880, 13.
27. *St. Louis Globe-Democrat,* October 17, 1880, 2; *St. Louis Globe-Democrat,* October 31, 1880, 12; Spink, 46.
28. *St. Louis Globe-Democrat,* March 17, 1881 3; *St. Louis Globe-Democrat,* March 27, 1881, 11.
29. *St. Louis Globe-Democrat,* April 7, 1881, 7; *St. Louis Globe-Democrat,* 25 April 1881, 3; *St. Louis Globe-Democrat,* May 23, 1881, 7.
30. Hy Turkin and S.C. Thompson, *The Official Encyclopedia of Baseball* (New York: A.S. Barnes and Company, Inc, Third Edition, 1963), 309;

31. *New York Clipper,* July 26, 1884; *New York Clipper,* May 28, 1881.
32. *Brooklyn Eagle,* March 25, 1881, 1; *Brooklyn Eagle,* April 26, 1896 16; Jack Kavanagh, "William Harrison Barnie (Bald Bill)," *Baseball's First Stars,* 6.
33. *New York Times,* 23 November, 1937, 23; Daniel E. Ginsburg, "Albert George Pratt (Uncle Al)," *Baseball's First Stars,* 128.
34. Peter Palmer and Gary Gillette, ed., 2489, 2492.
35. *The Sporting News,* 19 May, 1900, 1; Frank V. Phelps, "Henry Dennis McKnight (Denny)," *Baseball's First Stars,* 109.
36. Spink, 47, 48.
37. *St. Louis Globe-Democrat,* May 30, 1881, 3.
38. Spink, 48.
39. *St. Louis Globe-Democrat,* July 4, 1881, 7; *St. Louis Globe-Democrat,* July 18, 1881, 8; *New York Clipper,* August 20, 1881.
40. Spink, 48, 50.
41. *Brooklyn Eagle,* January 30, 1898, 9.
42. *New York Tribune,* July 28, 1881, 8.
43. *Cleveland Herald,* August 16, 1881; *New York Clipper,* September 10, 1881; *New York Clipper,* October 18, 1881.
44. *Cleveland Herald,* September 3, 1881, 4; *St. Louis Globe-Democrat,* September 4, 1881, 3; *St. Louis Globe-Democrat,* September 5, 1881, 5; *Cleveland Herald,* September 6, 1881; *St. Louis Globe-Democrat,* September 9, 1881, 7; *Cincinnati Commercial Tribune,* September 9, 1881, 5; *Cincinnati Daily Gazette,* September 9, 1881, 2; *New York Clipper,* September 17, 1881.
45. *Cincinnati Daily Gazette,* September 10, 1881, 8.
46. *Cincinnati Commercial Gazette,* November 18, 1882.
47. *New York Clipper,* September 17, 1881.
48. *Philadelphia Inquirer,* September 15, 1881 3; *Philadelphia Inquirer,* September 16, 1881. 2; *Cleveland Herald,* September 19, 1881, 3; *St. Louis Globe-Democrat,* September 9, 1881, 5; *New York Clipper,* September 24, 1881; *New York Clipper,* October 1, 1881; *St. Louis Globe-Democrat,* September 25, 1881, 7; *St. Louis Globe-Democrat,* September 26, 1881, 3; *St. Louis Globe-Democrat,* September 27, 1881, 7; *St. Louis Globe-Democrat,* September 28, 1881, 5; *St. Louis Globe-Democrat,* September 29, 1881, 6; *St. Louis Globe-Democrat,* September 30, 1881, 6; *St. Louis Globe-Democrat,* October 2, 1881, 3; *St. Louis Globe-Democrat,* October 4, 1881, 2; *St. Louis Globe-Democrat,* October 9, 1881, 6; *St. Louis Globe-Democrat,* October 22, 1881; *New York Clipper,* October 10, 1881.
49. *Buffalo Express,* citing the *Philadelphia Times,* September 14, 1881.
50. *Cleveland Herald,* citing the *Cincinnati Enquirer,* September 17, 1881.
51. *New York Clipper,* September 24, 1881.
52. *Cincinnati Commercial Gazette,* November 18, 1882.
53. *Pittsburgh Dispatch,* November 9, 1889, 6.
54. *Washington Post,* March 11, 1894, 6.
55. *Cincinnati Enquirer,* October 11, 1881; *Cincinnati Daily Gazette,* October 11, 1881, 9; *Chicago Tribune,* October 11, 1881, 7; (Chicago) *Daily InterOcean,* October 11, 1881, 7; *Cleveland Herald,* October 11, 1881; *St. Louis Globe-Democrat,* October 11, 1881, 6.
56. David Pietrusza, "John B. Day," *Baseball's First Stars,* 49; *New York Clipper,* March 19, 1892.
57. *New York Clipper,* February 23, 1879; Joseph M. Overfield, "Charles John Fulmer (Chick)," *Nineteenth Century Stars* (Society for American Baseball Research. Manhattan, Kansas: Ag Press, 1989), 49.
58. *New York Clipper,* October 22, 1881.
59. Seymour, 137–138.
60. *New York Clipper,* November 12, 1881.
61. *New York Clipper,* March 18, 1882.

Peter Palmer and Gary Gillette, ed., *The 2005 ESPN Baseball Encyclopedia* (New York: Sterling Publishing Co., 2005), 1294; *New York Clipper,* July 26, 1884.

The Jefferson Street Ball Parks (1864–91)

Jerrold Casway

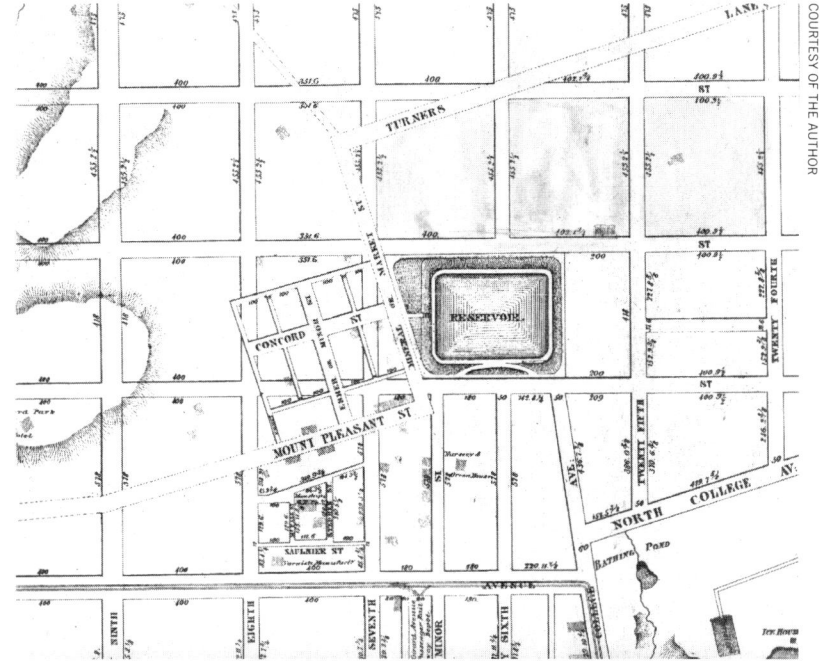

COURTESY OF THE AUTHOR

The Jefferson Street Neighborhood in 1860. From 24th Street to where Turner's Lane ends is the ballpark site.

The Philadelphia ballparks situated at Jefferson and Master Streets, between 27th and 25th Streets, have a significant historic importance for our national pastime. Originally, this plot of land was known as the Jefferson Parade Grounds. It was used as a bivouac and training site in the years leading up to the Civil War.[1]

In the antebellum era, the major Philadelphia teams, the Athletics, Olympics, Mercantiles, and Keystones, found it difficult to secure suitable playing grounds in the city. Because of the community's opposition to recreational sports, Philadelphia ball clubs were forced to play in Camden, New Jersey or across the Schuylkill River above the Fairmount Avenue Bridge near Harding's Inn and Tavern. With baseball's growing popularity, playing grounds soon encroached the outskirts of the city at 32nd and Hamilton and 11th and Wharton. It was not until the early war years that playing fields appeared at more accessible sites such as 10th and Camac Lane and 18th and Master Street. Eventually residential pressures compelled the Olympic and Mercantile ball clubs in 1864 to lease from the city "a handsome piece of ground at the north side of the Spring Garden Market" at 25th and Jefferson.[2]

Each club had two days a week for their practice. For a cost of about $1,500, the Olympics immediately built a clubhouse along Master Street and made substantial improvements by leveling and re-sodding the playing surface. The first game was played on Wednesday, May 24, 1864, between picked nines from Pennsylvania and New Jersey for the benefit of the United States Sanitary Commission. Without an enclosing fence, two thousand spectators, paying 25 cents for admission, established the field's boundaries. The only field-sitting was for ladies who sat behind the players' bench.[3] This ballpark was marked by certain features. Along the third base/Master Street side was the grass embankment of the old Spring Garden Reservoir. Trees also disrupted the playing site, and until the grounds were enclosed, neighborhood animals wandered onto the field of play. Parking for horse carriages was in the left field foul territory, and no elevated reporters' seating box existed until 1871.[4] Visible behind the 27th and Master home plate intersection on the Girard College campus was the towering Greek-styled Founders Hall with its Corinthian columns.[5]

The Jefferson Grounds experienced a significant overhaul when the city's best team, the Athletics, relocated there for the inaugural 1871 National Association of Professional Base Ball Players season. The Athletics had previously prospered at a popular site at 17th Street between Columbia and Montgomery Avenues before a housing development forced them to move to the Jefferson Grounds. Almost immediately, the Athletics tore down the old wooden grandstand

COURTESY OF THE AUTHOR

The playing field in 1865 looking southeast toward the reservoir at the corner of 24th and Master streets. On the left is Founders Hall of Girard College.

and the encircling fence that had been erected in 1866. The new tenants re-sodded and leveled the playing surface, erected a ten-foot vertical slatted fence, and built a pair of tiered pavilions that abutted near the original home plate area on the corner of 25th and Master. Bleacher benches extended along the outfield lines. This rebuilt ball field held over 5,000 fans. This figure doubled during major ball games, when spectators lined up in front of the outfield fences and stood on wooden boxes that supported unstable raised wood planks. Those attendees who could not gain admission purchased 25-cent roof-top seats on neighboring houses, or sat on the branches of overhanging trees. These fans were termed "tree frogs," and were likened to "living fruit."[6]

Initially, the ball park was popular with women, but they eventually were turned off by the cursing, drinking and the tobacco juice splashes on their dresses. Management tried to curb this rowdy behavior and attempted to attract fans with a music bandstand.[7] There was even talk in the off-season about having football games at Jefferson Grounds.[8] For the 1872 season, the champion Athletics resurfaced the infield, particularly the irregularly graded shortstop area. If these modifications were not completed in time for the new season the Athletics intended to schedule early season games across the Delaware River in Gloucester, New Jersey.[9]

During the Athletics' third season at the Jefferson Grounds, alarms were raised over the possibility that the site would be sold to housing developers. The Ath-

letics' directors were upset because they claimed to have invested over $7,000 on the ball field. After much debate and lobbying the politicians relented and the sale did not go through.[10] A subsequent concern was the building of additional cheap seats in the outfield. In 1874 this need intensified when the grounds welcomed a new tenant, the Philadelphia Centennials (also known as the Quakers or Fillies). The new club had the field every Monday and Thursday. The Athletics took the site on Wednesdays and Saturdays.[11] Prints of the playing grounds from a home plate perspective portrayed a wooden porched-styled construction.[12] In spite of the clubs' successes the ball park was losing money. The tenant teams compensated by raising ticket prices and erecting a new interior fence that could be plastered with paid advertisements. But the prevalence of gambling and drinking at the ball field kept people away.[13] Eventually, the expenses of park maintenance and renovation exceeded revenues. They could not even afford a tarpaulin to cover the infield.[14] It was hoped that the Athletics' affiliation with the new National League in 1876 might save the old ball field. But the well-worn Jefferson Park did not appeal to fans and with low income and poor attendance the Athletics could not afford to remain in the new League. The unaffiliated and homeless Centennials now shifted their games to Recreation Park at 24th Street and Ridge Avenue, and the expelled Athletics' rump team in 1877 played unsanctioned games wherever they could find a ball field. It was obvious that more revenue could be made by turning part of the Jefferson Grounds over to residential developers. It took the creation of the American Association in 1882 to revive the Athletics and the old Jefferson Park ball field.

The Athletics initially played their inaugural Association season at Oakdale Park at 11th and Cumberland. This leisure recreation site had a large lake and an adjoining playing field, used earlier for cricket. Some distance from the Jefferson/Columbia ball-playing corridor, the Oakdale grounds had been in use since 1866.[15] After nearly a decade the ball field became downtrodden until the displaced Olympics revived the grounds [1877–1881]. It was thus an ideal place for the revitalized Athletics to re-establish themselves.

Once the contracts had been signed, the Athletics razed the "old and unsightly" existing structure and replaced it with an upgraded wooden grandstand that held 2,000 spectators. The grounds were re-sodded and enlarged and open outfield benches were rebuilt for another 2,000 fans. A new fence was also erected for the start of the 1882 season.[16] Despite these renovations the ball field could not accommodate the large crowds that embraced the new Athletics. As a result, the Athletics decided to relocate back to the Jefferson Street ball field. Unfortunately, the original two-block 25th Street square site no longer existed. The city had committed the eastern portion to a new high school and 26th Street was cut through the original ball grounds. But the Athletics, recognizing the transportation convenience of the site, negotiated an initial lease for $1,000 for the remaining 27th Street remnant. As a result, the former centerfield space became the new home plate area for the Association's Jefferson Street ball field.[17]

Olympic Clubhouse near the 24th and Masters intersection, circa 1865–1866. Behind the clubhouse is the reservoir.

COURTESY OF THE AUTHOR

On the corner of 27th and Jefferson, the Athletics constructed "the handsomest ball grounds in the country."[18] The corner was backed up by a semi-circular two-tiered grandstand. Painted white and adorned in "ornamental...fancy cornice work," the pavilion featured arm-chair seating behind a wire-mesh screen. The structure eventually was topped by 32 private season boxes, each holding five people, and a 22-person press box. The grandstand sat 2,200 people and open benches bordering the outfield held more than 3,000 fans.[19]

After a successful 1883 championship season, the ballpark's capacity was increased to 15,000. Special features abounded. The Oakdale flagstaff was planted at the 27th and Master Street corner, a private external staircase for box ticket holders was erected, a ladies room, with a female attendant, was set up, and a bandstand, linking the third base pavilion and outfield seats, was erected.[20] The outfield benches were fronted by a horizontal slatted barrier and the left field fence held a scoreboard and advertisements. Towering over the left field benches was the Jefferson Street Mission Church. In the distance, beyond center field, was the still-visible Founders Hall on the Girard College campus.[21]

The new Athletics and their renovated ball field were overseen by a popular local triumvirate, Charles "Pop" Mason, Lew Simmons, and Billy Sharsig. They raised funds to finance the franchise and redesigned the grounds to suit their needs and limited budget. Each served a term as team manager, but Sharsig managed the ball club for five out of the eight years at Jefferson Street. The Athletics' record for these years

was 519–464 for a .528 percentage. For most of their tenure at Jefferson Street the team was competitive and held their own attendance-wise against the National League Phillies. Their popularity was due to ballplayers like Bobby Matthews, Henry Larkin, Harry Stovey, and Louis Bierbauer. But Mason and Simmons recognized that the financial well-being of the franchise would be enhanced by Sunday ball playing. Unfortunately, Pennsylvania "Blue laws" forbade games on the Christian Sabbath. To counter this restriction Mason and his partners revived an old practice of scheduling games in Gloucester, New Jersey. Fans would assemble early on a Sunday morning at the South Street ferry and take a 45-minute crossing to Gloucester. Games were contested at a site next to the centrally-located race track that was served by horse trolleys. Radiating from this sporting juncture were saloons, betting parlors, fishcake stands, and other hostelries. One editorial called Gloucester "a nineteenth-century Sodom."[22]

The Athletics began the 1886 season with an advertisement claiming to be the "oldest playing organization in the United States." They asserted that they gave the Jefferson Street patrons "honest ball playing" when they posted the opening season schedule of games. These contests began at 4:00 PM and admission remained at 25 cents. Even the train schedule from Broad Street was publicized.[23] Despite this confidence, the ballfield was again threatened by city officials. These ambitious politicians were deterred when they were reminded that no one except the Athletics was willing to pay the $2,000 lease for the grounds.[24] Once this issue was settled the Athletics re-dedicated their resources to repairing the grounds. They raised the infield, put in new cinder paths, and purchased "an immense canvas to cover the entire infield."[25] Two years later, Mason and Simmons, looking

COURTESY OF THE AUTHOR

1873 ballgame looking north, towards Jefferson. First base pavilion is on 24th.

for revenue, changed the ticket prices. General admission became 50 cents, and for an extra quarter women and their escorts could sit on cushioned seats in parts of the grandstand.[26] This new revenue was intended to cover the expenses of erecting a new fence, replacing old floorboards, and re-painting the pavilions.[27] In spite of these changes, the growing threat of a players' strike put the Athletics and their ball park in jeopardy.

In 1890, the players' Brotherhood union brought a player strike team to Philadelphia. This anticipated rivalry moved the Pennsylvania Railroad to offer the Athletics a new ball field at a more competitive location with easy access from the Broad Street Station. It was rumored that the club was offered a five-year free lease if they moved to a site in West Philadelphia on the other side of the river below the 40th Street Bridge.[28] Rather than lose or alienate their existing fan base, the Athletics turned down this speculative offer. Instead the Athletics, in grounds which had not been updated in a number of seasons, prepared for the 1890 strike season, competing against two Philadelphia ball clubs in different leagues. The season, as expected, was a hardship for the American Association Athletics. Attendance waned and expenses mounted. By the end of the year the Athletics had new management and the Jefferson Street grounds were on the verge of being eclipsed.

By the middle of the strike season the Athletics were plagued by pre-existing financial woes. In 1888, this condition moved Mason, Simmons, and Sharsig to seek new investors, like H.C. Pennypacker and his partner William Whitaker. But during the season of 1890 the club's problems mounted. In one instance, a suit for almost $300 was brought against the franchise in the Court of Common Pleas by carpenters who were not fully paid for their work on the pavilions.[29] The ball club also owed $1,200 in back rent and $1,435 for lumber purchases. To pay these outstanding debts the grandstand, inside fence, seats, flagstaff, ticket boxes, and office furniture, appraised at $765, were sold at the end of the season for $600.[30] Sometime during these dealings, the Wagner brothers, J. Earle and George, wholesale meat distributers, took over the defunct franchise. Previously, the Wagners were stockholders in the city's Players League team. After the Jefferson Street field's sheriff sale, the Wagners shifted players from the three city ball clubs and set up their reconvened team at the Players League ball field, Forepaugh Park and Broad and Dauphin Streets.

The Athletics played one more season in Philadelphia before merging with the new National League Washington ballclub. The Washington AA club joined the National League. It was a better end than what was in store for the Jefferson ball field. Vacant and partially denuded during the 1891 season, the ballpark was set ablaze by neighborhood youngsters in November. A good deal of lumber, stored for carpenters repairing the surviving outside fence, fed the flames.[31] A month later the Wagners' offices on Vine Street burned down. Fortunately, the office safe, with the club's records, tickets and contracts, survived the fire.[32] By the following summer the old Jefferson Street grounds, behind a new "substantial fence," were converted into an enclosed "pleasure park" and playground.[33]

By the mid-1890s there was speculation that a new baseball association would take over the Jefferson Street site.[34]

COURTESY OF THE AUTHOR

1883 ballgame at the new 27th and Jefferson Street field, looking north towards Jefferson street. Home plate is at 27th Street. The big building on the right is the Mission Church at 26th and Jefferson.

COURTESY OF THE AUTHOR

1884 ballgame looking southeast from the corner of 27th street and Jefferson. Founders Hall is at the top left of the picture.

COURTESY OF THE AUTHOR

Contemporary picture of the playground and softball field at the corner of 27th and Jefferson.

In 1900 the future owners of the American League Athletics, Ben Shibe and Connie Mack, pondered the advantages of revisiting the old 27th Street ball field.[35] Mack's Athletics offered to lease the grounds for $1,000 a year and signed a $30,000 lease to upgrade it. But neighboring residents and the new 25th Street School opposed the new ballpark and its anticipated crowds.[36] As a result, the inaugural American League Athletics located themselves at 29th and Columbia while the Jefferson Street site hosted leisure activities and an occasional Buffalo Bill Wild West Show.[37]

Today a memorial plaque to Billy Sharsig is mounted at the 26th Street recreation center and kids play on a softball field set on the grass and dirt of one of Philadelphia's oldest and most important ball playing sites. ∎

Notes

1. *Sunday Dispatch*, March 27, 1859.
2. *Sunday Mercury*, May 16, 1866; *Sunday Dispatch*, March 3, 1872.
3. Ibid., May 22, 1864; *Philadelphia Inquirer*, May 25, 1864. Olympics club house, c. 1866. Baseball Hall of Fame Library, Olympics Folder, B 13.55.
4. *Evening City Item*, May 15, 1871.
5. Painting by A. Kollner, 1865 in Logan Library, Philadelphia, PA. See also T. Eakins painting, 1875, "Baseball Players," at Rhode Island School of Design, Providence, Rhode Island.
6. *Sunday Dispatch*, September 15, 1872; 11 June 1871; *Philadelphia Inquirer*, April 11, 1871.
7. *Sunday Dispatch*, April 7, 1873.
8. Ibid., November 21, 1871.
9. Ibid., April 7, 1872; April 28, 1872.
10. *All Day City Item*, May 23, 1873.
11. *Sunday Dispatch*, January 25, 1874.
12. *The Daily Graphic*, April 30, 1873; April 18, 1874.
13. *All Day City Item*, February 10, 1875; February 28, 1875; May 3, 1875.
14. Ibid., July 30, 1875.
15. *Sunday Mercury*, November 4, 1866.
16. *Sunday Item*, March 26, 1882.
17. By the end of the first year the Committee on City Property gave the Athletics a three-year renewable lease at $2,000 a year. This agreement stood unless the new high school was built. In that case the city had to give the ball club a three month notice of the forfeiture. *Sunday Dispatch*, December 9, 1883. *Philadelphia Press*, January 17, 1883; *Sunday Dispatch*, February 4, 1883,
18. *Sunday Item*, April 8, 1883; April 1, 1883.
19. Ibid., April 8, 1883; *Sunday Dispatch*, January 14, 1883; *Philadelphia Record*, April 1, 1883.
20. Ibid., March 29, 1883.
21. *Frank Leslie Illustrated Newspaper*, October 6, 1883 and Gilbert & Bacon picture, 1884, Baseball Hall of Fame, B. 164.65. *Philadelphia Record*, March 29, 1883; March 31, 1883. The late Larry Zuckerman calculated that the ball park's dimensions were 288–440–352. Zuckerman to J. Casway, August 7, 1999.
22. *North American*, August 28, 1899; May 5, 1893. *Philadelphia Inquirer*, October 10, 1898.
23. *Sporting Life*, March 31, 1886.
24. Ibid., May 5, 1886.
25. Ibid., November 17, 1886.
26. Ibid., April 25, 1888.
27. Ibid., February 20, 1889.
28. Ibid., October 16, 1889; *Sporting News*, October 19, 1889.
29. *North American*, June 26, 1890; *Sporting Life*, June 28, 1890.
30. Ibid., October 18, 1890; *The Sporting News*, October 18, 1890; *Cleveland Plain Dealer*, October 15, 1890.
31. *Sporting Life*, November 28, 1891.
32. Ibid., December 12, 1891.
33. Ibid., June 18, 1892; *Sunday Item*, June 19, 1892; *The Sporting News*, October 27, 1894.
34. *Sporting Life*, October 27, 1894.
35. *The Sporting News*, September 23, 1900; November 24, 1900.
36. *Philadelphia Press*, December 20, 1900.
37. Ibid., May 13, 1901; *Sunday Item*, May 11, 1902.

Philadelphia—October 1866

The Center of the Baseball Universe

Jeff Laing

In the late nineteenth century, Philadelphia was a hotbed of baseball activity, and specifically of idiosyncratic match-ups. For three weeks in October 1866, Philadelphia was the scene of two "world" championship series that helped determine the future course of baseball in the areas of professionalism and race.

The 1860s were a decade of rapid social change and radical perceptions of what it meant to be an American. The growth of the railroads and affordable train travel; the development of communication services, such as the telegraph and the typewriter; and the end of the Civil War all aided in the growth and development of baseball into a shared national experience. The game was simple to understand, inexpensive, relatively easy to play, and, according to its most vocal proponents, American in origin and nature. With little competition from other team sports, baseball in the 1860s stepped into a nation searching for a means of reunification and dedication to American ideals.

Baseball was also ubiquitous in this era as a part of many school physical education programs because it was cheap to fund—a ball and a bat—with many possible participants. The US Military used the game to develop physical strength and dexterity, mental agility, and team cohesion while sharpening the soldiers' competitive skills. Local baseball associations developed personal camaraderie and civic devotion to town teams. The notion of baseball as a patriotic activity began in this decade and the flag was often presented by local groups to visiting clubs.

The 1866 Championship Match, a best of three affair scheduled for early October, between the six-time eastern champion Atlantics of Brooklyn and the up-and-coming Athletics of Philadelphia who arranged the competition, was a major event in the evolution of baseball into a professional sport: "The October 1866 series…was, to that point, the culmination of enticing players, arranging tours, promoting matches between top clubs and charging the public, all to maximize profit."[1] The first game was scheduled for October 1 at the Columbia Avenue and 15th Street grounds. Though there had been an advance sale of 8,000 tickets at 25 cents, Philadelphia was not prepared for the crowds that showed up for the ball game. The estimated attendance was in excess of thirty thousand spectators, many of whom were herded to the outfield. When the police force proved insufficient to the task of removing the fans from the playing field, the game was called in the second inning.[2] The Philadelphia papers went into a paroxysm of excess about the possibility that a fervid devotion to baseball by half-crazed cranks would lead to the eventual demise of the sport:

> Yesterday the base-ball fever culminated in a scene disgraceful to Philadelphia. The much-talked of game between the Athletics and Atlantics was prevented by the ignorant conduct of the vast crowd assembled to witness the sport. We do not overestimate when we say there were 30,000 people present, and of those 30,000 a large proportion lacked common sense. In their eager desire to secure advantageous positions, they sacrificed all propriety, and overreaching themselves, prevented the game which they all had come miles to see. It is a matter of extremely slight importance whether the game in question occurs or not, but an instructive lesson can be drawn from the conduct of those present on the occasion, We stated yesterday that the admiration felt for base-ball as for all physical sports, was a natural one; that it should be popular is proper. But at the same time we warned all lovers of the game that the excess to which it was being carried would prove its ruin.

The reporter discussed in depth the twin dangers that threatened baseball's growing popularity: gambling and drinking. The article concluded with an appeal for moderation among all elements of fandom:

> We like the game of base-ball. We think it calculated to strengthen the muscles, invigorate the system, and counteract the evils of the sedentary life lead [sic] by some many of our young men.

But at the same time it would be better to have no game than what we fear it will become. Let the nuisance be abated, for nuisance it has become. Let us have it in moderation; for as long as the fever does not cool, the whole sport will be ruined, and base-ball and cricket rank among the things that were.[3]

On October 15 in clear weather conditions, the return match at the Atlantics' Capitoline Grounds in Bedford, New York, was played with the home team winning, 27–17, after a close match through the first four innings. Equally important, the Brooklyn ownership organized the game effectively by decorating the 4,000-seat stadium in patriotic colors, selling no tickets in advance but insisting that all spectators that entered the grounds pay a quarter by exact change, providing dignitaries with special seating, and having a small army of police to ensure order with the crowd estimated to be in the neighborhood of 20,000.[4]

With the revenues from the first two meetings—the aborted game on October 1 ($2,000) and the Atlantics victory on October 15 ($1,000)—totaling $3,000,[5] the 1866 series was turning out to be a financial if not artistic success. The third (and what turned out to be the final) game of the series took place back in Philadelphia on October 22. The Athletics were much better prepared for the anticipated fan interest with a stronger police presence and a new fence built around their field to limit the attendance to 4,000 paying spectators. To increase profits, the Athletics charged a dollar a ticket, an exorbitant, previously unheard-of fee to attend a baseball game.[6] The actual game followed the same pattern as the October 15 match with a close game becoming a blowout for the home team in the later innings. Philadelphia outscored Brooklyn, 22–3 in the last three frames, before a downpour ended the game in the eighth inning with the Athletics leading 31–12.

A final deciding game was never played in this series due to a money dispute: The Athletics wanted to take the cost of their newly erected fence off the top of the revenues while Brooklyn wanted to share in the total gross profits.[7]

While the 1866 Match series was inconclusive in declaring an eastern champion, it did prove that there was enormous fan interest in championship level baseball and that a great deal of money could be made from such games, suggesting that baseball in the near future was a potentially solid business investment and profit-maker.

During the same week that the Atlantics were facing off against the Athletics, the African American

PHILADELPHIA HISTORICAL SOCIETY

Civil rights activist Octavius C. Catto founded the Philadelphia Pythians in 1866.

Albany (New York) Bachelors came to Philadelphia and laid claim to the first (unofficial) black baseball championship

Early in October the Albany Bachelor Base Ball Club headed the 260 miles south to Philadelphia to challenge the newly established black Excelsior and Pythian clubs. Eager to spread the gospel of baseball to African American organizations and communities, the Bachelors paid their own expenses and had a successful first-ever road trip for a black ball club. On October 3, 1866, the Bachelors met the Pythians at the Parade Grounds at 11th and Wharton Streets near the Moyamensing Prison.[8]

The Philadelphia Pythian Base Ball Club was founded in 1866 by civil rights activist and base ball star infielder Octavius V. Catto who recruited 50 percent of his middle class team from the Banner Institute (a literary and debating society that shared rooms with the ball club).[9] Catto's vision for the club was always larger than the won-loss column. He desired "equal participation and recognition" for African Americans in American society. He himself was instrumental in desegregating the city trolley cars. He believed base ball "built community ties, pushed racial boundaries, and established local and national networks of support."[10] (The Bachelors were led by a similarly motivated leader, James C. Matthews, who became the New York State Recorder on the Democratic ticket in

NEW YORK PUBLIC LIBRARY

This 1874 photo depicts Weston Fisler, who joined the Athletic Club of Philadelphia in 1866.

1895, and saw the national pastime as a means for African Americans to strive for equality.[11])

The result of the October 3, 1866, match game was a rout in favor of the Upstate New York visitors. The *Albany Evening Journal* was quick to reprint the results of the game: "Oct. 3—Philadelphia: A match game of base ball was played this P.M. between the Bachelors of Albany and the Pythians of this city, which resulted in a victory for the former by a score of 70 to 15." The *Syracuse Daily Standard* (October 4, 1866) published the fact of the Bachelors' victory and added that "this game attracted a large crowd of spectators." Word of the Albanians' resounding defeat of the Pythians was also reported in the *Nashville Daily Union and American* (October 4, 1866): "Philadelphia, Oct. 3—A match was also played between two negro [sic] clubs, the Bachelors of Albany, and the Pythians of this city [Philadelphia]. This game attracted a large number of spectators."

On the following day, the *Albany Evening Journal* reported another solid diamond victory for the Bachelors: "Philadelphia, Oct. 4—Another match was played this P.M. between the Bachelors of Albany and Excelsiors of this city, which resulted in another victory for the Bachelors, by a score of 44 to 28."

In 1867, the Pythians baseball club went 9–1. Trying to follow up on their on-field success, Catto's

club unsuccessfully attempted to participate in the Pennsylvania Convention of Baseball in Harrisburg on October 16 and, despite the support of Athletics of Philadelphia vice-president and president of the nominating committee E. Hicks Hayhurst, the Pythians were the only one of 266 clubs denied entry into the association. Later in the fall, the National Association of Base Ball Players (NABBP) upheld the Pennsylvania decision.[12]

In spite of their failure to enter organized baseball, Catto's Pythians were a major force in the attempted integration of the national pastime. The high visibility and political astuteness of its founder and the integrity and skill of its club members provided the Pythians a place of prominence in early black baseball's fight against racial bias. Yet, by the fall of 1867, less than two years after the conclusion of Civil War, baseball had officially established a color line that was not to be lifted on a full-scale basis for 80 years.

Within a few weeks of each other in 1866, two major baseball competitions were held in Philadelphia that would lead to radical changes. Baseball was becoming America's national pastime and a viable profession for talented players; the game was also doing so without the inclusion of African Americans. Money matters and racial prejudice, national issues that remain unresolved to this day, thus dominated the earliest years of our national pastime. ∎

Notes

1. Preston D. Orem, Baseball 1845–1881 from Newspaper Accounts, 54–55, cited in Eric Miklich's "Money Ball: 1866 Championship Match—Athletics vs. Atlantics" *The Base Ball Players Chronicle: 1–13.* http://vbba.org/newsletter/?p=36. (Accessed 10/20/2012).
2. Ibid, 2–3.
3. *Philadelphia Evening Telegraph* (PET), October 2, 1866, 4.
4. Miklich, 4.
5. Ibid, 5.
6. Ibid.
7. Ibid.
8. Jerrold Casway, "Octavius Catto and the Pythians of Philadelphia," Historical Society of Pennsylvania: www.hsp.org/print/node/2931.
9. George B. Kirsch, *Baseball in Blue and Gray: The National Pastime during the Civil War* (Princeton University Press, 2003), 128.
10. "Playing for Keeps: The Pythian Base Ball Club of Philadelphia," Historical Society of Pennsylvania. www.hsp.org/node/2937.
11. *The Hamilton* (Marion County, AL) *News-Press* (HNP), November 14, 1895.
12. For a comprehensive discussion of the life and untimely political murder of Octavius Catto and his Pythian Club SEE the following articles: Daniel R. Biddle and Murray Dubin, "An Early Quest for Equality on the Diamond," philly.com: 1–6. www.printthis.clickability.com/pt/cpt?action=cpt&title (Accessed 9/16/3010); Jerrold Casway, "Philadelphia's Pythians," *The National Pastime*, 120–123; "On the field, the Pythian Club…," Philadelphia Baseball Review: 1–2. www.philadelphiabaseballreview.com/pythian2.html. (Accessed August 20, 2011).

Did New York Steal the Championship of 1867 from Philadelphia?

Richard Hershberger

Baseball was booming in the years immediately following the Civil War. New clubs were forming in cities and towns across the country as established clubs created more excitement than ever. Major matches attracted unprecedented crowds. Competitive rivalries grew more heated.

This environment led inevitably to controversies. One of the greatest was the claim that the New York clubs colluded in 1867 to steal the championship from the Athletic Club of Philadelphia, to keep the pennant in New York. This charge was made in Pennsylvania, and some writers accept it to this day. But is it true? This article will assess the claim in the context of how baseball was organized at the time.

The story of this dispute centers on two institutions of the amateur era: the judiciary committee and the championship.

ORGANIZED BASEBALL AND THE JUDICIARY COMMITTEE

The National Association of Base Ball Players (NABBP) was the governing body of baseball in the 1860s. In 1857 a group of clubs in and around New York City held a convention for the purpose of promoting the game, primarily through the adoption of revised set of rules for inter-club play. The convention reconvened the following year and established itself as a permanent organization, the NABBP.

From the start, the rules included an administrative element in addition to playing rules. The 1857 rules required that "Any player holding membership in more than one club, at the same time, shall not be permitted to play in the matches of either club." The previous September, the Knickerbocker Club had arrived at their grounds in Hoboken for a match game against the Gotham Club. They found one Mr. Pinckney among the Gotham players, much to their surprise, as they knew perfectly well he was a member of the Union Club. Their protest was forestalled by the Gothams, who informed them that he had joined the club the previous Tuesday, though without resigning from the Unions. "The presumption prevailed that he entered the Gothams for the purpose of this match" but the game

went on. The Unions held a special meeting to condemn this, and Pinckney resigned from the Gothams the Tuesday following the match, "expressing his conviction of the impropriety of a person belonging to or playing matches in more than one club."[1] The practice had the double disadvantage of threatening the social structure of clubs and leading to the best players monopolizing match play. Thus, it was abolished.

There was obvious potential for a crafty player to get around this by resigning from his old club and rejoining it after the match. The following year this loophole was closed with the requirement that all players "must have been regular members of the club which they represent, and of no other club, for thirty days prior to the match." This would remain the standard throughout the amateur era.

There remained potential for disputes. Suppose a club showed up on the appointed day for a match and found the opposing club fielding an ineligible player. Its only recourse, should the opposing club refuse to withdraw the player, was to refuse to play or to play under protest. In fact, this happened on July 20, 1862, when the Mutual Club fielded two such players in a match with the Empire Club. The Empires played, losing 24–12, and protested to the NABBP convention the following December. A committee was formed to investigate the matter, and a year later reported in favor of the Empires, nullifying the match. Justice delayed is justice denied, and a year and a half was obviously too long for a satisfactory result. At its December 1863 meeting the NABBP also created a standing judiciary committee to investigate and report on any future disputes in a timelier manner.[2]

This judiciary committee was to be the body that ruled in that Athletics' dispute in 1867. It could not, however, overtly rule on the championship question.

THE AMATEUR CHAMPIONSHIP

The defining characteristic of the baseball championship in the amateur era was that officially there was no such thing. The NABBP declined to sponsor one, in the entirely reasonable fear that "matches, except with the club holding the champion ball, would sink into insignificance, and the popularity of the game would therefore decline."[3] However, an unofficial, but widely recognized, championship system arose.

This unofficial system copied the existing model of boxing championships, grafting it onto baseball. As with boxing, aspirants would challenge the champion for the prize, with the initial champion determined through a combination of self-promotion and popular acclaim. This was combined with the existing custom of a best-of-three series. Usually the first game would be played on the challenger's home ground (with the challenge likened to a social invitation), the second on the recipient's home ground, with the third game, if necessary, played on a neutral ground.

This system was rife with potential confusion. The championships were conventionally stated in terms of the pennant for the season, but series were sometimes played over the course of two seasons, it not being entirely clear whether a championship could be won based on a series partly played the previous season. Also, a club might win the championship while it had partially completed other series. However, there was no clarity whether these would then transform into a championship series. There also was a widely held opinion that a club was ineligible for the championship if it had lost a series against some other club: "...it is one of the customary rules governing the championship matches that the loss of a match–best two out of three– throws a club out of the ring for the season, as a champion club, in order to have the right to "fly the whip," must win every series of match games they play. They may lose a single game without invalidating their title, but two defeats out of three games with a club places them hors de combat for the season."[4]

Only through good luck did most of these problems fail to arise. There were numerous games which, had victory gone the other way, could have put the whole system in confusion. The requirement that the challenging club itself lose no series did, as we shall see, arise in 1867. But as every contender for the championship had lost a series, all parties conveniently forgot the requirement. Indeed, it likely was an attempt at artificially generating interest in matches involving potential challengers for the championship.

The championship system itself coexisted uncomfortably with the ideology of amateur baseball. The archetypal baseball club was a social organization formed as a vehicle for young men of sedentary occupations to take their exercise together in a congenial setting. The vast majority of ball games were intramural affairs. Match games, in which two clubs tested their mettle against one another, were comparatively rare and were as much social affairs as they were competitive. Rivalry was not the goal. Clubs often played each other year after year if they were socially compatible, even if they were completely mismatched competitively. On the other hand, clubs might also refuse to play if they found the experience disagreeable, even if they were well matched on the field.

Championship matches were the logical outgrowth of match games, but they still operated within the assumptions of social norms. This began to change in the postwar baseball boom. Spectators, it was learned, were willing to pay for the privilege of watching ball clubs compete. Clubs needed the revenue as they sought to attract top players by paying them (surreptitiously, as the practice was prohibited by the NABBP). Arrangements for matches grew less like social engagements and more like business contracts with penalty clauses for default. These gradual changes lead to confusion and dissension as they were sorted out.

THE ATLANTICS AND THE ATHLETICS

There were perhaps a half dozen serious championship contenders, but only two concern us here: the Atlantic Club of Brooklyn and the Athletic Club of Philadelphia.

The Atlantics were the powerhouse organization of the amateur era. They had held the championship every year since but two its inception. They were also notorious for pushing the limits of gentlemanly competition. As a modest example, the first known use of the hidden ball trick was by an Atlantic player.[5] More serious was the history of Atlantics supporters verbally abusing their opponents and, in an era when the spectators were not physically separated from the players, interfering with the course of play. While the Atlantic players could claim innocence on the grounds that they could not control their supporters, this did not stop them from accepting the advantage.[6]

Their reputation improved in the postwar years. Their continued success stifled criticism, while general standards within the fraternity lowered. In fairness, the Atlantics' behavior also improved, as did crowd control in a fully enclosed ball ground. In any case, they were the team to beat for clubs striving for the championship.

The Athletics of Philadelphia were the only serious contender for this outside of the New York region. The baseball craze came to Philadelphia in 1860. The Athletics were one of the first baseball clubs there. In the early years they were merely one of several pretty good clubs in Philadelphia, none of whom stood a chance against the best New York clubs. They pulled ahead of the pack in 1865 through aggressive recruiting, collecting the best Philadelphia players, making the club essentially a regional all-star team. They supplemented this with out-of-town talent in the person of Al Reach, formerly of the Eckford Club of Brooklyn. Professionalism was outlawed by the NABBP, so was exercised secretly. Reach holds the distinction of being the first undoubted professional, though almost certainly not the first actual one. He semi-openly marketed his services, with the Athletics placing the winning bid. He opened a cigar shop in Philadelphia and went on to become a baseball equipment manufacturer. The Athletics built on this, and by 1867 were said to have four professionals.[7]

That Atlantics and the Athletics already had a contentious history going into the 1867 season. They first competed in 1863, with relations amicable through 1864. They soured in 1865. The two clubs had scheduled a series, the first game for October 30 in Philadelphia and the second for November 6 in Brooklyn.[8] Then Matty O'Brien, a long-time member of the Atlantic Club, unexpectedly died. The Atlantics published a resolution of condolence, including a cancellation of all further play by the club for the season, in his memory. The Athletics followed with their own resolution of condolence.[9] A rumor then spread that the Athletics were planning on appearing at their grounds on the day appointed for the match and declare the Atlantics forfeit. The Atlantics responded to this by sending a telegram the afternoon of the 29th stating their intention to play the next day. This forced the Athletics to scramble to prepare for the match, which they had understood to have been cancelled. Both sides felt aggrieved. There is no knowing if there was anything behind the rumor, but it seems likely that this was a breakdown in communication.[10] The Atlantics went on to win both games, keeping their championship secure from Philadelphia's first serious challenge.

The interest—and potential income from gate receipts—was too high for them to not meet again the following year. But where 1865 saw miscommunication and hard feelings, 1866 saw farce. The first game was scheduled for October 1 in Philadelphia. A contemporary account vividly describes the excitement:

> In the meantime, as the hour approaches for the contest to commence, the steady tide begins to flow Columbia avenueward, until towards 1PM, when the mob of people, the crowd of vehicles, and extraordinary numbers of men, women and boys en route for the scene of action, is only equaled by the exodus from London on the great

NATIONAL BASEBALL HALL OF FAME LIBRARY, COOPERSTOWN, NY

London-born Al Reach played for the Eckford club of Brooklyn in the early 1860s before joining the Athletics of Philadelphia in 1865.

> Derby day. The ground reached, what a sight is presented! No such scene of the kind was ever before presented to the public eye in this country, and probably will not again for some time, certainly not this season. Within a radius of a quarter of a mile from the centre of the circle were collected nearly 40,000 people, it is thought. Every window of every house within sight of the field was crowded. The house tops were peopled to an extent endangering the roofs. Trees were loaded with human fruit, and vehicles of every description surrounded the field, filled with all who could get a foothold on them. Inside the enclosure, the pressure was immense, and by the hour appointed for commencing play standing room within fifty feet of the base lines was at a premium, and, as a consequence, there was no space for the players for field operations, at least to an extent admitting of an equal contest. At last, out of patience with the delay, an effort was made to begin...[11]

The pressure of bodies was too much. They pressed onto the field, and play had to be halted after one inning. As the crowd spilled onto the field "the whole affair broke up in a row and a number of heads had been smashed by the police, amidst the cries and screams of the ladies and children, the breaking down of fences, the throwing of stones..."[12] This left only the pointing of fingers. The Athletics claimed that ruffian

Atlantics supporters had started the trouble, pushing their way to the front of the crowd. The Athletics in turn were charged with allowing too many people within the enclosure in the quest for maximum gate receipts. The bottom line, though, was that the Athletics had failed their obligation as hosts to provide a clear field. They had allowed too many people into the enclosure and not hired enough police to control the crowd.[13]

The economics still called for the series to be salvaged, so the two clubs quickly negotiated a solution. The game scheduled for October 15 in Brooklyn went on, with extra precautions for crowd control including the presence of 100 policemen.[14] The Philadelphia game was rescheduled for October 22. This gave the Athletics time to repair the ground, constructing a new, stronger fence. Ordinarily the home club retained all the gate receipts, but agreement was reached to compensate the Atlantics for the failed game by splitting the October 22 gate with them equally, after expenses.

The games went off beautifully. The Brooklyn game saw a huge crowd: "the estimate of a veteran of the Potomac army, well versed in numbering large bodies of men, was that there was not less that from twelve to fifteen thousand people within the enclosure" with the Atlantics winning 27–17.[15] The Philadelphia game was thinly attended within the enclosure, as the Athletics experimented with a one dollar admission: a great leap from the usual twenty-five cents. They still attracted about two thousand paying spectators, as well as a large crowd gathered outside the fence. Best of all, the Athletics finally beat the Atlantics, 31–12.[16]

This would ordinarily have led to a third, and lucrative, game. But again some combination of miscommunication and bad faith intervened. The Atlantics understood their share from the Philadelphia game to be minus ordinary expenses, while the Athletics understood it to be minus all expenses, including the cost of the new fence, which ran to over half the gate receipts. The Atlantics refused their reduced share, regarding it as a swindle, while the Athletics saw the Atlantics reneging on a straightforward agreement. No third game was played in 1866.[17]

THE CAMPAIGN OF 1867

Once again financial demands overcame all obstacles. The two clubs in 1867 agreed to complete the previous season's series, followed by a new best-of-three series. Ordinarily the clubs would split three ways the receipts from the third game of a series, with the proprietor of the neutral ground taking a share. The Athletics agreed to compensate the Atlantics with their share from the belated final game. This game was played in Brooklyn on September 16, with the Atlantics winning 28–16. The critics of the Athletics were only too happy to point to the large crowd, and that the Atlantics came out ahead from where they would have, had they been paid in the first place.[18] The Atlantic victory also had the fortunate effect of avoiding any immediate claim by the Athletics to the championship pennant.

The first game of the new series came off successfully on September 23 in Philadelphia, the Athletics winning soundly by 28–8. The second game was scheduled for the following Monday, September 30, in Brooklyn. The Friday before, they requested the game be postponed, on the grounds that four of their first nine were injured. The Athletics refused to accept the postponement, and showed up in Brooklyn at the appointed time. A fiasco ensued. The Atlantics refused to play their first nine. After much discussion, they instead presented a "muffin" nine: the most inept amateurs on their club. There was a tradition of "muffin matches" which were considered the source of great hilarity. To play a muffin nine in a championship match was a mockery. There are two interpretations of this action. The more usual is that the Atlantics were shaming the Athletics to keep them from playing. There is also a claim that the muffin nine would play so incompetently that they would be incapable of getting the Athletics out (keeping in mind the requirement that the catcher hold a third strike for an out), and therefore of playing five innings before the game would be called on account of darkness. This claim is entirely plausible. Games in theory started at two o'clock, but this one obviously would start much later, and this being late September the sun would set around half past five. There also was ample precedent for clubs stalling, usually to force the score to revert to the last completed inning. So there was a reasonable argument that the Atlantics were not merely shaming the Athletics, but using an underhanded stratagem to avoid a complete game. In the end, the Athletics refused to play, claimed a forfeit, and thereby claimed the championship.[19] (There also was a later assertion that the Atlantics had offered a ball, i.e. a forfeit, which the Athletics refused. This is not credible, as it only arose later, and no one seemed to take it seriously.)

Claiming the championship was one thing, but getting the rest of the baseball fraternity to acknowledge it was quite another. The Athletics filed a complaint with the judiciary committee, demanding a ruling that they had won forfeit. The committee considered the question on October 30 and ruled that the Atlantics had indeed failed in their obligation, and ordered the game to be played within 15 days. The committee admitted that there was no rule granting them such authority, but foreshadowed the much later powers of the Commissioner of Baseball with the argument that "their powers should be liberally construed when a palpable injury may result to the interests of the game."[20]

This solution might seem as Solomonic. It was actually a repudiation of the Athletics, for the situation had changed. A forfeit as of September 30 would have given the championship to the Athletics. A victory by the Athletics in November would not. To everyone's surprise the Unions of Morrisania defeated the Atlantics for the second time on October 10, making them the champions. Morrisania was then a village in what is now the Bronx. The Unions played not far from the modern site of Yankee Stadium. The Unions were an old established club that had for years hovered just below the top level. Their winning the championship was not quite scandalous, but it was widely regarded as something of a lucky fluke. It also rendered any future game between the Atlantics and the Athletics irrelevant, so far as the championship went.

The New York clubs, it is claimed, colluded to steal the championship from Philadelphia. The judiciary committee was dominated by New Yorkers. The ruling was apparently equitable, but not made in a vacuum. The championship had no official standing with the NABBP, but the ruling was made with the full understanding of the championship implications. If the Athletics' complaint to the committee was justified, they should have been awarded the forfeit. If not, then there was no need to order the game be played. The ruling was crafted, it is charged, to ensure that the championship pennant stayed within the metropolis.

THE RECORD OF THE JUDICIARY COMMITTEE

The charge of collusion is plausible on its face because the ruling of the judiciary committee seems implausible. This presupposes, however, that the committee would have acted differently had it been a New York club making the charge. Quite the contrary, this would have been very much out of character.

The committee had an inglorious history from its inception, marked mostly by inactivity. In 1867 it had a sizeable docket of eleven cases, both large and small. Most were charges of a club using an ineligible player, usually on the grounds of a violation of the 30-day rule.[21] Its decisions show an unmistakable pattern. If the defending club was an unimportant one, the ruling might or might not go against it. If the defending club was an important one, some grounds would be found to acquit it, even if the accusing club was also important. So, for example, the minor Chestnut Street Theater Club played a match using two members of the Alert Club, and this game was declared null and void. On the other hand, the charge against the important Excelsior Club of using four players claimed to belong to the Star Club was overturned, with the individuals declared "regular members of the Excelsior Club, within the meaning of the Rules." It is possible that the evidence in each case supported the conclusion, but it is remarkable how well the conclusions correlate to the status of the defending club. Several cases with important defendants were also dismissed on technicalities, while those with minor defendants were uniformly free from such procedural defects.

The sole exception is a particularly illuminating case. The Unions of Morrisania charged the Mutual Club of New York—one of the top clubs—with playing one Tom Devyr. In 1865 Devyr had been expelled after confessing to accepting a bribe to throw a game with the Eckford Club. In 1867 he was reinstated with the Mutuals, contrary to the NABBP constitution. The committee ducked the issue once on procedural grounds, but when forced to make a decision, ruled against the Mutuals. Both the facts and the law were beyond question. Even at this early date the baseball community recognized the existential threat to the game of corruption by gamblers. This was a situation where the committee had to stand up to a powerful club.

What followed shows the realities of how the NABBP worked. For all that the committee acted like a judicial body, it was in fact a committee tasked to make a report to the convention. The convention as a whole would then accept or reject the report, in whole or in part. The Mutuals undertook a brazen lobbying campaign and used the convention to retry the case. The convention overturned the judiciary committee's decision by a vote of 451–143, and then promptly passed a motion to reinstate Devyr "in the position he occupied previous to the playing of the Eckford and Mutual match in 1865."[22]

This repudiation clearly shows the limits of the judiciary committee's power, and explains its reluctance to take a stand on any less vital issue. It also shows the NABBP devolving into a banana republic, with different de facto rules for powerful clubs than for weak ones.

In light of this reality, it is clear that the judiciary committee could not possibly have awarded a forfeit to the Athletics, and with it the championship. This would have outraged both the Atlantics and the Unions. It would also have offended the wider baseball fraternity by moving the championship contest from the playing field to the meeting room. None of this has anything to do with civic rivalry. It would have been the same had the dispute been between two New York clubs.

It is also clear that the committee believed that the Athletics had the law on their side, if not political realities. They had ample room to rule in the Atlantics' favor, in that the Atlantics had in fact presented nine players. The order that the game be played shows that the committee agreed that presenting a muffin nine did not fulfill the club's obligation. This order was the best outcome that the Athletics could realistically hope for. If they were cheated, it was by circumstances rather than any sort of conspiracy.

AND THE ATHLETICS FINALLY WIN THE CHAMPIONSHIP

The transformation of baseball from an amateur social exercise to a business took a decade to sort out. The story of the 1867 championship takes place early in the process. The business of baseball needed new rules for how clubs would interact. These new rules were not yet worked out, and no one really knew what the rules were.

The final game of 1867 was never played. Both clubs ignored the committee's order. The championship campaign of 1868 was even more convoluted. (An article could well be written titled "Did New York Steal the Championship of 1868 from Philadelphia?") The championship system was coming apart. The Cincinnati Red Stockings were clearly the best club in the country in 1869, but did not bother with the notional championship. That year the NABBP bowed to the inevitable and allowed open professionalism. The professional clubs in 1871 split from the NABBP to form the National Association of Professional Base Ball Players which established the first official national championship and the modern scheme of member clubs playing each other a fixed number of matches.[23]

This was the final era for the old clubs. New clubs, founded as joint stock corporations, were taking over. The old social-turned-professional clubs tried to adapt, but had too much institutional inertia to keep up. None survived the 1870s. The Atlantics faded fast, and stumbled through the 1875 season before disappearing.

The Athletics won their championship in 1871, making them the first official national champions of baseball. This was the high water mark for the club. They held out long enough to become a charter member when the National League formed in 1876, but they were on their last legs. They could not complete the season, and were expelled from the league. A derivative Athletics organization wheezed on a bit longer, but did not see the end of the decade. ■

Notes

1. *Porter's Spirit of the Times*, September 13, 1856; September 20, 1856.
2. *New York Sunday Mercury*, December 14, 1862; December 13, 1863.
3. *New York Sunday Mercury*, September 25, 1859.
4. *Ball Players Chronicle*, July 11, 1867.
5. *New York Sunday Mercury*, October 23, 1859.
6. The most famous example was a game in 1860 with the Excelsiors, which led to the Excelsiors refusing to ever again play the Atlantics. A less known, but vividly egregious example occurred two years earlier. As reported in the *New York Evening Express* of October 26, 1858, in a game with the Gotham Club: "The Atlantics won the game, the last two innings of the game being played under considerable difficulty on the part of the Gothams, who protested repeatedly—and justly, but without redress—at the unfair arrangements of the members of the Atlantic Club for keeping the field clear; while it was cleared most effectually to allow the fielders to follow the balls which were struck by the Gothams, and the openings in the fence in the left field were particularly left free and respected by the crowd of outsiders, yet no sooner was the Gotham side in the field and the Atlantics at the bat, than the crowd was allowed to close in on the openings in the fence, and become an impassable barrier. This was so barefaced in one instance, that the Gothams' fielder, finding the crowd not disposed to give way, sat down in front of them until the batsman had run home." The Gothams did not play the Atlantics again until 1864.
7. There is every reason to believe that other top clubs, including the Atlantics, were doing the same thing. The Athletics differed only in that they also had a running feud with one Thomas Fitzgerald, the former president of the club, and Fitzgerald owned a newspaper, the *City Item*, which he used freely to air their dirty laundry.
8. This late in the season was typical of the era, when serious play didn't get started until late May and ran through November. The major championship matches usually were played late in the season.
9. *New York Leader*, October 28, 1865; *Fitzgerald's City Item*, October 28, 1865.
10. *New York Clipper*, November 4, 1865; *Fitzgerald's City Item*, November 4, 1865.
11. *New York Clipper*, November 4, 1866.
12. *Fitzgerald's City Item*, October 6, 1866.
13. The event was widely reported. In addition to those cited above, see the *Philadelphia Sunday Mercury*, October 7, 1866.
14. *Philadelphia Sunday Mercury*, October 14, 1866.
15. *New York Sunday Mercury*, October 21, 1866. This game is also notable by including the earliest known called third strike to end an inning. The account in the *Philadelphia Sunday Mercury* of October 21, 1866 also includes a description of something very like the modern wave: "Directly in front of the Philadelphia delegation a number of planks had been arranged as seats, the same being packed full of interested spectators. Said seats being too low for comfort, several of their occupants arose and indulged themselves in a good stretch, accompanying the action with the yawning sound peculiar under such circumstances. The cue was taken by the opposite side of the field, and soon the entire assemblage became infected, producing a scene ludicrous in the extreme. The satisfaction produced by this little by-play was heartily and good-humoredly manifested by the crowd on the left side of the field waving their handkerchiefs, which was promptly returned by their friends opposite, and soon thousands of pieces of white drapery were floating in the air, creating a sight probably never before witnessed on a similar occasion."
16. *Philadelphia City Item*, October 27, 1866; *Philadelphia Sunday Mercury*, October 28, 1866.
17. Ibid.
18. *Philadelphia City Item*, September 14, 1867; *New York Sunday Mercury*, September 22, 1867.
19. *Philadelphia Sunday Mercury*, October 6, 1867; *New York Sunday Mercury*, October 6, 1867.
20. *New York Sunday Mercury*, November 3, 1867; *Ball Players Chronicle*, December 19, 1867.
21. *Ball Players Chronicle*, December 19, 1867.
22. Ibid.
23. This is still reflected in the official rules, which somewhat confusingly refer to "championship games" and the "championship series" in what is otherwise universally called the "regular season."

Mundell's Solar Tips
The Intersection of Amateur, Trade, Professional and Major League Baseball in Philadelphia

Paul Browne

In Philadelphia, Mundell's Solar Tips moved back and forth among the various levels of baseball during the 1880s and 1890s. Their history is illustrative of the more open and entrepreneurial baseball world that ended long ago.

John Mundell Jr. founded the Solar Tips baseball team in 1879. The first players were workers in the factory of John Mundell & Company, a shoe company founded by John Mundell, Sr. The Solar Tips were a company team established to promote the company's line of children's shoes with a patented tip to protect the shoes from the hard wear of children. One of the earliest mentions of Mundell's Solar Tips regards a game scheduled for Saturday August 11, 1883, at Recreation Park (a site also used by Philadelphia's new team in the National League) against a picked nine of striking telegraphers during a national telegraph operators strike. That a company team would play a strike team might seem unusual but John Mundell Sr. was a progressive business owner.

John Mundell Sr. was born in Ireland in 1829 of Scotch-Irish stock. He traveled from Belfast to New York as a stowaway at the age of 14 but became a cabin boy before the journey was over. He stayed at sea and became an able seaman, working at that job until 1847, when he arrived in Philadelphia. While working in the Quaker City fisheries he met a former apprentice of his father's who was a shoemaker, and learned that trade from him and opened his own shoe shop in 1848. In 1870 he opened the larger firm of John Mundell & Company, where he developed his patented shoe tip and became wealthy.

Mundell and his employees were exceptionally loyal to one another. He is quoted as saying, "(L)et all who employ people look into the grievances of his employees, for in a great many instances, to my knowledge, the employees are right, but instead of listening to their workmen's complaints many employers give them the cold shoulder, which they are apt to resent, and thus bring about strikes and lockouts."[1] Mundell's company was home to strikes and labor unrest from time to time despite his attitude towards labor. In most cases, however, the problems occurred after Mundell and his employees had reached a frequently novel solution to a problem only to have the union's regional officers outside the company reject it.

In 1884, Mundell's employees formed the Solar Tip Mutual Improvement Land Association. Their plan was to purchase farmland a half-hour's trip by rail from the city, build affordable homes, and sell them to the members, who made periodic contributions to pay them off.[2] Mundell was an active member of the Republican Party when it was the party of "Free Soil, Free Labor, Free Men" and was a member of the Electoral College that elected Benjamin Harrison in the 1888 presidential election.

John Mundell Jr. apparently did not have as good a relationship with labor. He was once arrested, tried, and convicted, along with an associate, for beating up a former employee after an argument ensued while the ex-employee was picking up his last check. He became a member of the joint arbitrators' board of the Philadelphia Shoe Manufacturers Association in 1885. This body's purpose was to arbitrate between management and labor.

The company team that promoted Mundell's "Solar Tip" children's shoes played two games on July 4, 1884, before crowds of over 2,000 people. The morning game was against Wanamaker's Grand Depot team and the afternoon against Hood, Bonbright & Co. The Solar Tips won both games.

Another important game that season occurred in September against the American Association Athletics. The American Association was the major league rival of the NL at that time and the Athletics had won the AA championship in 1883. The Athletics won the game 8–2 with both Tip runs coming in the fifth inning. The Athletics had most of their regulars on the field with their second regular battery of pitcher Billy Taylor and catcher Jack O'Brien. Harry Stovey led the victors with a double and shortstop Kelly led the Solar Tips with a triple.

Young Mundell and his friends had ambitious plans for 1885. Meeting "at the base ball headquarters, 139

North Eighth Street," Mundell, Fulmer of the Quaker City team, and Doyle of the Somerset team agreed to play nine games apiece against each other.[3] The winner would receive $250 plus the local championship of Philadelphia and would be expected to challenge the Athletics and Philadelphia National League club at the end of the season.

This corporately sponsored amateur team continued on its usual path into 1888. They started the season as a member of the Philadelphia area trades league, consisting of teams formed by the 12 largest manufacturers in Philadelphia, ostensibly from among each company's employees. The Tips' opening game was at Recreation Park against Laird, Schoner & Mitchell's team on April 28. The Solar Tips continued undefeated in this league into the end of May as did the McNeely Club. These two teams met on May 30 before a crowd of over 7,000 fans at Recreation Park, a site presently being called the Solar Tip grounds; the Philadelphia National League club had abandoned the field at the end of the 1886 season. Unfortunately for the Solar Tips, they lost their undefeated status and first place to McNeeley & Co., 4–3. The defensive play of the McNeeleys was credited for the victory.[4] Other members of this league were Gumpert Brothers, Hastings & Co., American Sewing Machine, J.W. Cooper, the Allen Grays, and the Richmonds.

In this same period, John Mundell Jr. was exhibiting leadership in Philadelphia's amateur baseball world. He was elected president of the Amateur Base Ball Union of Philadelphia at their organizational meeting on May 29, 1888, at Industrial Hall. The organization consisted of 62 amateur clubs (whose players were over 17), and was intended to form leagues from among the clubs, secure and maintain a clubhouse for transaction of business among the clubs, arrange a series of games for the amateur championship of Philadelphia, and establish an annual amateur day at which a baseball parade was to be held.[5]

The amateur season moved very quickly and plans for the amateur day parade were finalized at a meeting at Earley's Hall, Arch Street, above 13th, on June 18. Fifty clubs had paid their dues and 19 more were in the application process. One hundred twenty-five clubs were signed up to participate in the parade, including junior clubs and visiting teams from other parts of Pennsylvania and New Jersey. The parade was to take place on Saturday, June 23. The parade was to begin formation at Industrial Hall at Broad and Vine Streets. The parade was then to proceed down Broad Street to Chestnut, turn on Fifth from Chestnut, up Fifth to Market, Market back to Broad, up Broad to

Columbia and from Columbia to 24th, at which point they would enter the old Recreation Park. Here a game for the championship of Philadelphia was to be played between the Solar Tips, champions of the Trades League, and the Young Americas, which had been considered the amateur champions for some years.[6] By the date of the parade a large banquet at Industrial Hall had been added as an evening event.[7]

The Young Americas held onto their championship, beating the Solar Tips 10–5 (though the two teams would have a rematch on the following Wednesday). The Solar Tips continued to make a strong showing in the Trades League.

On July 5, the Solar Tips played Easton of the Central League. The Central League was one of the top minor leagues in the country that year. The amateur Solar Tips acquitted themselves well in this game against a higher-level club, losing by a single run, 9–8. Attendance was reported at 2,500.[8] Four of Easton's players had brief major league careers. Buck Becannon had played for the AA Metropolitans in 1884 and '85 and the Giants in 1887. Thomas "Sandy" McDermott played with the AA Baltimore Orioles in 1885. John Deasley, who was also a member of the Solar Tips in 1888, had been with Washington and Kansas City in the 1884 Union Association. Jim McKeever had also played in the Union Association for the Boston Reds. The Solar Tips had future major league players on the field that day. William "Bad Bill" Eagan would play with the AA St. Louis Browns in 1891, Chicago of the NL in 1893 and Pittsburgh in 1898. John Riddle would play with the Washington Nationals of the NL in 1889 and the AA Athletics in 1890.

About this time Camden withdrew from the Inter-State League (now sometimes called the Philadelphia Region League). The Inter-State League, operating in and around Philadelphia, started as a semi-professional league in January 1888. When Harry Wright's Philadelphia Reserves announced their intention to join this league, the semi-pro status of the league began to look suspicious. The league's other teams began to make announcements of players signing contracts. The large number of contract signings that continued to be reported with some teams also brings the organization's status into question. The Philadelphia Reserves were all contract players; Frankford reported 14 players signed by late March, Somerset had 13, and Houston six. Camden and the Quaker City teams had also reported some paid players by this time.

James Farrington had been managing Camden when the Solar Tips brought him over to manage their team as it moved from an amateur league to—

LIBRARY OF CONGRESS

"John Mundell & Co's solar tip shoes Lead All in bright Dongola solar tip, pebble goat solar tip, pebble grain solar tip," proclaims this 1889 advertisement.

in theory, at least—a semi-pro league.[9] Young Mundell's take on this change is not known. Farrington had been a player/manager for Camden in 1883 and managed the Wilmington/Atlantic City team in the Eastern League for part of 1885. He would manage several Pennsylvania state league teams over the rest of his career.

The Solar Tips continued to play trade league clubs during their time in the Inter-State League. On July 21 they played a doubleheader, facing the non-league Keystones at 1:30 PM and the other new ISL team, the Kensingtons, at 4 PM. In a quirk of the times, the Solar Tips would be listed in first place in late July with a 2–1 record, followed by Houston at 12–6, Camden at 10–6, Brandywine at 8–5, Frankford at 11–7, Kensington at 1–1, Norristown and Germantown, both at 9–11, Somerset at 8–11 and the Quaker City in last at 7–14. It was not unusual at this time for even recognized minor leagues to have teams with very different totals of league games throughout the season or for new teams to enter a league without being credited or charged with the records of teams they replaced.

On July 23 the Solar Tips played Frankford. Down 2–1 in the ninth, Eagan walked, Graham of Frankford muffed a double play attempt, Clark singled and Deasley, now back with the Tips, hit a triple and drove in the tying and winning runs.[10] On July 24 it was announced that the Solar Tips would again be playing the Young America for the amateur championship of Philadelphia. The first game was to be Saturday, July 28.

By August 7, the Solar Tips withdrew from the Inter-State League. They had compiled an impressive record of 10 wins and 2 losses (while their record is now sometimes listed as 8 and 2). They indicated their intention was to play all the leading amateur teams of the region. They also announced their plans to play the Cuban Giants on Thursday and Friday of that week. The teams were said to be evenly matched.[11]

This was a strange choice for a team wishing to play with amateurs. The Cuban Giants were the first fully-salaried black professional team. That the Tips were thought to be evenly matched with the Giants, and that they had players on their roster (not just pitchers and catchers) who had played minor league ball before and/or during the 1888 season, makes one wonder how the term "amateur" was being defined in Philadelphia at this time.

The Cuban Giants were a frequent rival of ISL teams in 1888. The Solar Tips met the Cubans on August 9. The "colored champions" opened the scoring, jumping out to a two-run lead in the bottom of the first. The Tips responded with a single run in the top of the second, narrowing the gap. Pitchers Rittenhouse for the Solar Tips and Stovey for the Cuban Giants then held their opponents scoreless for the next three innings. Stovey would go his opponents one better, silencing the Tips bats in the top of the sixth. Rittenhouse then gave up two runs in the bottom of that inning, the final tallies of the game. Clarence Williams and Jack Frye each had doubles to lead the Cuban Giants. Koons led the Solar Tips with a triple. The fielding of both teams was said to be very good and the 4–1 victory was placed in the hands of Stovey's pitching.[12]

The Solar Tips faced a very good team that day. Bob Davids (SABR's founder) once ranked the best black players of the nineteenth century. The pitcher, Stovey, and seven of the eight other players on the field that day, were on this list.[13]

On the other hand, the Solar Tips' two key players that day, pitcher Rittenhouse and catcher Koons, had less auspicious careers. Rittenhouse was a mainstay of Pennsylvania state leagues but would see no major league action. There is no link to this Mr. Koons and any team but the Solar Tips of 1888 at this time.

When the two teams met again the next day, the Solar Tips were minus a manager. Criticized by president Mundell after the loss to the Cuban Giants, Farrington immediately resigned.[14] The change in management didn't help and the Solar Tips fell to the

Cuban Giants 6–4 the next day. William Whyte and Clarence Thomas were the Cubans' battery that day. Whyte had the highest winning percentage of the best black pitchers of the nineteenth century and many feel that Thomas's exclusion from the Hall of Fame is an injustice.

The Solar Tips would continue to play, and frequently defeat, Philadelphia area teams for the rest of the 1888 season. The Interstate League was expected to fold shortly after the Solar Tips withdrew but certain teams continued to be referred to as members of that league until the end of the season. Frankford and Norristown of the ISL initiated efforts to form a new league for 1889. While Frankford would never play in this league, which became the mostly Pennsylvania-based Middle States League, the Cuban Giants, playing out of Trenton, becoming the first black team to play in a mostly white minor league. Before the 1889 season was over, they would be joined by another black team, the Gorhams, headquartered in Easton.

Many Solar Tip players would also make their way into the MSL. Catcher Rigby, first baseman O'Donnell, shortstop (and captain) Clark, and pitcher Rittenhouse would join Lancaster. Samuel Hoverter, another one-time Solar Tip, would play for York.[15] It would also be reported that pitcher Smith of the Philadelphia Giants had played for the Tips the previous year.[16]

After the 1888 season the Solar Tips confined their activities to the Philadelphia regional circuit. They made no attempt to enter the MSL but Mundell Jr., along with N.B. Young, were at the head of an effort to form a semi-professional league. Former ISL teams Norristown, Brandywine, and Houston, and future MSL member Wilmington were targeted as potential members.[17] Nothing appears to have come of this effort. The Solar Tips ceased play for a period after the 1890 season, a decision that was reportedly based on the Players' League's impact on the American Association.[18]

Coverage of the Solar Tips activities appears again in 1892. There are reports of losses to Camden and Burlington, New Jersey, and a victory over Rowlandville that year. In 1893 the Solar Tips reportedly lost to Trenton, Royersford, and Camden, and Camden would again beat the Solar Tips in 1894. The team lost its patron that year as John Mundell Sr. passed away on September 2. John Mundell Jr. continued to operate the company and sponsor a baseball team. There was a report of the Philadelphia-area Wyoming team defeating the Solar Tips in an 1899 game.

Young Mundell initially experienced success leading his father's company. In 1900 they won the Franklin Institute ribbon and medal at the Export Exposition. On the day the prize was announced it was also reported that the company was expanding its plant on Market Street.[19] In February 1901, Mundell had to make corporate and personal assignments to creditors, Charles F. Walton of England and Bryan & Co. leather merchants of Philadelphia. The cause of the failure was attributed to loss of government work which the company had become dependent on, its children's shoe business no longer its strength.[20]

The Solar Tips team history exemplifies the fluid nature of baseball competition at this time. Major league teams frequently played teams from much lower level organizations. Teams formed as, or proclaiming to be, amateur sometimes included paid players, most often pitchers and catchers but the virus of professionalism often spread to additional position players quickly. Sometimes pay was in cash, other times it was hidden in a company payroll which carried players who supposedly had other jobs but whose real purpose was to promote the company by playing baseball. In the 1880s and 1890s the Solar Tips of Philadelphia began as a team of company employees, appear to have progressed to paying players and then returned to their amateur roots. They played against all levels of competition and showed well against all comers. No such team today could ever hope to test itself against the quality of competition the Solar Tips were able to face. ■

Notes

1. "John Mundell Has Passed Away," *Philadelphia Inquirer*, September 2, 1894.
2. *Philadelphia Inquirer*, July 23, 1884.
3. *Philadelphia Inquirer*, June 15, 1885.
4. *Philadelphia Inquirer*, May 31, 1888.
5. *Philadelphia Inquirer*, May 30, 1888.
6. *Philadelphia Inquirer*, June 19, 1888.
7. *Philadelphia Inquirer*, June 23, 1888.
8. *Philadelphia Inquirer*, July 6, 1888.
9. *Philadelphia Inquirer*, July 7, 1888.
10. *Philadelphia Inquirer*, July 24, 1888.
11. *Philadelphia Inquirer*, August 7, 1888.
12. *Philadelphia Inquirer*, August 10, 1888.
13. Sol White Introduction by Jerry Malloy, *Sol White's History of Colored Base Ball with other documents of the early Black game, 1886–1936.* (Lincoln, NB & London: University of Nebraska Press, 1995) p 161.
14. *Philadelphia Inquirer*, August 10, 1888.
15. *Philadelphia Inquirer*, April 17, 1889.
16. *Philadelphia Inquirer*, May 20, 1889.
17. *Philadelphia Inquirer*, March 22, 1889.
18. James Hampton Moore, *History of the Five O'clock Club of Philadelphia*, (published for private circulation, 1891). 268.
19. *Philadelphia Inquirer*, Mach 30, 1900.
20. *Philadelphia Inquirer*, February 3, 1901

Tuck Turner's Magical 1894 Phillies Season

Or, Whatever Happen to Tuck?

Peter Mancuso

Bill James observed and commented, "At the age of 21, Tuck Turner hit .416 and scored 91 runs in 80 games, he also drove in 82 runs. His career degenerated quickly after that. I can't remember that I ever read anything about him, and I have no idea what the story was."[1]

James was referring to George A. "Tuck" Turner a member of the National League and American Association for seven seasons (1893–98) and a utility outfielder for the Phillies for the first five of those big league seasons.

Turner was born on Staten Island on Cherry Lane, the same street his father George, a laborer, and mother, Caroline, a house keeper, had both been born.[2] Cherry Lane is in the West New Brighton community on the Island's north shore. According to every baseball reference until recent times, Tuck Turner was born there on February 13, 1873.

How Tuck Turner became a major leaguer and a member of the Philadelphia Phillies is an unusual story. Before joining the Phillies and appearing in his major league debut on August 18, 1893, Turner never played organized professional baseball, but he had played on some of the best amateur teams on Staten Island, and we know that he was on the island's best semi-pro team of his day, the West New Brighton Corinthians, and several other highly respected semi-pro clubs in the greater New York City area.

In 1892, and for the start of the 1893 season, Turner played on one of the very best of these semi-professional teams, the New York State Asylum team in Middletown, New York. Some of the players worked at the asylum and others came to play on the team; patients did not play. The Asylum team would also be a stopping off place in 1894 for pitching great Jack Chesbro en route to his hall-of-fame, major league career.

Before Turner's mid-August major league debut with the Phillies in 1893, he played for another excellent semi-pro team, the Plainfields of New Jersey.[3] Like the New York Asylum team, this team played against top competitors, including exhibition games with major and minor league teams, top college clubs and other semi-

pro organizations, including racially segregated African American teams like the great Cuban Giants.

In 1893, two other Staten Islanders were playing for the Philadelphia Phillies; both were from Turner's West New Brighton neighborhood. The first was right hand pitcher John "Brewery Jack" Taylor, who was in his first full season with the club, and who would, in just another year, become the Phillies' top ace for several seasons. Taylor would be traded from the Phillies to St. Louis after the conclusion of the 1897 season and then on to Cincinnati for one season before a tragically young death at age 26 in February 1900.

The other was former New York Giants pitcher, then Phillies utility player, Jack Sharrott. Sharrott had come to the attention of New York Giants' manager Jim Mutrie in early 1890 as Mutrie was in desperate straits to field a team as a result of the players' rebellion that particularly decimated the New York roster. Mutrie's "discovery" of Sharrott, who turned out to be a surprisingly good pitcher, is a story in itself, involving a mugging, a police intervention, a cop whose son was a pitcher, a tryout with the Giants, and a degree of entertaining speculation.

Sharrott had a brief, sometimes headline-grabbing, career as a Giants hurler before a base-sliding injury to his shoulder ended his days as a pitcher. He was a skilled enough athlete and hitter, however, to remain a Giant for another season before he was sent to the Phillies in 1893 in a high profile trade which included Giants future Hall of Famer Roger Connor.

It was in that season (1893) when Sharrott called to the attention of Phillies' manager Harry Wright the presence of a young guy from his neighborhood back on Staten Island. This young man, Tuck Turner, now had a chance to show his skills. Playing only semi-pro ball at the time, Turner was free to try out for the Phillies. Harry Wright liked what he saw and immediately signed Turner and inserted him into the Phillies line-up every chance he had for the remaining six weeks of the 1893 season. Turner played in 36 games with 155 at-bats, which resulted in a very impressive .323 batting average; not too shabby for a 20-year-old rookie.

In one of those ironies of baseball and life, it was Jack Sharrott's fate to be replaced on the Phillies' roster by the person he scouted, his old friend, Tuck Turner. Sharrott was cut from the team's roster shortly before opening day of the 1894 season, ending his four-year major league career. His departure, however, did not take place until the end of spring training and not before the taking of a team photo showing Turner and Sharrott (along with fellow Staten Islander Jack Taylor), causing endless confusion for modern researchers who do not understand how an 1894 Phillies team photo depicts all three players, while team records show Sharrott was not on the Phillies that year.

Although his major league career was over, Sharrott was an enterprising young man and remained attached to baseball for another two decades, mostly in the New England minor leagues. He even served on occasion as a baseball scout and signed a couple of players for the Detroit Tigers in the early twentieth century.

Not unnoticed by baseball historians, in 1893 (Turner's debut season) the pitching distance was moved back. The pitching rubber was set 60 feet, six inches from home plate, instead of the forward line of the old pitcher's box, 50 feet away. The new rule mandating that the pitcher keep a rear foot on this rubber slab resulted in a net difference of approximately four and a third feet further from the pitcher's new release point to the plate.

Today's observer might be shocked by the style of play in Tuck Turner's era. Legendary baseball analyst Bill James describes baseball of the 1890s as:

Dirty. Very, very dirty. The tactics of the eighties were aggressive; the tactics of the nineties were violent. The game of the eighties was crude; the game of the nineties was criminal…. Players spiked each other. A first baseman would grab the belt of a base-runner to hold him back a half-second after the ball was hit. Occasionally, players tripped one another as they rounded the bases. Fights broke out from day to day. Players shoved umpires, spat on them, and abused them in every manner short of assault. Fans hurled insults and beer bottles at the players of opposing teams.[4]

Imagine Tuck Turner, at five feet, six-and-one-half inches and 155 pounds out there in the rough and tumble baseball world of the 1890s, competing with the best of them. And, compete he did!

After his August 1893 debut, he appeared in 36 games with 155 at bats. In addition to his .323 BA, he hit four doubles, three triples, and one home run. He stole seven bases and struck out only 19 times, while driving in 13 runs and scoring 32. Not bad for a short season rookie.

There remained a problem for manager Wright: Turner was an outfielder, and not a very impressive defensive one but adequate enough given his lively bat. Wright had arguably the finest starting outfield in all of major league history: "Big Ed" Delahanty in left field, "Sliding Billy" Hamilton in center field, and "Big Sam" Thompson in right field. All three would eventually be inducted into the Baseball Hall of Fame and all three were at the prime of their careers in Philadelphia in the early and mid 1890s. Utilizing Turner as a Phillie, particularly as an outfielder, would be a challenge, but the opportunity would unexpectedly present itself the very next season.

After spring training in 1894, the Phillies were about to embark on the finest offensive season in major league history. The team's record-breaking collective season batting average of .350 has never been surpassed.[5] Leading the way in 1894, of course was that incredible Hall of Fame outfield: Delahanty, .404; Hamilton, .403 and Thompson, .415. Amazingly, however, Tuck Turner outdid all three of them, hitting .418.

In 1894, the Phillies would set the record for collective team batting average for a season at .350. Tuck Turner hit (back row, far right) .418, better than all three members of the "Hall of Fame" outfield, Ed Delahanty (.404), "Sliding Billy" Hamilton (.403), and "Big Sam" Thompson (.415).

COURTESY OF BOB MAYER

Turner's .418 was not just a pinch hitter's batting average. Due to injuries suffered by two of his outfield teammates, particularly Thompson (102 games) and Delahanty (116 games), Turner managed to play in 82 games and had 347 at bats.

From 1876 through 1920 the accepted standard for a player to qualify for the batting title was that a player had to appear in at least 60 percent of his team's scheduled games.[6] Tuck Turner met that standard in 1894. In that same season, however, Boston's Hugh Duffy of that city's National League team hit for the highest single season batting average in major league history, .440. This effectively gave Tuck Turner the first of his three major league records, the highest single season batting average not to win the league batting title.[7]

Unlike a streak, when a player grows hot for a few weeks or even a few months and attains an exceptionally high batting average over that one portion of the season, Turner's ability to hit at such a high level was sustained throughout the entire season, giving some savvy baseball observers reason to suspect that "park effect" might explain his level of sustained performance. That would be a reasonable speculation given that at the start of the 1895 season the Phillies moved into their new home field, Philadelphia Park (later known as Baker Bowl and the team's home field through 1938). However, SABR researcher Trent McCotter's paper, "The .400 Club," which is a comparative analysis of all .400+ season batting averages, puts the "park effect" theory to rest. One of McCotter's findings is that Turner achieved the highest on-road single season batting average in major league history, a sizzling .443.[8] This is the second of Turner's two records. As it turns out, there was no "park effect" in Philadelphia; it was all Turner, hitting at a record pace across 11 other major league cities.

Although outpaced by Duffy's .440, Turner ended up ninth on the all-time highest single season batting averages list.[9] He set a third record which is likely to remain unbroken. Turner's .418 season average is the highest single season average ever recorded by a switch hitter.[10]

In 2010 the Staten Island Sports Hall of Fame inducted Turner posthumously and installed a plaque honoring this native son. In considering the six inscriptions on that plaque, two of these career accomplishments deserve further comment:

"Hit .323, .416, .386 in first three seasons with 1890s Philadelphia Phillies" and "Had 11 straight multiple-hit games, third best all time."

Had there been a bigger plaque, two more inscriptions might have been included; one to give credit to his highest season average for a switch hitter and the

other for Turner's 12 consecutive games with at least one RBI, tying him with ten other players for eighth overall among all major leaguers.[11] There are only seven players above him on that RBI list.[12]

Although we may never know the full story of Tuck Turner's obviously short career, there is something we do know today about Tuck Turner that Bill James and everyone else before him didn't know; that is, when Tuck Turner hit .418 and scored and drove in all those runs in 1894 he was not a 21-year-old kid in his second big league season. He was actually 27 years old.

Turner had been practicing one of baseball's oldest traditions, lying about one's age. To all in the baseball world, Turner was born in 1873, when in reality he was born in 1867 making him a slightly less impressive 26-year-old freshman whose image was featured on the front page of *The Sporting News*.[13] Naturally, Turner's West New Brighton teammates knew he was considerably older than they were, but this was baseball, and the practice of presenting one's self as younger was so much a part of the game it was almost expected.

This tongue-in-cheek approach to lying about one's age, however, didn't keep Turner from giving up the charade after baseball. When he died on July 16, 1945, at his son's home in Staten Island it was even recorded on his death certificate that he was born on February 13, 1873, which would have made him 72.[14] His obituary in the local newspaper was even more lenient about his age, it was headlined "New Brighton Ex-Ballplayer Dies at 70."

Turner, however, was not going to mess with the US government. When the census taker visited the Turner household in 1900, 1910, 1920, and 1930, Turner told Uncle Sam his true age, which was always six years older than his baseball age. In addition, George Turner Sr., Tuck's father, not knowing in 1870 and 1880 that his son would be trying out for the Phillies in the future, reported in those years' censuses that his son George's ages were three and 13 respectively. Finally, we arrive at the Turner family plot in Oceanview (formerly Valhalla) Cemetery in Staten Island where he was laid to rest beside his wife Louise (Kiley) Turner, who predeceased him in 1942 (they had been married for 52 years). The family headstone is inscribed, "George Turner 1867–1945", making him 78 years old at the time of his death, which matches the census data.

Age was probably only part of the explanation of Turner's major league decline. Part of the story seems to be playing time. His outfield teammates were three future Hall of Famers. He was not going to replace any of those stars. And, even though the Phillies completed one of the worst trades in baseball history in 1896, sending Billy Hamilton to Boston, they did acquire (in a different deal) another future Hall of Famer, second baseman, Napoleon Lajoie, who as a rookie they used mostly at first base.

The final blow for Turner might have been his transfer to St. Louis, which in 1896 was "baseball hell." The National League and American Association Browns (later to be known as the Cardinals) were at the mercy of their megalomaniac owner, German beer baron Chris von der Ahe. Von der Ahe, who made, spent, and lost a fortune was, by 1896, the most erratic owner in all of baseball. His wife was suing him for divorce, his mistress was suing him for false promises, he had been "kidnapped" by agents of Pittsburgh Pirates owner Barney Dreyfus to stand trial for "kidnapping" Pirates pitcher Mark Baldwin, whom he tried to drag into State Court for breach of contract.

Von der Ahe, now cash strapped, was wheeling and dealing players like Monopoly properties. When Turner arrived in St. Louis, before he could put on a Browns' uniform, he immediately found himself in St. Paul, Minnesota, as a minor leaguer, another Von der Ahe deal.[15] He returned to St. Louis in time to play in 51 games, where he hit only .246. He followed up nicely, however, in 1897 with a .291 average, playing in 103 games. But, after a slow start in 1898, he was released after 35 games. He was now 31 years old, not very old, but not young by baseball standards.

Turner continued to play baseball in the minor leagues for another eight seasons, but never returned to the major leagues. His first year in the minors was in 1899 with Kansas City, of the top minor circuit Western League, which in 1900 would become the American League. From 1900 through 1906 Turner played in the competitive Eastern League, Connecticut State League, and New England League.

On July 16, 1905, Turner played in one of the finest displays of baseball in the era of racial segregation. Playing for his old Hoboken club, Turner accepted a challenge from the African American Philadelphia Giants and their great pitcher "Rube" Foster. Foster, a legendary pitcher in the early twentieth-century, later founded the Negro National League but on that July day in 1905, 38-year-old Tuck Turner had one of the only four hits that Foster allowed in a 2–1 Hoboken victory.[16]

With his playing career behind him in the first decade of the twentieth-century, Turner worked as a laborer in various locations throughout New York City. He and Louise and their two sons, who were separated by 22 years (Harry, born in 1892 and Wilfred [a.k.a. Charles] born in 1914), lived both in Manhattan and Brooklyn. In the early 1930s, due to Louise's declining health they returned to Staten Island and lived an almost invisible but idyllic life on a houseboat in a tidal estuary known as Lemon Creek on the island's eastern shore. By World War II, Tuck and Louise were living not far from his old neighborhood on Staten Island's north shore in the house of his now married younger son, Wilfred. With Louise's passing in 1942, Turner remained at his son's home where he died on July 16, 1945.

At the time of his death, Turner had not only survived his two Phillies Staten Island teammates, Jack Taylor (d. 1900) and Jack Sharrott (d. 1927) but he also survived all of Staten Island's 19th-century major leaguers: Dude Esterbrook (d. 1901), George Sharrott (d. 1932), Jack Cronin (d. 1929) and major league manager Jim Mutrie (d. 1938). Only Esterbrook and Mutrie were born before Turner. ∎

Notes

1. James, Bill, *The New Bill James Historical Baseball Abstract*, New York, *The Free Press*, 2001; 62.
2. Obituary of George A. Turner, *Staten Island Advance*, Staten Island, NY, July 17, 1945.
3. Mayer, Robert, email, Turner's minor league teams; unpublished; January 9, 2007. In 1893 Turner played for the Plainfield Club in the New Jersey League (*The Sporting News*, August 25, 1894) which was most likely the Central New Jersey League. On July 13 and August 16, the team traveled to Middletown where the Asylums defeated the club 10–7 and 17–8 with Turner playing in the first game against the Asylums. The Middletown newspaper report referred to the team as the Crescents of Plainfield. Turner also played in several games for the Asylum team that year. In 1904 and 1905, Turner played for Hoboken, and on September 29 played with the Asylum BBC in their reunion game against the Cuban X Giants with Chesbro pitching against Frank Grant and Clarence Williams. (Phil Dixon, *Phil Dixon's American Baseball Chronicles Great Teams: The 1905 Philadelphia Giants, Vol. 3*, (Charleston, SC: BookSurge, LLC 2006), 83, and Robert Mayer; email; unpublished, March 24, 2013).
4. James, *Bill James' Historical Baseball Abstract*, New York, Villard Books, 1998, 38.
5. Westcott, Richard and Bilovsky, Frank, *The Phillies Encyclopedia*, Philadelphia, Temple University Press, 2004, 17.
6. Daniels, John E., "Where Have You Gone, Carl Yastrzemski?: A Statistical Analysis of the Triple Crown," *The Baseball Research Journal*, vol. 37, Cleveland, SABR, 2008, 107.
7. Dewey, Donald and Acocella, Nicholas, *The Biographical History of Baseball, Chicago*, Triumph Books, 2002, 428.
8. McCotter, Trent, "The .400 Club," *The Baseball Research Journal*, Vol. 33, Charlton, Jim, Ed.; Cleveland, SABR; 2004; 64–70.
9. McCotter, Ibid.
10. McCotter, Ibid.
11. McCotter, "The .400 Club," Ibid.
12. McCotter, "Record RBI Streak Discovered," *Baseball Digest*, Vol. 67, No. 3, Ibid, May 2008, 62–64.
13. Image of George A. (Tuck) Turner, *The Sporting News*; August 25, 1894, 1.
14. Certificate of Death #1625, Borough of Richmond [Staten Island], Bureau of vital Statistics, Department of Health, City of New York, filed July 18, 1945.
15. *Brooklyn Eagle*, "Base Ball Notes," June 29, 1896, 5.
16. Dixon, Phil S., *Phil Dixon's American Baseball Chronicles Great Teams: The 1905 Philadelphia Giants, Vol. III*, Charleston, SC, Book Surge, LLC, 2006, 83.

Columbia Park II

Philadelphia American League: 1901–08

Ron Selter

Columbia Park was the second ballpark in Philadelphia to carry the name. The first Columbia Park had been used by the National Association Philadelphia Centennials for all of two months in 1875. Columbia Park II opened for baseball on April 26, 1901, as the first home park of the American League Philadelphia Athletics. The wooden ballpark had been quickly built before the start of the season on a vacant lot that had been leased for 10 years by the A's manager and part-owner Connie Mack. Columbia Park was built almost entirely of wood–only the front or street side of the main entrance was brick. Unlike many of the other Deadball Era wooden ballparks, this one never burned.

The park site consisted of an entire rectangular-shaped city block located in North Philadelphia. The ballpark site was bounded on the north by Columbia Avenue, on the south by Oxford Street, on the west by 30th Street, and on the east by 29th Street. The location of the ballpark was not far from downtown Philadelphia. The grandstand and home plate were located in the southwest corner of the park site. This park site, although consisting of the entirety of one city block, was not large: 400 (east-west) by 455 feet (north-south) and amounted to 4.2 acres. By comparison, other wooden Deadball Era major league ballparks occupied sites ranging from 3.9 acres (League Park III in Cleveland) to 9.6 acres (American League Park in New York). The 400 foot (east-west) dimension, along Oxford Street on the south and Columbia Avenue on the north, limited the extent of the ballpark's right field dimension.

For Opening Day 1901, the ballpark's seating areas consisted of a single-deck covered grandstand that extended from first base to third base, and sets of bleachers down both foul lines. Behind home plate, there was a short diagonal section of the grandstand that formed the backstop. On the roof of the grandstand were both a small press box and a wire screen on each side of the press box to try to keep foul balls from leaving the ballpark. There were short gaps between the grandstand and both sets of foul line bleachers. Both the first base and third base bleachers ran parallel to the foul lines—thus creating an ample amount of foul territory. The first base bleachers reached nearly to the right field corner, and the third base bleachers extended all the way to the left field perimeter fence on Columbia Avenue and then hooked around as far as the left field foul line to face home plate. There was a wire screen erected on top of the right field perimeter wall that was intended to keep home runs and foul balls from hitting vehicles in and possible pedestrians along 29th Street. As home plate was in the southwest corner of the park site, the left field line ran due north-south, and right field was thus the sun field for afternoon games. There was a modest-

View of Columbia Park from Deep Left Field

SABR BALLPARKS COMMITTEE COLLECTION

sized scoreboard in right-center field that was set into the right field-center field fence. There was one small clubhouse (for the use of only the home team), but no dugouts—the players sat on benches in front of the grandstand. On Opening Day 1901, Columbia Park had seating for 5,000 in the grandstand, and 4,500 in the bleachers, for a total of 9,500. Capacity was expanded by a small amount in 1903 by adding seats to the foul area first base bleachers.[1] Additional unspecified foul area expansion raised the seating capacity to 13,600 for the 1905 season. In the Deadball Era, capacity was an elastic concept. The all-time record attendance at Columbia Park—for a crucial game against the White Sox late in the 1905 season when 25,187 were in attendance—was far in excess of the park's seating capacity of 13,600.

The A's won two American League pennants playing at Columbia Park, but hosted only one World Series, in 1905 against the New York Giants. The A's other pennant was in 1902, a year before the American and National Leagues agreed to a post-season series. Columbia Park was also used by the National League Phillies for 16 games in 1903 while the Phillies home park (National League Park, later known as Baker Bowl) was temporarily under repairs after a portion of the stands tragically collapsed.

Columbia Park was abandoned after the 1908 season when the A's moved into the first of the Classic ballparks—Shibe Park. When the A's left, the park was used by a circus and for other events for several years before being demolished. The site is now a mixed commercial and residential area.

THE BASIS OF COLUMBIA PARK'S CONFIGURATIONS AND DIMENSIONS

No listed dimensions for Columbia Park were found in any of the usual ballpark reference books.[2,3] The 1901 dimensions: LF 340, CF 396, RF 280 (all dimensions are in feet), were derived entirely from a finely-detailed 1907 Philadelphia City Atlas.[4] This atlas provided the size of the park site, and the location and extent of the grandstand and bleachers. The foul lines were not shown. A diagram of the park and the dimensions of the park site were copied from the 1907 atlas. The details that were copied from the atlas included the location of the grandstand, bleachers, and the main entrance to the ballpark (located at the corner of 30th Street and Oxford Street). The location of home plate was based on photos of the park, and was estimated to have been 72 feet from the diagonal section of the grandstand that formed the backstop. Given the location of home plate, all of the outfield dimen-

sions were then calculated from the park diagram. Because the shape of the land plat was a rectangle and the foul lines were parallel to 29th Street, the outfield fences were aligned at 90 degrees to the foul lines in both left field and right field. Based on research into home runs at Columbia Park, it was found that there had been home runs hit over an interior fence in right field and right-center.[5] From the 1901 Opening Day photo in the Philadelphia Inquirer, this interior fence was quite close to the perimeter right-field wall and screen and included a modest sized scoreboard in right-center.[6] The right field screen was constructed of chicken wire and was an estimated 25 feet in height. The screen was mounted on top of the perimeter right-field wall. This screen, as it was erected on the exterior wall, located behind the interior fence, was out-of-play and extended all the way to the center-field corner.

In summary, all of the Columbia Park dimensions were estimated from the 1907 Philadelphia City Atlas. As neither the foul lines nor the home plate locations were shown in the atlas, these dimensions contain a small amount of uncertainty. All dimensions were checked against, and are consistent with, the available photographic evidence and the home run data. Park data and dimensions for Columbia Park are shown in Table 1.

THE IMPACT OF THE PARK'S CONFIGURATION AND DIMENSIONS ON BATTING

Columbia Park, in its limited lifetime of eight American League seasons (1901–08), was the smallest ballpark in the American League. Over the ballpark's eight major league seasons, Columbia Park was above average for batting average, on-base percentage, slugging percentage, and doubles. (See table below of Batting Park Factors.) In the 1902 season, the A's compiled a .322 home batting average (highest in the American League) at Columbia Park, while hitting only .249 on the road. This 73-point difference was the largest home/road differential in batting average for any team in the Deadball Era.

As the smallest American League ballpark, Columbia Park was a poor park for triples and inside-the-park home runs (IPHRs). There were only 4.25 IPHRs per season at Columbia Park while the average American League ballpark had more than twice that number per year in the 1901–08 seasons. At Columbia Park, the large majority of IPHRs were hit to CF, as that was the only deep part of the ballpark. Bounce home runs were rare–less than one per season because (1) the stands were not close to the foul lines (except in deep left field), and (2) the outfield fences were a minimum of

Table 1. Dimensions, Fence Heights, and Outfield Distances

Dimensions (All Calculated from Park Diagram)

Years	LF	SLF	LC	CF	RC	SRF	RF
1901–08	340	352	392	396*	323	290	280

LF: Left Field
SLF: Straightaway Left Field
LC: Left Center
CF: Center Field
RC: Right Center
SRF: Straightaway Right Field
RF: Right Field
* Deepest point in the ballpark was 440 at the CF corner located to the left of dead CF.

Fence Heights (Estimated from Photos)

Years	LF	CF	RF
1901–08	8	8–11*	8

* The 11 foot height was only the scoreboard in right-center field.

Average Outfield Distances

Years	LF	CF	RF
1901–08	358	385	295

Capacity: 9,500 (1901–02), 10,000 (1903–04 Est.), 13,600 (1905–08)
Park Size-Composite Average Outfield Distance: 346
Park Site Area: 4.2 acres
Deadball Era Run Factor: 108 (Rank: AL 5)

Table 2. Home Run Data and Batting Park Factors

Home Runs by Type at Columbia Park

Years	Total	OTF	Bounce	IP
1901–08	197*	163	5	34

Bounce: Bounce Home Runs
IP: Inside-the Park
OTF: Over-The-Fence (Includes Bounce)
* Includes four National League home runs in 1903.

Revised Data

OTF Home Runs by Field at Columbia Park (Excluding Bounce)

Years	Total	LF	CF	RF	Unknown
1901–08	158	47	21	80	2

Inside-the-Park Home Runs by Field at Columbia Park

Years	Total	LF	LC	CF	RC	RF	Unknown
1901–08	34	2	3	26	2	1	0

Batting Park Factors at Columbia Park

Years	BA	OBP	SLUG	2B*	3B*	HR*	BB**
1901–08	104	103	104	125	79	108	99

* Per AB
** Per Total Plate Appearance (AB+BB+HP)

eight feet in height. Of the five bounce home runs hit at Columbia Park, four were into the foul area third-base bleachers and one bounced over the interior fence in fair right field. The distribution of over-the-fence (OTF) home runs reflected the outfield dimensions. Left field (340 feet) had 47 OTF home runs, while right field (280 feet) had 80 OTF home runs. The batting Park Factor for home runs during the eight-year life of Columbia Park was only 108, a surprisingly modest value for the smallest ballpark in the American League and one with a composite average outfield distance of only 346 feet. This result occurred because while OTF home runs were relatively numerous with this small park size, there were not many IPHRs. Throughout the Deadball Era, and especially before the introduction of the cork-center ball, there was no relationship between park size and home runs. ∎

Notes

1. Bevis, Charlie. *Sunday Baseball* (Jefferson, NC, McFarland, 2003).
2. *Washington Post*, July 5, 1903.
3. Lowry, Philip J. *Green Cathedrals* (New York, Walker Publishing Company, 2006), 209; Gershman, Michael. *Diamonds: The Evolution of the Ballpark* (Boston: Houghton Mifflin, 1993), 247.
4. *Philadelphia City Atlas 20th and 29th Wards*, (Philadelphia PA, Elving Smith, 1907), Plate 1.
5. *Philadelphia Inquirer*, May 8, 1902; June 26, 1906; April 22, 1907.
6. *Philadelphia Inquirer*, April 27, 1901, "Panoramic View of the Opening Game of the American League Season at Columbia Park."

The Long Way to Philadelphia

The Strange Route Leading Rube Waddell To Join The Philadelphia Athletics

Joe Niese

George Edward "Rube" Waddell was an original oddball lefty, who could endear himself to fans, provide fodder for sportswriters, and alienate his teammates and manager. He was also immensely talented. Hijinks notwithstanding, he was the premier power pitcher in the opening decade of the 1900s. The enigmatic Waddell struggled during the first few years of his professional career though, and was lucky just to be a .500 pitcher. It was not until Connie Mack coerced him into coming to the Philadelphia Athletics in June 1902 that Waddell was finally able to harness his talents, becoming one of the first great left-handed pitchers the game had seen.

Born on a small farm on the outskirts of Bradford, Pennsylvania, Waddell's journey to Philadelphia began in August 1901, when he went missing from the National League Chicago Orphans.[1] His absence came as no surprise to many in the Chicago organization. After all, he had been obtained from Pittsburgh in May for a cigar after Pirates manager Fred Clarke marched into owner Barney Dreyfuss's office. "Sell him; release him, drop him off the Monongahela Bridge," ranted Clarke. "Do anything you like, so long as you get him the hell off my ball team!"[2]

In the few months he was in Chicago, Waddell often argued with his manager (Tom Loftus) and teammates, was clawed in the (right) arm by a lion at a sideshow, frequently showed up to games intoxicated, and often skipped practice to go fishing. As the last place team's only drawing card, Waddell's eccentricities were initially overlooked, but his output began to drop. He seemed to be bored with the game. Rumors swirled as to Rube's whereabouts. A lover of libations, it was said that he had quit to enter the saloon business. Some said that he would return to the team after tracking down a dog that had been shipped to him from St. Louis. Others sniffed a conspiracy, noting that Charles Comiskey was trying to lure him to Chicago's South Side to the White Sox. To stoke the flames, Waddell was seen on the roof of South Side Park taking in a ball game, while the Orphans were playing across town.

It soon became known that Waddell hadn't given up baseball after all. He was making the rounds in the town ball circuit, playing for teams in northern Illinois and southeastern Wisconsin. Although he was playing under the assumed name of Brown, Waddell was anything but inconspicuous. In one game, it was reported "every time Brown, alias Rube, came up to bat, he was wagering he could make a hit. Sometimes he won and oftener he didn't."[3] In another, Waddell ordered his infield to stand behind him at the mound. His teammates initially protested, but "Rube declared that if he did not have his way he would throw up the game right there as he was not accustomed to being disobeyed."[4] They finally conceded, watching Waddell strike out the next three batters. His bragging grew more audacious the next inning, when he ordered everyone but the catcher to sit on the bench. Once again, he struck out all three batters.

In early October, Waddell was in Kenosha, Wisconsin, playing for a team from nearby Burlington. He gave up four hits, but 13 errors led to an 11–5 Kenosha victory. Following the game, he decided he wanted to play for the Kenosha Athletics. All he had to do was play one more game for Burlington—against Kenosha. This time, Burlington prevailed with a 6–5 win, as Waddell "struck out seventeen batters and didn't exert himself to any great degree."[5]

It was apparent that Waddell had an affinity for Wisconsin. He first fell in love with the state in the summer of 1900, when he spent several weeks throwing for Connie Mack's Milwaukee Brewers of the newly named American League. It was Mack who sought out the talented, yet erratic Waddell, traveling to Pittsburgh to obtain Pirates owner Barney Dreyfuss's permission to pursue the lefty. Waddell was still under contract with the Pirates (whom he had pitched for earlier in the year), but was then playing for semipro teams in the Punxsutawney area. Waddell had been nothing but a headache for Dreyfuss and Pirates manger Fred Clarke. "Go ahead. We can't do anything with him—maybe you can," was the owner's response.[6]

In their initial contact, made by phone, Mack made the crucial error of calling Waddell "Rube" (he preferred to be called "Eddie"). The conversation was brief and ended with the pitcher saying he was staying put in Punxsutawney. For the next two weeks Mack sent Waddell daily telegrams and letters. Finally, Waddell wired Mack: "Come and get me."[7] The next morning Mack was in Punxsutawney. He woke Waddell and took him out to breakfast. They then went about town settling up Waddell's debts. Before noon Mack had spent nearly $100 on a bar tab, fishing gear, a dry goods store bill, a watch, and the shipping of a dog Rube had received. Finally, Mack began to worry that they were causing such a stir around town that someone might alert the local baseball club, so they retreated to a hotel. Finally, at 2:45, they headed for the train depot for the 3:00 train.

Mack and Waddell weren't at the platform for more than five minutes when a large group of men converged on them. They motioned Waddell over for a brief talk and then a man, who turned out to be the head of the local ball club, approached Mack.

"You Connie Mack, manager of Milwaukee?" asked the man gruffly.

"Yes," replied Mack. He was certain that they were there to talk Waddell out of leaving, and worried for his own safety.

"Well, I want to shake your hand," said the man, extending his hand to Mack. "My friends and myself have come down here to thank you. You are doing us a favor. Waddell is a great pitcher, but we feel that Punxsutawney will be better off without him."[8]

Mack was still trembling as they boarded the train.

Waddell immediately took to his surroundings in Wisconsin, especially the plentitude of fishing holes. Fishing was one of his favorite hobbies, and the one that he was least likely to injure himself doing, so he was encouraged to indulge. Indulge he did; spending every moment that he could doing so. He traveled all over the area, finding a favorite spot when he took the trolley to Pewaukee.

In just over a month's time, Waddell went 10–3, including throwing 22 innings in a doubleheader against the Chicago White Sox. After throwing 17 innings in the opening game, Waddell turned handsprings when he struck out the final batter. In between games Mack and White Sox owner Charles Comiskey decided to play an abbreviated 5-inning affair for the second game. Seeing Waddell showing no signs of being worn down, Mack approached the lefty about pitching Game 2. "Rube, how would you like to go to Pewaukee for a few days instead of going to Kansas City?" asked Mack. "Pitch the second game and win it for us and you can have a few days off, and can rejoin is in

Indianapolis."[9] Waddell took the ball and won the second game 1–0, allowing just one Chicago hit.

During his brief hiatus from the Brewers, Waddell was also able to partake in another hobby—fighting fires. On his way back to Milwaukee, word spread that a barn had been hit by lightning and was engulfed in flames. Waddell jumped off the trolley and headed for the smoke. Upon arrival, he found farmers standing around watching the $5,000 barn burn. Waddell snapped into action, rushing into the barn and hitching a piece of wire to a wagon. Salvaged from the fire were "forty head of stock, wagons, buggies, machinery and other things."[10] In the process Waddell badly burned his non-throwing hand.

When asked about what took place, Waddell responded nonchalantly. "I'm a peach at a fire. There is nothing I like better than to fight fires. I was a fireman for seven years at Pittsburgh. I'm glad I was able to help the old farmer out some."[11]

Shortly thereafter, Pirates owner Barney Dreyfuss heard about how well Waddell was performing, and recalled him to Pittsburgh. Despite finishing with an 8–13 record for the Pirates, his 2.37 ERA was tops in the National League.

With Waddell on the mound in 1901, the Kenosha Athletics made plans to play Appleton for the unofficial 1901 Wisconsin state title. The dream of a state championship was put on hold when the Appleton team asked to be released from their agreement to play. Their reason was that they were playing Racine in a three game series—for the state championship. Rube and the Athletics would have to wait two weeks before they would have their shot at a title.

In the meantime, Waddell immersed himself in happenings around Kenosha. He officiated boxing matches at the Kenosha Opera House and tended bar at the Grant Hotel (often in full uniform, including spikes). He had big plans for the future. Not only did he want to start a football team, but he was looking ahead to next year's baseball season. He proclaimed that he "planned to remain here for a year and that he would like to have a team here next year."[12]

While waiting for a shot at the Wisconsin state title, Waddell struck out 16 in a 7–2 defeat of the Chicago Spaldings, regarded as "the crack amateur team of the west."[13] Finally, after much back-and-forth, a date was set for the postponed game with Racine, which by then had defeated Appleton.

On the morning of October 20, Racine's Athletic Park filled up fast. Kenosha sent a dozen train cars, and by game time an estimated 5,000 packed into the grandstands, bleachers, and along the foul lines. Waddell's

CLEVELAND PUBLIC LIBRARY

Born on a small farm on the outskirts of Bradford, Pennsylvania, Waddell's journey to Philadelphia began in August 1901, when he went missing from the National League Chicago Orphans. (Pictured here during his time with the Los Angeles Looloos.)

mound opposition was Addie Joss, a Woodland, Wisconsin native who had gone 25–18 for the Toledo Swamp Angels of the Western Association.

Addie Joss and Rube Waddell could not have been more different. The spindly Joss was a former schoolteacher. Waddell was broad-shouldered and uneducated. What they had in common was that few people could throw a baseball like them. The game in Racine was the start of a long professional rivalry.

Joss had helped Racine win the three-game series from Appleton, but in the top of the first, he showed some nerves. The first three Kenosha batters reached base. Aided by a double play, Joss and Racine escaped unscathed. Waddell then showed his all-around game. After striking out the first three Racine batters in the bottom of the first, he drove in the first two runs of the game in the top of the second when he launched a deep fly ball over a bicycle track in right field. He could have had an easy inside-the-park home run, but loped into third base with a triple, giving Kenosha a 2–0 lead.

Neither team scored in the next two innings. Waddell struck out each of the batters he faced, giving him nine straight to start the game. Racine took advantage of Waddell's wildness (he walked five in the game) and four errors by Kenosha's second baseman. The result was four unearned runs—one each in the fourth, fifth, sixth and eighth.

After eight innings, Waddell had struck out 19, yet his team trailed 4–2. Still, he had a chance to win the game in the top of the ninth, when he came to the plate with two out and runners on first and second. He overswung at all three of Joss's offerings. According to Joss biographer Scott Longert, when the final out of the 4–2 Racine victory was recorded, "Delirious rooters dashed en masse out of the grandstand, hoisted Addie on their collective shoulders, and carried him around the park on a jubilant victory lap."[14] Longert called it called it "probably the greatest semi-pro game ever staged in Wisconsin, and one of the greatest played anywhere."[15] Joss called it, "One of the greatest games I ever pitched in my life."[16]

The next weekend found Waddell on the gridiron for the Kenosha Regulars football team. A bruising fullback, he scored the only touchdown of the game, an 80-yard scamper, in a 10–0 defeat of a team from Chicago.

A week later Waddell was found living in Racine and tending bar at Sugden's saloon and billiards room. He gave no reason for his move from Kenosha other than "Tisn't what it's cracked up to be down there."[17] Once again, Waddell had long-term plans to settle in Racine. He went about forming a football team and talked about plans for the next summer's baseball team. A few weeks later it seemed his plans had changed. The football team he put together disbanded. By December, all that remained of Waddell in Racine were his clothes at the Drexel Hotel. He had headed to the warm weather of California to play baseball on a major league barnstorming tour set up by Joe Cantillon.

Cantillon, who had umpired in the American League during the 1901 season, got the idea to take two teams made up of players from each league (All-Americans and All-Nationals) on an ambitious 76-game schedule. They started "in Chicago on October 12 and soon moved across the country—meeting, for example in Louisville, Denver, Albuquerque, and Las Vegas—before arriving on the West Coast."[18] There was even talk of playing games in Honolulu.

Problems arose for Cantillon when the Boston Americans' Cy Young, their primary pitcher, dropped

NATIONAL BASEBALL HALL OF FAME LIBRARY, COOPERSTOWN, NY

It was not until Connie Mack coerced him into coming to the Philadelphia Athletics in June 1902 that Waddell was finally able to harness his talents, becoming one of the first great left-handed pitchers the game had seen.

out before the team headed west. The promoter scrambled to find a replacement, before cajoling Waddell, who was more than happy to see himself out of the situation he had created in Wisconsin. It didn't take Waddell long to make an impression. As in most places he went, Waddell wowed locals with his baseball prowess. At Recreation Park in San Francisco, he won a game for the All-Americans with a long home run to center field.

Waddell did little wrong during the trip and was courted by all four teams in the California League. When the rest of the barnstormers returned east, Waddell stayed in the Bay Area. Unable to make up his mind, he agreed to terms with three of the league's four teams: the Oakland Mud Hens, the Sacramento Mosquitos, the San Francisco Has Beens, and the Los Angeles Looloos. All three wanted him in camp immediately, so Waddell "told the three club owners to shake the dice for him."[19] Los Angeles won, so he headed south.

Waddell was an instant fan favorite for the Looloos. Barely a month into the season, he established the league's single-season strikeout record. He loved batting and was ecstatic to play the outfield or first base when he wasn't pitching. In Oakland, he was rewarded for hitting the first home run of the season at Freeman's Park with "several prizes in the way of shoes, clothes, and many other articles donated by charitable shopkeepers, who like to see the ball-tossers dress like members of the swagger set."[20]

Of course, it wasn't all baseball for Waddell. Beyond frequenting the local taverns and fishing holes, he was able to partake in another of his endless hobbies, boxing. Before a game in Oakland, he sparred with heavyweight champion Jim Jeffries. As with most everything, Waddell was good at it. He was described as having a "stiff punch and a block that is said to be a wonder."[21]

Waddell was also able to show his firefighting prowess. During another game in Oakland, a mattress that was being used as a backstop caught fire. The fans and players scattered, and Freeman Park's wooden bleachers looked as if they would burn to the ground. Waddell swooped into action. "He ran over and tore the burning mattress from its moorings and plopped it on the field, where it burned harmlessly."[22]

Word of Waddell's on-field success reached the east. One day, Connie Mack, now manager of the Philadelphia Athletics, was lamenting the state of his pitching staff to umpire Jack Sheridan.

"Why don't you get Waddell back?" replied Sheridan. "He's pitching in San Francisco."[23]

Mack tracked down Waddell and invited him to join the Athletics, then in their second year of existence. The two worked out an agreement. Mack sent Waddell $100 and a train ticket, but the pitcher never arrived. The Philadelphia manager wasn't alone in being stood up. The same thing happened to Fred Clarke, the manager of the Pittsburgh Pirates, who also tried to woo Waddell.

While in Chicago, Mack was approached by a man who had some firsthand information about Waddell.

"I saw him get on the train at Los Angeles. Some men got on after him and talked to him for about ten minutes. He started to cry and I heard him say 'I never did want to leave you, you have been so good to me,' and he got off the train."[24]

Immediately, Mack went to Ban Johnson, American League president, whose office was in Chicago. After hearing the story, Johnson took Mack to the nearby Pinkerton Detective Agency. There, a plan was hatched for detectives to track down Waddell in San

Francisco, where the Looloos were playing, advance him $200, and bring him to Kansas City. From there, Mack would personally escort Waddell to Baltimore, where Philadelphia was scheduled to play next. Things didn't go as planned.

The Pinkerton detectives found Waddell in his hotel room in San Francisco, despondent over a loss earlier that day. He gave little resistance. They traveled without incident to Kansas City, where the detectives ran into a problem. It was there Waddell met boxer William Rothwell, known as Young Corbett II. Rothwell had just defeated Terry McGovern for the featherweight title. Waddell became enamored with the newly crowned champion. He wanted to impress Rothwell, so Waddell decided to seek out one of the two Kansas City teams to pitch for in the coming days. Both would have gladly snatched up a talent like Waddell. The detectives called Mack and told him to come to Kansas City immediately.

When Mack arrived in Kansas City, Waddell refused to come with him, insisting on going to the park.

"I agreed to take him to the park and he came along with his $1 suitcase and $40 fishing outfit," recalled Mack. "I don't know how I did it, but I talked Rube out of pitching that day and got him on the train for Baltimore before anyone could grab him."[25]

Mack and Waddell arrived in Baltimore on the morning of June 26. Waddell implored Mack to let him pitch later that day. Initially, Mack refused, wanting Waddell to become acclimated, but finally, he gave in.

John McGraw was player/manger for the Baltimore Orioles. Having faced Waddell previously, he knew one of the few ways to beat him was to be in his head. From the Baltimore bench, McGraw jockeyed him relentlessly, agitating the big lefty. In addition, Philadelphia catcher Mike "Doc" Powers had trouble catching Waddell's hard breaking pitches. Consequently, Baltimore won 7–3.

That same year, McGraw played a role in the Athletics franchise. In mid-season, he left the Orioles and the American League to manage the National League's New York Giants. Speaking to a reporter about how much money the Athletics were losing, he said that Ben Shibe had "a big white elephant on [his] hands." Mack, who had a good sense of humor, immediately ordered a white elephant to appear on all Athletics' gear and apparel.[26] To this day, it remains emblematic of the team, now based in Oakland.

The magic of Rube Waddell in an Athletics uniform began on July 1 at Philadelphia's Columbia Park against Baltimore. Mack inserted catcher Ossee Schrecongost, whom he had recently signed as a free agent from the Cleveland Bronchos.[27] The pitcher and catcher tandem became instant friends—not an easy thing for Waddell to manage. "They were roommates, drinking buddies, hunting and fishing pals, general partners in crime."[28]

Waddell and "Schreck's" first game together was near perfection. In the second inning, Orioles right fielder Cy Seymour dribbled one past third baseman Lave Cross. On the next pitch, Seymour bluffed a steal. Still in his crouch, Schreck fired a perfect throw to first baseman Harry Davis, who slapped on a tag for the out. In the next inning Waddell set down the Orioles batters on nine pitches, his first documented "perfect inning."

In the fifth inning, Baltimore's Wilbert Robinson singled with one out. Trailing 1–0, McGraw, desperate to put a runner in scoring position, sent the 38-year-old catcher on a steal. It wasn't even close at second base.

In the sixth and eighth innings, Waddell struck out the side. In the bottom of the seventh, he had added an insurance run with a booming double. When he took the mound in the top of the ninth, Waddell gave the crowd a playful wave, yelling "It's all over, go on home."[29] He struck out the final three batters, giving him 13 for the game, in facing the minimum 27 batters. Many of the 2,500 in attendance rushed the field and hoisted him onto their shoulders, parading him around the ballpark.

In just over three months with Philadelphia, Waddell amassed a 24–7 record. His 2.05 ERA and league-leading 210 strikeouts helped Mack's Athletics to an 83–53 record, and the 1902 American League pennant (the World Series was one year away from being re-established).

Over the years, the line between fact and fiction has blurred. Waddell's bizarre antics overshadowed his abundant skills. Waddell's tenure in Philadelphia was mind-boggling. In six seasons he amassed 131 wins, including four straight 20-win seasons (24, 21, 25, and 27). He led the American League in strikeouts in all six years, and the major leagues in the last five (including an astonishing 349 in 1904, still an American League record).

Befittingly, Waddell was never the same after he suffered a serious shoulder injury when trying to punch a hole through a teammate's straw hat in September 1905.[30] He won 15 and 19 games over the next two years (and his last two strikeout titles), before being purchased by the St. Louis Browns in February 1908. He won 19, 11, and three over the next 2½ years in St. Louis, before spending parts of the next four seasons in the minor leagues.[31] In early 1913, he contracted pneumonia after spending hours stacking sandbags in icy waters in flood-ravaged Hickman, Kentucky, where he was living with Joe Cantillon. The pneumonia proved to be a symptom of tuberculosis which lead to his death on April 1, 1914, in a San Antonio sanitarium. ■

Notes

1. The franchise became the Chicago Cubs in 1902.
2. Alan H. Levy. *Rube Waddell: the Zany, Brilliant Life of a Strikeout Artist* (Jefferson, NC: McFarland and Company, Inc. Publishers, 2000), 77.
3. *The Daily Northwestern* (Oshkosh, WI), September 6, 1901, 8.
4. *The Decatur Review* (Decatur, IA), September 20, 1901, 5.
5. *Kenosha Evening News* (Kenosha, WI), October 7, 1901, 1.
6. *The Sporting News* (St. Louis, MO), November 19, 1942, 4.
7. Ibid.
8. Ibid.
9. Fred Lieb. *The Pittsburgh Pirates* (Carbondale, IL: Southern Illinois University Press, 2003), 71.
10. *Milwaukee Sentinel* (Milwaukee, WI), August 22, 1900, 7.
11. Ibid.
12. *Kenosha Evening News* (Kenosha, WI), October 4, 1901, 1.
13. Ibid.
14. Scott Longert. *Addie Joss: King of the Pitchers* (Cleveland, OH: The Society for American Baseball Research, 1998), 33.
15. Ibid.
16. *The Toledo News-Bee* (Toledo, OH), August 22, 1905, 7.
17. *The Racine Daily Journal* (Racine, WI), November 8, 1901, 8.
18. Thomas Barthel. *Baseball Barnstorming and Exhibition Games, 1901–1962* (Jefferson, NC: McFarland and Company, Inc. Publishers, 2007), 27.
19. Levy, 95.
20. *The San Francisco Call* (San Francisco, CA), June 19, 1902, 4
21. *The San Francisco Call* (San Francisco, CA), May 10, 1902, 4
22. Levy, 96–97.
23. *The Sporting News* (St. Louis, MO), November 19, 1942, 4
24. Ibid.
25. *The Sporting News* (St. Louis, MO), November 19, 1942, 10
26. Charles C. Alexander. *John McGraw* (New York, NY: The Viking Press, 1988), 91.
27. The Cleveland American League franchise has used the nicknames Blues (1901), Bronchos (1902–1904), and Naps (1905–1914).
28. Levy, 104.
29. Ibid.
30. It was ritual for any ballplayer that saw a teammate wearing a straw hat after Labor Day to nab it off the offender's head and break it. When Waddell saw fellow pitcher Andy Coakley show up at the train station with one, Rube saw an opportunity to have some fun. Coakley tried to conceal the hat, but Waddell would not let that stand in the way. Trying to avoid the charging Waddell, Coakley tossed his bag at Waddell. In the bag was Coackley's spikes, which hit Waddell in the chin. Waddell's jovial mood turned to anger. It took several teammates to restrain Waddell from pulverizing the shocked Coakley. In the process, the peace-keeping scrum stumbled over a suitcase, with all the weight coming down on Waddell's left shoulder. That night, he rode the train with his left arm hanging out the window, taking in a stiff breeze. A few days later he could not raise it above his shoulder. The zip never returned to his fastball, or the snap to his curve.

Sources–Newspapers

The Daily Northwestern (Oshkosh, WI)
The Decatur Review (Decatur, IA)
Kenosha Evening News (Kenosha, WI)
Milwaukee Sentinel (Milwaukee, WI)

The Strangest Month in the Strange Career of Rube Waddell

Steven A. King

Hugh Fullerton has a theory regarding left-handed pitchers that their left arms affect their hearts and that affects their brain which is why they're all eccentric. Waddell is, of course, the synonym for eccentricity in baseball.

— *Cleveland Plain Dealer*, January 21, 1906

One controversial aspect of Rube Waddell's career, while he was still playing and a century later, is what happened during the last month of the 1905 season that resulted in his missing the World Series. This was the first played by Philadelphia and would be his one opportunity to pitch on the grand stage.

A story has been told about a bit of horseplay when Waddell tried to destroy the straw hat worn by Philadelphia Athletics teammate Andy Coakley at the train station in Providence, Rhode Island, on September 8, 1905, resulting in Rube injuring his shoulder, causing him to miss most of the last month of the regular season, and the whole World Series versus the New York Giants.

Whether Waddell was actually injured as he claimed, or was bribed to fake an injury, has remained at the core of the controversy. Biographies of Waddell and Connie Mack, his manager, have described it, and it has even been the subject of a mock trial staged at the National Baseball Hall of Fame in 2008.[1] A majority of those who voted on the verdict in this trial acquitted Waddell of the charge of bribery and faking the injury and most writers on the subject have generally taken a similarly sympathetic view.

However, by returning to the newspapers of the period, it is apparent that important evidence has been overlooked that may offer a different view of Waddell and what occurred in 1905. This may burst many of the widely held myths about what is supposed to have happened.

RUBE WADDELL BEFORE SEPTEMBER 8, 1905

Before discussing the final month of the 1905 season, it is useful to review his career.

By 1905 Waddell had established himself as one of the finest pitchers in baseball in the eyes of most observers, second only to Christy Mathewson in terms of greatness. From the time he made his debut with the Athletics at the end of June 1902, he dominated American League hitters. He led the league in strikeouts in 1902 and 1903 and in 1904 he struck out 349 hitters, a post-1900 major league record that lasted until broken by Sandy Koufax 61 years later.[2]

Although his strikeout total declined to a league-leading 287 in 1905, that season is generally considered the greatest of his career. He won the AL pitching triple crown. Along with Eddie Plank, he was one of the Athletics' two most important starting pitchers and also the team's top relief pitcher.[3]

Although Waddell's pitching skills were apparent from the time he reached the major leagues, he was always a difficult person to handle. First the Louisville-Pittsburgh combination, and then the Chicago team of the National League gave up on him because of his behavior and undependability. Connie Mack, for whom Waddell had pitched in the then minor league American League in 1900, was willing to take another chance on him in 1902 and, for at least a few seasons, was able to tame Waddell's behavior to a certain degree.

Mack was willing to put up with Waddell's antics that he would not have tolerated in any other player because of his pitching greatness and his ability to bring fans to ball parks. In 1911 Alfred Spink, the founder of *The Sporting News*, described Waddell as the greatest crowd draw in baseball history.[4]

However, even Mack could not always control Waddell. In 1903, Mack suspended him for the last month of the season for missing practice and pitching for semipro teams. Mack would attribute the Athletics' failure to win the AL pennant that year and missing the chance to play in the World Series to Waddell's absence.[5]

Throughout most of the 1905 season, Waddell generally behaved himself. He had an incentive to do so because that season he was under indictment for assault with a deadly weapon.

During the winter of 1904–1905, Waddell lived

with his wife's parents in Peabody, Massachusetts (although, curiously, his wife was living with friends in nearby Lynn). Waddell did little work during that period, preferring to spend his time telling stories about his baseball feats to the locals at a general store. He did receive adulation for putting out a potentially dangerous fire.[6]

One night in February, Waddell returned to his in-laws' home and announced he was leaving. Newspaper stories of the time indicate that he had been drinking heavily during the previous few days and suggest that he was drunk that night. When his father-in-law inquired about the money for board that he felt Rube owed him, Waddell took a flat iron and beat the man about the head, knocking out several of his teeth. When his mother-in-law tried to intervene, he beat her over the head with a chair. The only family member who managed any blows against him was his in-laws' Newfoundland dog who sunk his teeth into Rube's pitching arm before he punched the animal, causing it to release him from its grasp. Waddell realized that he was in trouble, and almost immediately grabbed a train out of town before a warrant could be issued for his arrest. He did not stop running until he made it back to Philadelphia.[7]

Initially, there was concern that if he tried to play in Boston once the season began he would be arrested, but it appears that some arrangement was made whereby any legal proceedings would be held in abeyance until the end of the season, and he pitched there several times in 1905 without hindrance from the law.[8]

Although most descriptions of the 1905 season indicate that Waddell's trouble began on the train platform on September 8, there were earlier signs that his behavior was again problematic.

In St. Louis in late August, Waddell, after spending the night at an amusement park, showed up at 1AM, knocking on Connie Mack's hotel door. When the manager opened it, he found Rube standing there offering him what was called a "pazzazza" sandwich, consisting of limburger cheese and stale onions. Not surprisingly, Mack turned down the offer and went back to bed.[9] Stories of the incident either implied or stated that Waddell had been drinking.[10]

From then on, Mack kept a close eye on Waddell, taking the berth below Rube's on the Pullman car when they were traveling, and the adjacent room at hotels.[11] Mack also appointed the team's trainer, Frank Newhouse, to be what the newspapers described as Rube's "keeper."[12] Newhouse had been appointed as trainer on the recommendation of Waddell, whom he

had befriended when they met on the train when Rube came east from California to join the Athletics in 1902.[13] Newhouse's job to keep Waddell out of trouble meant keeping him from drinking and thwarting attempts to keep him from pitching.

For the rest of the season, Mack gave Newhouse Waddell's per diem travel money, requiring Rube to ask Newhouse to pay for anything Rube wished to purchase. Waddell made attempts to ditch Newhouse. While the Athletics were playing in Detroit, Mack gave Waddell time off to go fishing, which according to the manager was (along with drinking) the thing he loved most.[14] Waddell tried to take off without Newhouse knowing it. However Newhouse tracked him down and visited as many places as he could in the area that served alcohol to warn them that Waddell had no money and therefore not to serve him. One hotel did serve Rube beer. When Newhouse found him there, Waddell told the owner to obtain the 30 cents he owed from Newhouse, who refused to pay, resulting in a fist fight that Newhouse, a former fighter, won.[15]

Mack may have also been sending a message to Waddell in his treatment of Waddell's friend, roommate, and favorite catcher, Ossee Schrecongost, whose last name was usually shortened in newspaper stories and box scores to "Schreck." When, at the end of August, Schreck was in no condition to catch after a drinking binge, Mack decided to suspend him. It was only when the other players, knowing that Waddell did his best work with Schreck, begged Mack to change his mind that Mack relented.[16]

Despite his problematic behavior, Waddell continued to pitch well. On September 5 in Boston, he threw one of the best games of his career. He extended his scoreless inning streak to 43⅔, and carried a one-hitter into the ninth inning before giving up two runs to tie the score. He ended up losing 3–2 in 13 innings, giving up three hits and eight walks while recording 17 strikeouts. (Cy Young was scheduled to oppose him but sat out due to a sore arm.)

Waddell next pitched on the day he was supposed to have been injured in his scuffle with Andy Coakley, September 8. Coakley had pitched and won the day before. He had been given permission by Connie Mack to spend that night and the next day with his family in Providence, Rhode Island, and to join the team when its train stopped there on its return to Philadelphia after the game.

WHAT HAPPENED ON SEPTEMBER 8, 1905

Virtually all discussions of Waddell and September 8, 1905, have focused on the purported incident with

Coakley. However, another key event in the story, what occurred in the game against Boston that day, has largely been ignored. Biographies of Waddell and Connie Mack and most baseball histories either do not mention it at all, or note it only in passing.[17]

Waddell started opposite Cy Young, and set Boston down in order in the first inning. In the Boston second, Jimmy Collins led off with a double, followed by a home run by Kip Selbach that went over the head of center fielder Danny Hoffman and rolled to the fence. Waddell appeared to recover, striking out Moose Grimshaw. Hobe Ferris followed with a single that most newspapers attributed to miscommunication between second baseman Danny Murphy and right fielder Socks Seybold.[18] Lou Criger then flied to center and Young struck out, ending the inning.

What happened next is a matter of controversy. It is certain that Waddell was pinch hit for in the top of the third, but why this occurred remains unclear. Most newspaper coverage of the game did not immediately offer any specific explanation for Waddell's removal, choosing to instead focus on Jimmy Dygert's excellent major league debut in relief. The next day, the *Philadelphia Inquirer* reported that Waddell had "demonstrated that he was not himself." Horace Fogel of the *Philadelphia Evening Telegraph* briefly discussed what had happened, reporting that Waddell "had one of those off days which all pitchers have occasionally. He felt good but for some inexplicable reason could not reach any speed in practice" and that catcher Schreck had noted the problem, but that Waddell thought once he warmed up, he would be all right.[19]

Several newspapers subsequently published stories that he was relieved in the September 8 game due to a sore arm.[20] Of course, this raises the question: if he already had a sore arm in that game, then how could he have developed it after the purported struggle with Coakley?

There was some difference of opinion as to whether Connie Mack took Rube out of the game or if Waddell removed himself. Newspapers did agree that after he left the game, instead of joining his teammates on the Philadelphia bench, or going to the clubhouse, Waddell sat in the bleachers. This behavior appeared curious even for Waddell. At least one newspaper attributed it to "being ashamed of being knocked out of the box," certainly a strange explanation considering that Waddell was never noted for either being introspective about or ashamed of any of his behavior, no matter how bizarre, at any time in his life.[21]

Some newspapers did comment that it was unusual for Waddell not to finish a game. The *Philadelphia Inquirer* noted the following day, "That Waddell, the man who always stood by in the hour of distress ready and willing to step into the breech [sic] after others have failed, should himself feel the need of succor is one of the rare incidences of the national pastime."

It was certainly "rare" for Waddell to be taken out of a game he started in 1905. Until that game, he had finished all but five of his starts:

- Against Boston on July 7, he was struck in his pitching hand in the seventh by a ball off the bat of Freddy Parent. He completed the inning and started the eighth, but swelling in his hand prevented him from continuing and he was relieved.
- In his next start on July13, he appeared to still suffer from the effects of this injury. Although he gave up four runs in the first inning, Connie Mack did not take him out until the fifth, when he gave up two hits and a walk.
- On August 11 against Cleveland, Mack relieved him in the middle of the sixth inning while losing 5–3.
- On August 20 against St. Louis, Waddell went to field a bunt by Tom Jones. As he bent down, Jones ran into him, hitting Rube behind the ear with his knee and knocking him out.

Even when Waddell appeared to be on the ropes early in a game, Connie Mack always gave him the chance to right himself as in the game on July 13. On August 2 against Chicago, Waddell gave up four walks and a hit and hit a batter in the first inning, resulting in three runs. He proceeded to strike out the next three batters and went on to a complete game victory to put the Athletics in first place.

The most famous example of Mack's patience with Waddell that year occurred in the second game of the July 4 doubleheader versus Boston when he gave up four hits and two runs in the first inning. Waddell settled down and pitched all 19 shutout innings, beating Cy Young, who also threw a complete game. Each would subsequently describe this as the greatest game of their careers.[22]

If it was Mack's decision to remove Waddell from the September 8 game, he would seem to have been taking a risk. Chief Bender, who together with Waddell, handled most of the relief duties for the Athletics that season, was ill, leaving the manager limited options. Mack turned to Jimmy Dygert, a spitballer who had joined the team on August 31 from New Orleans of the Southern Association, and had yet to pitch in the majors.[23] Dygert gave up one run against Boston the rest of the game, and beat Cy Young in what would be his only win for the Athletics that season.

THE FIGHT WITH COAKLEY: FACT OR FICTION?

The story of Waddell's fight with Andy Coakley over his straw hat has become widely accepted. There is much to suggest that it never happened.

Even before the alleged incident on September 8, there were suggestions that attempts might be made to keep Waddell from pitching in the World Series. An article in the September 2, 1905, issue of *The Sporting News* by a Philadelphia correspondent writing under the name "Veteran," reported a story from someone described as a gambler and friend of John McGraw, the manager of the New York Giants, that if the Athletics won the pennant, friends of McGraw would finance a fishing trip for Waddell that would last until the end of the series, causing Waddell to miss it.[24]

Skepticism about the straw hat story is supported by the prominent identities of the reporters who expressed doubt about its veracity. Although Joseph Vila of the *New York Sun* is often credited as most vocal in doubting the story and raising the possibility that Waddell may have been bribed, in reality Horace Fogel of the *Philadelphia Evening Telegraph* and Charles Dryden of the *Philadelphia North American* were the most vociferous. Fogel and Dryden were traveling with the Athletics, and would have had first hand knowledge if a fight had occurred.[25]

Dryden and Fogel were also the first to report the straw hat incident. Dryden, in the *Philadelphia North American* of September 10, in explaining why Waddell had been unable to relieve Bender in the second game of a double header when the Philadelphia fans had called for Rube, wrote: "In a straw hat smoking tournament on the way here from Boston the noble southpaw jammed his pitching shoulder." Fogel would fill in some details in the *Philadelphia Evening Telegraph* on September 13. In this initial telling, the event occurred on the platform at the Providence train station when Waddell tried to grab Coakley's hat and bumped his shoulder against the side of the train.

Both Fogel and Dryden began to express doubt about the story when they accompanied the Athletics to New York for a three-game series on September 19–20 and found its gambling and sporting circles awash with stories that arrangements had been made to ensure that Waddell would not pitch in the World Series. Bets were being taken on his not pitching.[26]

In a September 20 article in the *Philadelphia Evening Telegraph*, Fogel wrote that Mack and most of the Athletic players "are beginning to feel a bit dubious about there being much if anything the matter with Waddell's shoulder." The next day, devoting virtually his whole column to it, he stated that Mack had never believed the Coakley fight story. That New York men without any apparent inside knowledge of Waddell's health could be so certain that he would not be able to pitch in the World Series was especially unsettling to Fogel.

Waddell wrote a response to Fogel that was published in the *Evening Telegraph* on September 22, stating that his shoulder was injured, and emphatically denying that he had been bribed.[27] Fogel expressed appreciation for Waddell's willingness to address the rumors, but noted that Rube held the key to terminating them; all he had to do was to start pitching again. Mack did at least publicly defend Waddell and stated his belief in the straw hat fight story and that Waddell had perspired as a result of it and "caught a cold" in his shoulder.[28]

What also troubled both Fogel and Dryden was that details of the incident with Coakley varied from telling to telling. In some, it was in the train station in Providence, in others, on the platform or on the train. Dryden even noted that some reports placed it in the station at New London, Connecticut rather than Providence.[29]

Even more disconcerting was that they were unable to find any of the Athletics or apparently anyone else who reported witnessing a fight that supposedly had occurred in a public place. And, although Waddell stated that it had happened, there is no record of the one other person who could have verified it, Coakley himself, making any statement at the time. In fact he made no public comment at all about it until almost 40 years later when, in 1943, he did so in response to a letter from J.G. Taylor Spink, the publisher of *The Sporting News*, who was writing a series of articles on Rube Waddell, asking about the incident.[30]

Spink could have saved the effort as Coakley's rendition of the event was essentially the same as that provided by Connie Mack in his syndicated memoir *My Fifty Years in Baseball*, published in 1930, and in an article he published on his relationship with Waddell in the *Saturday Evening Post* in 1936.[31]

Nowhere in contemporary accounts or in either of these remembrances did Mack explain why Waddell was removed from the game of September 8. Mack noted in the 1936 article that some reporters thought that he might have been behind creating a phony story so Waddell could sit out until the World Series to "throw the Giants off guard," but denied there was any truth to this or to the rumors that gamblers had gotten to Waddell.

If Coakley lied in his response to Spink, he would certainly have had good reason. If he had given a significantly different story from Mack's, he would have appeared to be accusing his former manager, who by 1943, was already considered the grand old man of baseball, of either being unaware of what was going on with his team, or of participating in a cover-up of a possible bribe.

Also, if Coakley had admitted to knowledge of such a cover-up, he might have faced his own problems. Kennesaw Mountain Landis was still the commissioner of baseball at the time, and anyone closely associated with the game would have been well aware of his banning of Buck Weaver from organized ball for life for not reporting knowledge of the 1919 World Series game fixing, although there was no evidence Weaver had participated in it. When he replied to Spink, Coakley was already 60 years old and was not going to play again, but he was the baseball coach at Columbia University (where he coached for another nine years before retiring after 37 seasons), and had an insurance business that might have also suffered.[32]

Perhaps the most suspicious of all events occurred at the end of September. By then, Mack had publicly stated that he had become disgusted with Waddell who, instead of taking care of himself, was spending most of his time drinking. Determining that Waddell was no longer of any benefit to the team that season, Mack informed him: "I won't need you anymore Rube. You can spend the rest of the season among the breweries or any where you want."[33]

Within one to two days, Waddell suddenly announced that while he was shaving, he had heard something click in his left shoulder, and he was able to move it freely without any pain. He immediately rushed to the Athletics' ball park to convey the good news, bringing his wife with him so she could confirm that she had also heard the click.[34]

Despite the reports that Waddell had regained his health, Mack remained skeptical. It appears that this may have less to do with how Rube was throwing the ball and more that his manager had lost trust in him. Waddell's teammates believed he was physically able to pitch in the World Series. Team captain Lave Cross, on the opening day of the series said: "I'd like to clock him [Waddell] on the head with a bat. His work out yesterday on the quiet had both speed and curves. There is no reason why he should not pitch. He's jeopardizing our chances of getting the bulk of the money, and is not there for the team."[35]

Connie Mack, 1905 Philadelphia Athletics manager.

NATIONAL BASEBALL HALL OF FAME LIBRARY, COOPERSTOWN, NY

One final factor suggests the straw hat story was false. In September 1920, in the wake of the indictment of the eight White Sox players for fixing the 1919 World Series, Horace Fogel filled in more details of his story about 1905. He told of how a New York politician with significant financial interests in the gambling business, "Little Tim" Sullivan, and two New York gamblers met Waddell in a Boston hotel during the September road trip and offered him $17,000 to fake an injury and sit out the World Series.[36] Because the Athletics left Boston following the game of September 8, if such an episode had occurred, it would have had to take place before that game. Thus, if Waddell faked an injury to force his leaving the game that day, it would have fit in with the timeline provided by Fogel, and not the story involving Coakley and the straw hat.

That Fogel did not reveal these details until 1920 raises questions about the veracity of the claims. However we might understand this better in light of an account from 1908. The New York Giants and Chicago Cubs tied for the National League lead on October 7, 1908, at the end of the season. The teams met on October 8, 1908, in New York for a scheduled make-up game that would decide the pennant. It was later revealed that the game's umpires were approached and offered a bribe. Fogel reported in 1908 that he consciously had withheld details from 1905 stories to prevent him or his paper from being sued for libel. Fogel wrote in 1908, "Let's wait and see what the present investigation will show, and if I deem it necessary to take a hand in it for the good of base ball, I'll tell a few things I know, later."[37]

It was not only the writers, Mack, and his teammates who grew skeptical that Waddell was in fact injured. Despite Waddell being the most popular of all the Athletic players, Philadelphia fans also began to voice disbelief about Waddell's injury. During the third game of the World Series in Philadelphia, one fan mocked Waddell by throwing a straw hat onto the field.[38]

TWO VEXING QUESTIONS

There are two questions that have troubled those who believe Waddell was bribed to sit out the World Series:

(1) If he was bribed, why have him sit the last month of the season, before the Athletics had captured the AL pennant and were still engaged with the Chicago White Sox?

(2) Gamblers benefit by keeping private inside information they have. If Waddell was on the take, what was gained by pretending he was injured which would have prevented him from pitching the Series as well?

While we can never know with any degree of certainty the motives of those who bribed Waddell, if there was a bribe, it is possible to speculate on several that would provide answers to both questions.

As it turned out, the Athletics did not need Waddell to win the American League championship. His sitting out the last month did not markedly imperil its chances. Even when Waddell was out of action, most observers still felt that the Athletics were going to win the pennant. The team was never out of first place during the rest of the season, although for one day, September 27, Philadelphia fell into a virtual tie with Chicago. Furthermore, in mid-September, there were some who thought that while both the Athletics and Giants were the betting favorites to win their respective league pennants, the latter might have had a tougher row to hoe as they faced an extended road trip. It was also noted that Pittsburgh, the Giants' chief competitor for the pennant, was playing better ball than the White Sox, who were chasing the Athletics.[39]

As to the timing of a possible bribe, baseball historian Steve Steinberg has suggested that one possible explanation is that bets may have been placed on the Giants winning the World Series before the season and that gamblers were making sure that Waddell would not be available to pitch against them.[40] If this was all bribers cared about, obviously it would not have made any difference when Waddell stopped pitching. Furthermore, having several weeks to observe that he did so would have given them some degree of assurance that he intended to keep his agreement.

An alternative and not necessarily contradictory explanation regards the fact that for gamblers it is not only who wins that is important, but also the odds gamblers will accept. Anyone who could manipulate these would clearly have a significant advantage.

It is important to remember that Waddell was not shut down completely after September 8 and did pitch in three more games that season. On September 27, he relieved Weldon Henley, but was taken out after having difficulty putting the ball over the plate and giving up a hit to the only Detroit hitter he faced. However, in his next appearance on October 6, when the Athletics captured the pennant due to a White Sox loss, he did better, pitching six innings in relief of Andy Coakley versus Washington, although he did give up six runs, while walking five and throwing two wild pitches.

On the surface, Waddell's performance in that game appeared to be quite poor, but observers actually felt that, apart from diminished control attributed to his being rusty, he pitched well. In its coverage of the game, the *Philadelphia Public Ledger* the next day noted "he demonstrated that he is the same wonderful mechanism of speed and curves that has gained him a reputation second to none as a pitching marvel. But his work clearly showed his absence from the diamond. He not only lacked confidence, but was as erratic as an unbroken yearling."

On October 7, the last day of the regular season, Mack started Waddell in the first game of a double header and relieved him after he gave up two runs in the first inning.

Until the World Series began, the public was uncertain whether Waddell would pitch at all. Some newspapers warned their readers against bets on the Series until they knew whether Waddell would be available. On October 9, the opening day of the series, the *Cleveland Plain Dealer* warned, "To those who wish to wager money on the result of the series or on a single game this is good advice: wait until the teams are lined up before you bet. This is based on the admitted fact that the Athletics will be at least 20 percent stronger if Rube Waddell is able to pitch two or three of the games." The *Philadelphia North American* of October 7 would note that after the Athletics had won the pennant the day before, gamblers considering backing the team in the World Series were hesitant until they knew whether Waddell would be able to pitch.

There is also another possible sinister explanation for why Waddell might have been bribed to not only sit out the World Series, but also the final month of the season. If Waddell had pitched effectively in his regular spot in September, the Athletics most likely would have run away with the pennant. *Sporting Life* expressed an opinion after the season that if Waddell had not sat out during that time, the Athletics would have clinched the pennant at least one to two weeks before the end of the season.[41]

The Giants had won the National League pennant a week before the season end and were rested for the Series. Even before he knew whether the Athletics or the White Sox would win the AL pennant, John McGraw noted that it did not matter. No matter the winner, the players would be worn by the pennant race and the Giants would "just walk in" to the world championship.[42]

The details of the 1905 World Series are beyond the scope of this paper. Many observed at the time the poor play of the Athletics both in the field and at bat. There were undertones that things might not be on the level in the Series, although most observers attributed the poor performance to exhaustion from playing the next to last day of the season before clinching the American League pennant.

After the Series, Ban Johnson, the disappointed president of the American League, said, "It seems to me that the Athletics did not play up to the excellent form they showed toward the close of the American League season. They played with lightning speed then, but there was a noticeable diminution in the rapidity of play this week. Perhaps the defection of Rube Waddell discouraged the players."[43]

Suspicions that the World Series might not have been on the level were heightened when it was revealed later that the Athletic players and most of the Giants had agreed beforehand to split the players' share of the receipts 50–50, instead of abiding by the official split of 75 percent for the winners and 25 percent for the losers. *The Sporting News* felt the need to publish an editorial denying that this should be interpreted as indicating that the players might have not done their best.[44]

POSTSCRIPT: AFTER THE 1905 SEASON

Despite Waddell's phenomenal pitching record in 1905, reports appeared during the off-season that Mack was trying to move him to another team. There were stories of him being traded or sold to the Boston Americans or to Cincinnati, but how plausible any such deal might have been is unknown.[45] Mack may have been unable to find anyone willing to give anything close to the value that a star pitcher would warrant if he was able to find any takers at all. Alluding to Waddell's diminished reputation, Frank Navin, the then secretary and later owner of the Detroit club, stated after the series that he "wouldn't give 30 cents for Waddell."[46]

After the season, there were reports that Ban Johnson was trying to have the National Commission, the then ruling body of organized baseball, initiate a formal investigation of the bribery charge, perhaps scaring potential buyers or trading partners away.[47]

In his defense of Waddell, Mack stated many times over the years that followed that Rube did not care about money, and that what was most important to him was winning. Many never believed this.[48] Even before the 1905 World Series, Charles Dryden wrote that "Rube Waddell does not care so much for the pennant but he would like to get one of the $50 diamond studded buttons [that the National Commission had promised to members of the World Series winning team]. It can be soaked [a synonym for pawning]."[49] Throughout Waddell's career there were stories of schemes he invented to wrangle money out of others. That he was chronically short of money is indicated by the fact that even though he received well over $1,000 as his share of the money from the 1905 World Series, by December of that year, he was already asking Connie Mack for money.[50]

In later writings, Connie Mack forgave Waddell for being unable to play in the World Series, but Mack's response afterward was to punish him the only way he could without hurting himself. In 1906, after Waddell's wife sued him for non-support and desertion, a court required that he show his contract for that season so the amount he had to provide to her could be decided. It showed that the Athletics were paying him a mere $1,200, half of what he had earned in 1905.[51]

Despite the reduction in salary, Mack continued to use Waddell in 1906 much as he had the previous season. For most of the season, Waddell pitched well, starting 6–2 with four shutouts before injuring the thumb on his pitching hand in a carriage accident on May 22. He missed most of the next month, but returned to his pre-injury form until the last month of the season, when he again let his teammates down, going 2–6, a major factor in the Athletics' failure to challenge for the pennant. He lasted one more season with the Athletics before Mack sold him to St. Louis before the 1908 season, explaining, "While I still consider Waddell a great pitcher, I figure my team has been considerably strengthened by his sale. There was not the best of feeling between Waddell and several of the players, and as harmony is the chief essential to success he was disposed of to St. Louis."[52]

CONCLUSION

It is unlikely we will ever know for certain whether Rube Waddell was bribed to sit out the last month of the 1905 season or that year's World Series. However, there is a great deal of evidence to suggest that the whole story of his fight with Andy Coakley over a straw hat, and an injury resulting from it, can itself be knocked into another type of hat, the proverbial cocked one. ■

Notes

1. Roger I. Abrams and Alan Levy, "The Trial of Rube Waddell," *Seton Hall Journal of Sports and Entertainment Law* 19, (2009): 1–30.
2. Except as noted, player statistics are from Baseball-Reference.com.
3. Baseball-Reference.com names Jim Buchanan of St. Louis as the American League leader in saves in 1905 with two, and Waddell none. A review of the 1905 season indicates that Waddell had at least four. John Thorn, in his book *The Relief Pitcher* (New York: E.P. Dutton, 1979) also credits Waddell with four and a tie for the league lead. The only other pitchers since 1900 who appear to have won this unofficial quadruple crown are Christy Mathewson of the New York Giants in 1908, and Lefty Grove for the Philadelphia Athletics in 1930.
4. Alfred Spink, *The National Game* (St. Louis: The National Publishing Company, 1911), 160.
5. Paul Proia, *Just a Big Kid: The Life and Times of Rube Waddell* (Baltimore: Publish America, 2007), 155.
6. *Boston Herald*, February 9, 1905.
7. Ibid.
8. It is possible that either Waddell or someone else eventually paid off his in-laws. When the case finally went to trial in January 1906, they did not appear to testify against him and it was dismissed. (*Wilkes-Barre Times*, January 12, 1906).
9. *Philadelphia North American*, August 21, 1905.
10. Waddell's drinking habits were sufficiently known that in late August 1905, Charles Dryden of the Philadelphia North American, upon learning that Rube had been asked to write an advertisement endorsing Coca-Cola as his favorite drink, reported; "We marvel much because a bolt of lightning did not enter the window and strike Mr. Waddell dead in the midst of his mendacious testimonial." (*Philadelphia North American*, August 26, 1905.) The advertisement appeared in *The Sporting News* on September 16, 1905.
11. *Philadelphia North American*, August 23, 1905.
12. *Philadelphia North American*, August 25, 1905.
13. Frank Newhouse is often described as the trainer of a boxer who fought under the name Young Corbett. In fact, he was more of a gofer. Corbett's actual trainer when he was the featherweight champion was Harry Tuthill, the New York Giants trainer in 1905. When Corbett was no longer able to make weight as a featherweight his title was claimed by the boxer Abe Attell who would come to have a more infamous association with baseball of any professional fighter.
14. Connie Mack, "The One And Only Rube," *Saturday Evening Post*, March 14, 1936, 12–13, 106, 108–110.
15. *Philadelphia North American*, August 27, 1905.
16. *Philadelphia North American*, August 27, 1905. Schreck caught almost every inning Waddell pitched in 1905 and when Waddell was called on to relieve, Schreck would enter the game with him.
17. See Proia, *Just a Big Kid*; Alan H. Levy, *Rube Waddell: The Zany Brilliant Life a of a Strikeout Artist* (Jefferson, NC: McFarland & Co., 2000); Fred Lieb, *Connie Mack: Grand Old Man of Baseball* (New York: G.P. Putnam's, 1945); Connie Mack, *My 66 Years In the Big League* (Philadelphia: Winston, 1950); Norman Macht, *Connie Mack and the Early Years of Baseball* (Lincoln, NE: University of Nebraska Press, 2007). The SABR Baseball Biography Project biography of Waddell incorrectly states that Waddell defeated Cy Young in the game.
18. *Philadelphia Inquirer*, September 9, 1905.
19. *Philadelphia Evening Telegraph*, September 9, 1905.
20. For example, see Associated Press report in the *Richmond Times Dispatch*, September 29, 1905.
21. *Pawtucket Times*, September 9, 1905.
22. *The Sporting News*, December 16, 1905.
23. Mack wanted Dygert to join the Athletics by August 31 so he would be eligible to play in the World Series. This proved to be no easy task as New Orleans was under quarantine for a yellow fever epidemic, and Dygert reported he had to elude inspectors on the train en route to join the Athletics. (*Philadelphia North American*, September 7, 1905).
24. The identity of "Veteran" remains a mystery. Other *Sporting News* correspondents at the time reported that it was unknown to them. I believe it was most likely Horace Fogel, who was noted to be its correspondent at various times during the first decade of the twentieth century, though I was unable to find specific evidence that he was "Veteran" in 1905. If it was Fogel, he was being disingenuous, for several times he praised Fogel's writings. I thank Norman Macht and Steve Steinberg for their opinions on Veteran's identity.
25. Dryden, who only reported on baseball, had traveled with the team for most of the season, while Fogel only did so after September 1. Contrary to reports that it was Vila who initiated and spread the rumor about Waddell being bribed, in *The Sporting News* of October 7, 1905, he actually expressed skepticism about it, asking "does anybody believe the story that 'Rube' Waddell has been fixed to keep out of the world's [sic] series?"
26. *The Sporting News*, September 30, 1905.
27. *Philadelphia Evening Telegraph*, September 22, 1905.
28. *Cleveland Plain Dealer*, September 28, 1905.
29. *Philadelphia North American*, September 21, 1905.
30. J.G. Taylor Spink, "Rube Waddell," *Baseball Register* (St. Louis, C.C. Spink & Son, 1944), 5–21.
31. Connie Mack, "My Fifty Years in Baseball," *Albany Evening News*, October 5, 1930; Mack, "The One And Only Rube."
32. If Coakley was willing to go along with Connie Mack on perpetuating a falsehood, it would not have been the first time he did so. In September 1902, a pitcher named McAllister made his debut with the Athletics. After the season, it was revealed that he was really Coakley, then one of the top collegiate pitchers in the country. When the college he was attending, Holy Cross, learned of his playing professional ball, it terminated his collegiate athletic eligibility. Mack admitted he had known McAllister's true identity all along and was trying to protect Coakley's eligibility through the use of the pseudonym. That Mack had no compunction about participating in future falsehoods is indicated by his similar willingness to have Columbia University student Eddie Collins play under the name Sullivan in 1906. For details on Coakley's post-major league career, see his obituary in *The New York Times*, September 28, 1963.
33. *Philadelphia North American*, October 1, 1905.
34. *Philadelphia North American*, October 1, 1905. Some newspaper stories reported that Waddell went to his doctor first.
35. *New York Evening World*, October 9, 1905.
36. *Philadelphia Inquirer*, September 30, 1920.
37. *The Sporting News*, December 17, 1908.
38. *New York Sun*, October 13, 1905.
39. *Cleveland Plain Dealer*, September 17, 1905.
40. Steve Steinberg, "Horace Fogel: The Man Who Knew (and Talked) Too Much." *Base Ball: A Journal of the Early Game*, 6 (2012):33–50.
41. *Sporting Life*, October 21, 1905.
42. *Sporting Life*, October 7, 1905.
43. *Cleveland Plain Dealer*, October 15, 1905.
44. *The Sporting News*, November 11, 1905.
45. *Baltimore American*, November 21, 1905; *Boston Daily Globe*, December 31, 1905.
46. *Grand Rapids Press*, October 27, 1905.
47. *Cleveland Plain Dealer*, January 8, 1906. Johnson may have had suspicions about Waddell's honesty and tried to distance himself from Waddell even before September 8. In August 1905, at a meeting of the National Commission, he and National League president Harry Pulliam chose all-star teams of the best players at each position in their own leagues. At pitcher, Johnson chose Jack Chesbro over Waddell. Although Chesbro had gone 41–12 in 1904, it is doubtful that by August of the following year many knowledgeable people would have rated him as superior to Waddell. *New York Press*, September 3, 1905.
48. Lieb, *Connie Mack*, 93.
49. *Philadelphia North American*, September, 17, 1905.
50. *Washington Post*, December 9, 1905.
51. *Trenton Times*, May 4, 1906. For Waddell's 1905 salary see Proia, *Just a Big Kid*, 147.
52. *Chicago Inter Ocean*, April 12, 1908.

Tim Hurst's Last Call

Rick Huhn

It was an unlikely time for a post-game riot, even in a baseball-crazy city like Philadelphia. Yet that is exactly what occurred at newly-minted Shibe Park on the afternoon of August 3, 1909. Moments earlier, the hometown Athletics had completed an exciting come-from-behind 10–4 victory to sweep a doubleheader from the Chicago White Sox. The pair of wins served as further notice that this team, fielding a number of young players, was becoming a force to be reckoned with in the American League. The wins that day lifted the record of manager Connie Mack's charges to 58–38, leaving them a mere two games behind the defending two-time AL champion Detroit Tigers. Not a bad day's work for a squad that finished in sixth place just one season before. Nonetheless, as the final White Sox out was recorded in the top of the ninth, several hundred Athletics fans, instead of celebrating, rushed the field as others, in the upper tier, threw seat cushions, bottles, and even their straw hats. The target of their anger was veteran umpire Tim Hurst. Only the intervention of several members of the Athletics, including Mr. Mack, and eventually the police, saved Hurst from serious physical harm. Hurst did not know it at the time, but as he was escorted from the field he had just umpired his last game in the major leagues.

The call that served to end Tim Hurst's storied career in baseball occurred late in the day's second game. When 23-year-old third baseman Frank Baker, batting with the bases full of Athletics and one out, lifted a fly ball to center field, it started a chain reaction of relay throws that eventually saw A's second sacker Eddie Collins attempt to advance from first to second. The action that unfolded at that point was described in one Philadelphia newspaper as follows:

> It was in the [bottom of the] eighth inning when the White Sox were throwing the ball around in reckless fashion that Collins saw a chance to get to second and availed himself of it, though it were patent to all that he was only safe because [Sox second baseman Jake] Atz dropped the ball. To every one's surprise Umpire Hurst called

him out, claiming that he [Collins] knocked the ball from the Chicago fielder's hand. As a matter of fact, Atz dropped the ball before Collins reached the bag. What Collins said to Hurst is not known, but it is claimed that when he came over to where the umpire was standing the latter spat at him.[1]

Hurst's actions, post call, were more colorfully portrayed by sports writer Jimmy Isaminger of the *Philadelphia North American*. He was uncertain if Hurst acted intentionally or not, but told readers "it is a fact that the umpire distributed a mouthful of moistened union-made tobacco in the direction of youthful Eddie, who immediately called Tim's attention to the Board of Health ordinance which prohibits expectorating in public places."[2]

Whether Hurst's actions violated any ordinances or not, it did violate the sensibilities of those locals who later rushed the field and threw Hurst's way any and all objects close at hand. Not long thereafter it caught the attention of one Byron Bancroft Johnson, the AL's president and baseball's major domo. Johnson took special pride in his umpires. He had a short fuse for any indiscretions. The next day, Johnson relieved Hurst from duty indefinitely pending a report of the incident.[3] There can be little doubt Hurst was suspended for spitting on Collins and not for his call. The reason for Hurst's overt reaction to Collins's protest is of interest. A more intriguing and less analyzed question is: Why had Hurst made what almost everyone agreed was such an egregious call? The question begs a closer look at Mr. Hurst.

According to Ring Lardner, describing the day's activities for the "bugs" back in Chicago, the call, "[p]robably the worst decision Tim ever made in his life, and that means a pretty bad decision, stopped Philadelphia in the midst of a rally…."[4] Lardner seems to be asserting that Hurst's miscall was just another of many made over the course of his career. The writer, even in these years prior to *You Know Me Al* and national repute as a writer of short stories and plays, seldom missed a chance to interject some dry wit into

THE RUCKER ARCHIVE

Tim Hurst circa 1904. Said umpire Billy Evans of his colleague, "[Hurst] had the implicit confidence of every player in the majors."

his work. This might have been just one more instance. On the other hand, if Lardner truly believed Hurst was a subpar arbiter, it was not an opinion generally shared by others. In fact, it was just the opposite.

Timothy Carroll Hurst was known far and wide for his fairness as a signal caller. He made a bad call every once in a while, but far fewer than most. Tim was born into a large Irish family in Ashland, Pennsylvania, on June 30, 1865. His father had been in the wholesale liquor business. In the 1870s the elder Hurst purchased a horse and wagon and eked out a meager living delivering coal from local mines to customers in the area. A childhood friend had this to say about Tim's turbulent early years:

> As youngsters, Timmie and I worked picking slate in a colliery in Ashland. When we knocked off for lunch, there was always a fight or two between employes [sic] to see who was the better man. That is where Tim learned to handle his fists and got a love for fighting. But Tim was too smart to stay in the mines. He saw there was no future there for him.[5]

This same friend introduced Hurst to a career in umpiring when the friend's nose was broken as he umpired a local game. The friend quit on the spot. When no one stepped forward to take his place, Tim,

playing second base for one of the teams at the time, volunteered and finished the game as the ump. He received a dollar for his troubles and decided it might be an easy way to make more.[6]

In 1888, at age 22, Hurst began his professional umpiring career in the Central Pennsylvania League. A stint in the Southern League followed a year later. When that league broke up in mid-season 1889, he transferred his skills to the Western Association. Hurst, who was once described as a "bandy-legged, sorrel-topped, five-foot-nine-inch 175-pound bit of dynamite," had the familiar combination of a keen Irish wit and the short, sharp temper to go with it.[7] During his brief time in the Western Association, he impressed the owners of the Minneapolis Millers so much as an umpire that in June 1890 he was hired as their manager. Hurst's Millers almost won the league championship, but Hurst fell out with team management and did not return as manager in 1891. Instead, he was hired as an umpire by the National League. He was now in the big time.

Plying his craft at baseball's top level, Hurst developed a reputation for his dim view of players who questioned his calls, preferring to use his fists to cut arguments short. According to baseball historian David Fleitz, "(t)hey called him 'Sir Timothy' for his bearing and 'Terrible Tim' for his temper, and few players elected to punch it out with him."[8] That probably cut down on arguments, but he garnered even more respect for his knowledge of the rules and the way he applied them.

Over the years, perhaps owing to his own attempts at a professional boxing career, Hurst developed a reputation for refereeing boxing matches. He was known for calling a fair fight. As his reputation as referee spread he began working some highly publicized fights, mostly during baseball's off-season but a few in the summer. This opened the door to offers to officiate bike races, running races, and even marathons. The men in charge of baseball were not impressed. In 1895 the magnates rose up and ousted him from the league. However, high-quality umpires like Hurst were difficult to find. After a season in the Eastern League, he was back in the NL, but not for long. On August 4, 1897, Tim was under heavy verbal assault from the fans during a game he umpired in Cincinnati. All at once, what had been mere verbiage turned physical when a beer bottle was heaved from the stands, striking Hurst in the back. He reacted quickly and violently, hurling the bottle back into the stands where it struck a city fireman over one eye and broke his skin. Fans immediately leaped from the stands onto the field and charged the fuming umpire. It took a police cordon to escort him safely from the field. Fortunately, the fireman's cut did not prove serious. Hurst was charged with assault and battery, paid a fine and served no time in jail. Although he was not dismissed at the time, at season's end he was quietly shuffled out of the league.

Hurst reappeared in 1898 as manager of the St. Louis Browns, a posting that did not survive a last-place finish. Interestingly, as a manager Hurst was a notorious umpire-baiter.[9] His managerial career at an end, Hurst sat out a year then returned to umpire in the National League on a sporadic basis. In 1904 he umpired only one game.[10]

In 1905 Hurst resurfaced in the American League umpiring for Ban Johnson. The Irishman's return to baseball was facilitated by Johnson's desire to field a superior team of umpires who would lend reliability and credibility to the game. According to one writer, "Under Johnson the many-lived umpire was to be reborn again, and this time to a position of authority, dignity and secularity."[11] Hurst liked the sound of it. He enlisted and Johnson had an authority figure to add to a growing list of first-class signal callers, albeit one who carried the risk of an explosion every once in a while.

For the most part, Hurst toed the company line during his AL tenure, adding to his credibility and delighting fans with the spirited way he approached his trade. Nevertheless, there were those occasional bumps in the road. One such incident occurred in May 1906 in New York during a contest with the visiting Washington Nationals when Highlander manager Clark Griffith protested a Hurst call in a close play at first base. Griffith reportedly rushed toward Hurst waving his hands and flinging his cap into the air. Hurst ordered him away. Instead, Griffith moved closer and stepped on Hurst's shoe. Hurst reared back to strike Griffith, before several players intervened. When Hurst grabbed Griffith by his lapel, intending to lead him off the field, the latter pushed Hurst's hand aside. As Griffith's men took control and led him toward the dugout, Hurst again approached and drew his fist back ready to take a swing. Order was eventually restored and Griffith ejected from the game.[12] Spotted later with a swollen lip, Griffith denied it came from Hurst.[13] Although various reports have Ban Johnson disciplining both men over the incident, Hurst umpired the

next day in a ballgame featuring the same teams.[14,15]

Another significant bump occurred on May 7, 1909, in New York, three months before the spitting incident involving Eddie Collins. This time Hurst's opponent was Highlander third baseman Kid Elberfeld. The Highlanders beat the Boston Red Sox in the bottom of the 12th, and the play that caused the ruckus occurred in the bottom of the 11th with the teams knotted at three apiece. Elberfeld stood at third with one out when teammate Joe Ward lifted a fly ball to left. Following the catch—or perhaps as one report had it, a little before—Elberfeld steamed for home. In his mind, he had beaten the throw from Red Sox left fielder Harry Niles and the game was over. He was stunned when Tim Hurst called him out, sending the game into yet another inning. Elberfeld had skirmished with Hurst before and was unwilling to back down. He rushed Hurst and jabbed him in the side. Hurst picked up his mask and swung away, striking Elberfeld in the jaw. After several Red Sox players intervened, Hurst tossed Elberfeld from the game.[16] Hurst was suspended by Ban Johnson until May 13.[17]

By August, Hurst was in the eye of the storm that would end his career. To a casual observer, a pattern seemed to be emerging: in both skirmishes the individual called out was irate and argued strenuously with Hurst. The incidents, however, bore significant differences. The first call was made in a tie game. Had Elberfeld been called safe at home, the game was over, his Highlander team victorious. The call at second base in the August contest occurred with Collins's Athletics team safely ahead, merely seeking to add to what appeared to be an insurmountable 10–4 lead. Where Elberfeld's game was played right in New York, Hurst's home base, the Collins dispute occurred in Philadelphia, a train commute for Hurst to his residence. While no one seriously disputed that Elberfeld's play at the plate was a close call, almost every observer agreed that Jake Atz dropped the ball and Collins was clearly safe at second. Thus, in the first instance as opposed to the second, Hurst's decision was justifiable.

Even the characteristics and circumstances of the two aggrieved ballplayers differed. Elberfeld had legitimately earned his nickname, "The Tabasco Kid," by his presence at the center of controversy throughout his career. Two of his more noteworthy skirmishes with umpires occurred in 1906, each involving highly-regarded signal caller Silk O'Loughlin. In the first, The Kid went after Silk with a bat, while in the second, he attempted to kick and spike O'Loughlin in the foot. This second incident, described by *The New York Times* as "one of the most disrespectful exhibitions of rowdyism ever witnessed on a baseball field," moved Ban Johnson to suspend Elberfeld for seven games.[18] It is not so surprising then, if still not appropriate, that when Elberfeld rushed at Hurst in May 1909, the latter might strike back. On the other hand, three months later, when Eddie Collins attempted to advance to second following Frank Baker's fly out, he carried none of Elberfeld's baggage. At the time Collins was only 22, in his first full season as the A's second sacker. There is no question that Collins played the game with a competitive spirit that at times—particularly on the base paths—seemed aggressive. In fact, only a couple of weeks before the row with Hurst, Collins had vigorously protested to no avail a call by rookie umpire Fred Perrine.[19] But throughout a long and illustrious career his disputes over calls were brief and relatively few. Disputes he was involved in did not rise to the level of all-out war as did Elberfeld's. He would eventually earn the nickname "Cocky" more for an attitude of quiet assurance than for any negative connotation.

Unlike "The Tabasco Kid," Collins did not physically assault Tim Hurst on August 3, although there were some who said the young infielder kicked dust on Hurst's patent leather shoes. This might have been enough to set off Hurst, a man known to buff his shoes prior to games until they glared back at him. Nonetheless, those wondering why Hurst, who did not eject Collins, went so far as to spit on him that fateful day need look no further than Sir Timothy's own words. When he was eventually confronted by Ban Johnson for an explanation of his actions, Hurst supposedly told his boss, "I don't like college boys."[20] Eddie Collins was a graduate of Columbia University, just one of a growing number of college-educated young men signed to a contract by the refined Connie Mack.

That might explain why Hurst spit on Collins. It does not explain why he made perhaps the worst call of his career. Hurst never spoke about the matter publicly. Thus we will never know the answer for sure. A reasonable explanation can be pieced together by a look at the timing of the call and revealing statements Hurst had made on earlier occasions.

The Collins incident occurred in the bottom of the eighth inning of game two of a twin bill. By this time, Hurst and his colleague Silk O'Loughlin had been umpiring for 17 innings. Game one had taken almost two hours to complete. The second game was heading toward the two-hour mark. (Today a two-hour game is considered short, but not so in 1909.) In the sixth inning the White Sox seemed to be in control, leading 4–0 behind veteran flinger Doc White. Then the A's

turned things around, scoring one in the bottom half of the sixth and five more in the seventh. They had pushed four more runs across by the time Collins tagged up and chugged toward second in the A's half of the eighth. By that time the game was solidly in hand, the play of little consequence. When Sox second baseman Atz dropped the relay throw representing the third out, Hurst must have groaned. He had seen enough. Instead of calling Collins safe and allowing the inning to continue, he called the base runner out. A half-inning later, the game was over. So, it would prove, was Hurst's long, storied umpiring career.

Hurst's intentions that day did not go unnoticed by that keen observer, Ring Lardner. At one point in his game summary he wrote that "Hurst must be thanked for the fact that they are not out there playing yet...." Later he opined that the umpire "to the amazement of every one ruled Collins out at second on the ground that it was almost supper time."[21] This was not a far-fetched assertion regarding Hurst. One time when Hurst's buddy O'Loughlin complained that an umpire leads a "dog's life," Hurst reportedly responded, "Sure it is, Silk, but you can't beat the hours." [22] On another occasion Hurst heard that Ban Johnson was interested in ways to shorten ball games. According to umpire Billy Evans, Hurst wrote Johnson suggesting the games be reduced to seven innings.[23]

It is said that when Hurst umpired in Philadelphia he would often call games due to darkness. The reason: He wanted to catch the commuter train back to his home in New York City.[24] According to sports columnist Joe Williams, who called Hurst "the most colorful" of umpires, "Whenever he [Hurst] was assigned to Philadelphia he would always catch the train back to New York after the game. If the lure was particularly fascinating, as it was on the occasion when he was to have refereed a marathon race, he would cut the game short himself."[25]

Of course, these statements and stories could be apocryphal, as are so many tales of the diamond's early days. However, a pattern seemed to emerge that fit perfectly Sir Timothy's ministrations of the late afternoon of August 3. In the crafty arbiter's mind he could make a call on Collins at second that affected not a whit the outcome of the game. In so doing he greatly increased his chances for a pleasant night in his cozy abode. When Collins protested and Hurst reacted by spitting at him, it was to be the umpire's undoing.

On August 5 Ban Johnson indefinitely suspended Tim Hurst pending an investigation into his actions. In announcing the suspension, the league president stated that any final decision would await his receipt

During a Hall of Fame career that spanned 25 years and 2,826 games, Eddie Collins (shown here) had few disputes with umpires. His face-off with Tim Hurst on August 3, 1909, was the exception and not the rule.

of a report of the incident. It is said that neither Eddie Collins nor Connie Mack, who held Hurst in high esteem, ever wanted charges against Hurst.[26] The way was clear for Hurst to explain his actions. He never offered an explanation—perhaps because there was none plausible—taking the same road he took when Johnson asked him to explain why he struck Kid Elberfeld in May. Johnson liked Hurst very much, and recognized his ability and valuable service to his infant league. But Johnson could not abide by this sort of repeated conduct from an official. When questioned on August 16 about reports that Hurst was still on the active list, he replied, "Hurst was dropped from the American league [sic] staff immediately after I investigated the charges against him and found them to be true."[27]

Reports that Hurst's unseemly deportment and seeming indifference in 1909 stemmed from an increasing weariness with umpiring were dispelled in 1910 when he returned to the minor leagues, umpiring in the Eastern League. That stint proved his last in baseball, although in 1914 he was mentioned as a candidate to umpire in the outlaw Federal League.[28] In the ensuing years from 1911 until his death at age 54 on June 4, 1915, reportedly from ptomaine poisoning following an attack of acute indigestion, he continued to referee boxing matches—many at Madison Square Garden. He also acted as manager and matchmaker of the Garden Athletic Club, and in his last years sold real estate in Far Rockaway, New York.[29]

In 1946, before election of umpires to the Baseball Hall of Fame was permitted, Tim Hurst was recognized among some 39 managers, executives, sportswriters, and umpires named to the newly instituted Honor Rolls of Baseball. Hurst's colleague and friend, Hall of Famer Billy Evans, would have seconded the nomination. According to Evans, "While Hurst hardly

measured up to Jack Sheridan, Hank O'Day, Tommy Connolly, or Bill Klem as to perfection, he had the implicit confidence of every player in the majors. They accepted his decisions with respect, firmly convinced that he called the plays as he saw them without fear or favor."[30] No doubt Eddie Collins was of that mind as he approached second base in the eighth inning on August 3, 1909. Thus his uncharacteristic reaction when that confidence was shattered, as in turn was the illustrious career of an umpiring legend. What a shame if it all ended for Sir Timothy Hurst because were he to call Eddie Collins safe at second, he might just miss the 5:25 to Grand Central Terminal. ∎

Notes

1. *Philadelphia Record*, August 4, 1909.
2. *Philadelphia North American*, August 4, 1909.
3. "Athletics Cop Two From The Chicagos," *Philadelphia Inquirer*, August 5, 1910.
4. Ring Lardner, "Sox Fall Twice; Fans Mob Hurst," *Chicago Tribune*, August 4, 1909.
5. Edward Burkett Price quoted in "Terrible-Tempered Tim—Fighting Umpire (Part One)," column "Three and One" by J. G. Taylor Spink, *The Sporting News*, April 8, 1943, 4, 6.
6. Ibid.
7. Ibid.
8. David Fleitz, "The Green and the Blue: The Irish American Umpire, 1880–1965," *The Baseball Research Journal*, 39 (Summer 2010): 28.
9. J. G. Taylor Spink, "Terrible-Tempered Tim—Fighting Umpire (Part Two)," *The Sporting News*, April 15, 1943, 4, 10.
10. Tim Hurst's entry in www.retrosheet.com. See also Larry R. Gerlach, "Timothy Carroll Hurst," Frederick Ivor-Campbell, Robert L. Tiemann, Mark Rucker, eds., *Baseball's First Stars* (Cleveland: SABR, 1996), 80.
11. James M. Kahn, *The Umpire Story* (New York: G. P. Putnam's Sons, 1953), 50.
12. "Umpire And Player Clash," *The New York Times*, May 8, 1906.
13. "Orth Scattered Hits," *Washington Post*, May 8, 1906.
14. For example see Eugene C. Murdock, *Ban Johnson: Czar of Baseball* (Westport CT: Greenwood Press, 1982), 101, citing *The Sporting News*, May 19, 1906, 4.
15. "Batted Out A Victory," *Washington Post*, May 9, 1906.
16. "Cree Drives Home The Winning Run," *The New York Times*, May 8, 1909.
17. *Sporting Life*, May 22, 1909, 11.
18. "Americans In The Lead After Stormy Series," *The New York Times*, September 4, 1906.
19. "Browns Hand Out Jolt To Mackmen," *Philadelphia Inquirer*, July 18, 1909.
20. Murdoch, *Ban Johnson*, 101-102, citing Kahn, *The Umpire Story*, 46.
21. Lardner, *Chicago Tribune*, August 4, 1909.
22. Tim Hurst's quote is variously reported, including Kahn, *The Umpire's Story*, 10.
23. Billy Evans quoted in ibid., 70.
24. Ibid., 41.
25. Joe Williams, "Some Umps Who Stood Out: Hurst, Evans and Klem, They're All Honest—Sure!" *New York World-Telegram*, date unclear, Tim Hurst's clippings file, National Baseball Library, Cooperstown, NY.
26. Tim Murnane, "Murnane's Baseball," *Boston Globe*, August 22, 1909.
27. "Hurst Surely Out," *Boston Globe*, August 17, 1909.
28. "Three National League Umpires With Federals," *Los Angeles Times*, June 15, 1914.
29. Bill Lee, *The Baseball Necrology* (Jefferson NC: McFarland, 2003), 194. See also "Old Tim Hurst Dies," *Cleveland Leader*, June 5, 1915.
30. Billy Evans quoted in Kahn, *The Umpire Story*, 43.

LIBRARY OF CONGRESS BAIN COLLECTION

The Delaware River Shipbuilding League, 1918

Jim Leeke

Baseball leagues flourished in American shipyards during World War I as legions of workers built warships and troop transports to safeguard the Atlantic sea lanes and carry men and materiel to Europe. Among the best of these circuits was the Delaware River Shipbuilding League of 1918. Centered in Philadelphia, it represented eight shipyards operating along the river in Delaware, New Jersey, and Pennsylvania:

CHESTER SHIP – Chester, Pennsylvania
HARLAN & HOLLINGSWORTH – Wilmington, Delaware
HOG ISLAND – Philadelphia
MERCHANT SHIP – Bristol, Pennsylvania
NEW YORK SHIP – Camden, New Jersey
PUSEY & JONES – Wilmington (replaced League Island Navy Yard after two games)
SUN SHIP – Chester, Pennsylvania
TRAYLOR SHIP – Cornwells, Pennsylvania

"The Delaware River Shipbuilding League is due for a successful season in its first year on the baseball diamond judging by the results of Saturday's games," the *Philadelphia Public Ledger* commented after opening day.[1]

The newspaper also pointed out what it considered "a defect in one of the rules of the organization which is entirely too stringent." A worker had to be on the job for 40 days before he was eligible to suit up for his shipyard team. The *Public Ledger* thought 10 days would have been wiser.

"For the opening any player should have been eligible up until Saturday," it declared, "and in order to avoid disputes all men who were in uniform on Saturday should be declared eligible, especially so because of the shortness of the season."[2] The stricter requirement remained in place, and would bedevil the league the rest of the season.

Only two of the four opening games drew sizeable crowds. The Traylor-Hog Island turnout was especially disappointing. Traylor had a "class infield, but... should hunt up an entire new outfield," the *Public Ledger* opined. A shipyard official brushed aside any

such worries. "We are in this for the sport alone," he said, "and if some other fellow gets Ty Cobb and (Grover Cleveland) Alexander, let him trot them out and, win or lose, we will be shouting just the same."[3]

The Traylor man was perhaps clairvoyant. On May 13, the same day that his comments appeared, a Selective Service board in South Carolina notified Joe Jackson, of the champion Chicago White Sox, that it had reclassified his draft status. "Shoeless Joe" was suddenly set to join the next group to be called for military service, a situation that Jackson initially seemed to accept.

"Well, the old boy will be out there slugging the Dutchman pretty soon," Jackson said in Philadelphia, where the White Sox had just played the Athletics. "And if I ever draw a bead on one of them birds, it'll be all off with him."[4]

The next morning, however, at the urging of his wife, Jackson instead reported for work as a painter at the Harlan yard in Wilmington, a subsidiary of mighty Bethlehem Steel. Shipyard workers, like those in other vital war industries, were usually exempt from military service. Although the outfielder was illiterate, the shipyard not only accepted Jackson, it immediately promoted him to painting inspector.

"If Jackson should stay at the shipyard as an employe [sic] he would be eligible to play in the Bethlehem Steel Baseball League as a member of the Wilmington team," a wire service reported. "This organization has teams at Bethlehem, Lebanon and Steelton, Pa., Fall River, Mass., Wilmington, Del., and Sparrows Point, Md."[5]

The Delaware River and Steel leagues both played their games on Saturdays, and Harlan had a team in each. Jackson suited up for Harlan's Steel League nine, and appeared in his first game on June 1. Fans of the company's Delaware River team would have to wait until the end of the season to see him.

Any big-league player who sought a shipyard job in 1918 heard abuse from many fans and sportswriters. A former St. Louis player serving in the Navy saw the phenomenon first hand in a shipyard game featuring

LIBRARY OF CONGRESS BAIN COLLECTION

Charles "Chief" Bender's major league career was essentially over when he pitched for the Hog Island team. The Hog Island yard employed 35,000 workers at the time.

several ex-Giants. "Nothing was too mean to call them," he wrote, "and if they got a dollar for every time some one called them 'slackers' or 'trench-dodgers' they must have gotten round-shouldered carrying their money home."[6]

Jackson, especially, became a lightning rod for condemnation, but many people defended him. Former Chicago teammate Alfred "Fritz" von Kolnitz, a major in the wartime Army, insisted that Shoeless Joe had every right to hold a shipyard job. "During the draft period, I will venture, there were thousands of men walking the streets in civilian clothes with exemption papers in their pockets with far less claims than Joe," he later wrote to a sportswriter.[7]

The Delaware River League had about two dozen recent or retired big leaguers on its rosters, most of them journeyman players. Among the better-known players was former Athletics star Charles "Chief" Bender, whose time in the majors was over (although he would pitch one final inning for the White Sox in 1925). With Joe Jackson watching from the stands as a spectator, Bender made his league debut the second weekend of play, appearing on the road in relief for Hog Island. The enormous Hog Island yard employed 35,000 workers on the site of what is now the Philadelphia airport.

"'Chief' Bender has at last broken into the box score of the Delaware River Shipbuilders' League," the

Public Ledger reported. "He accepted the mound for the final three innings of the Harlan-Hog Island encounter at Wilmington, which the former captured by 6–4."[8] Although later claimed on waivers by the Yankees, Bender didn't report to New York and would remain in the shipbuilding league until hurt in a car crash in August.

Despite having Bender and other experienced players, the Delaware River Shipbuilding League was still an industrial circuit. The hot club early in the season was Chester Ship, which played in nearby Upland on a field called White Hip. Chester fielded perhaps the river league's most colorful and diverse team, with one player who had once been under contract to the Browns, another to the Athletics, a pair of ex-minor leaguers from the New York State and North Carolina leagues, and a former player from Colby College. Its roster also included three Chinese ballplayers from Hawaii, who "put up a brand of base ball that Chester fans like to see."[9]

Widespread national criticism of shipbuilding leagues grew as the season progressed. New York Yankees manager Miller Huggins let loose a tirade in mid-May, after pitcher George Mogridge jumped the team for a shipyard job.

"A half dozen players on my club have been approached by men who presumably are conducting the welfare work for the Bethlehem Steel Company," Huggins charged, "and I have authoritative knowledge that players on virtually all the big league clubs who thus far have played on the Atlantic seaboard, have received offers similar to those made to my men." The outraged manager added that one Yankee "was offered more money for going to one of the Atlantic Coast shipbuilding yards to play baseball and learn a skilled trade than his American League baseball contract called for."[10]

The government looked into this and similar allegations, including one made by a US senator. Officials yanked at least two ballplayers from the so-called "paint and putty" leagues and sent them to an Army training camp on Long Island. Otherwise, little appeared amiss in the shipyard leagues. A vice president of the US Shipping Board Emergency Fleet Corporation, Howard Coonley, later announced that the number of ballplayers "camouflaging" as shipyard workers was actually negligible.

"The stories that all ball player workmen at $500 a month have to do is punch a clock in the morning is false, says Coonley," *The Sporting News* reported. "He says 'with very few exceptions' everyone [sic] of them does a full day's work. Furthermore, he praises the efforts that have been made to make baseball the main recreation for the ship yard workers and says an even more expansive sport program is being planned, to include soccer, football, trap shooting, and other activities."[11]

Significantly, directors of the New York shipyards voted to limit teams in their league to two ex-major leaguers apiece. "In the Philadelphia district there seems no limitation to the number of former major leaguers on a ball team, as there apparently are enough to go around," *The Sporting News* tartly added.[12]

By the middle of June, as controversy still bubbled, Chester Ship led the Delaware River league with a 6–0 record. New York Ship was a game back with one loss. Although eligible to play, Shoeless Joe hadn't yet taken the field for Harlan's river club. "Manager [Fred] Gallagher, of Harlan-Bethlehem, of the Ship League, will find it necessary to requisition the services of Joe Jackson if the Wilmington aggregation is to stay in the running at all," the *Public Ledger* commented. "They dropped to fourth place by losing to Hog Island, 4–3. It was the first game for Hog Island on its new grounds at Brill Park."[13]

The following Saturday featured an important Chester-Harlan matchup. The *Public Ledger* expected "the largest crowd that ever witnessed a game in Wilmington," and added that it was "almost a certainty that Joe Jackson and other big leaguers will appear."

"I don't care who they play. We are going to win," Chester Manager Frank Miller confidently promised. Fred Gallagher, skipper of the Harlan nine, said that his club "must win (this) game or quit the league."[14]

Chester took the highly anticipated contest, 3–0, in front of 5,000 fans, besting the former White Sox battery of Claude "Lefty" Williams and Byrd "Teddy" Lynn. Williams had won 17 games for Chicago in 1917 and six more early in 1918, and had unwisely speculated on what he would do to poor Chester, "but bragging doesn't win games, and Williams soon found it out."[15] The league leaders plated all three runs in the third inning before chasing Williams in the sixth. Jackson, Williams's former Chicago teammate, didn't appear—and regardless of Gallagher's bold statement, Harlan stayed in the league.

Chester finally lost a game on July 6, bowing 7–5 to New York Ship at Camden. The *Chester Times* acknowledged the loss, but devoted more space to describing Chief Bender leading Hog Island to a 6–3 win over Merchant Ship the same day. "Bender Does the Trick," the headline read. "Chief Bender, doing the twirling for the Islanders, showed all of his old-time cunning, and had the Bristol boys at his mercy all during the game."[16]

Dan Griner had been a pitcher for the Cardinals and the Dodgers, but gave up two home runs to "Shoeless" Joe Jackson in the final game of the 1918 shipbuilding league playoffs.

Hog Island now trailed Chester by only half a game. "When Hog Island started the season it looked like anything but a ball team that played the opening contest against Traylor at Franklin Field, but hard work has molded together one of the best clubs hereabouts," the *Public Ledger* declared. "Great interest is centered in next Saturday's game between Hog Island and Chester."[17]

More than 2,000 fans watched the thriller the following week at Upland. Ebullient headlines in the *Chester Times* told the tale: "Chester Wins Thrilling Game From Hog Island/Shipmakers Stage Wonderful Rallies, Tieing [sic] the Score in the Eleventh and Chasing the Winning Run Over in the Next Period—Long, Miller's Southern League [sic] Heaver, Pitches Great Ball."[18]

Chester's record now stood at 9–1. "Chester Ship virtually won the pennant of the Delaware River Ship League by defeating Hog Island, 4 to 3," the *Public Ledger* opined.[19]

Despite the wonderful game, the real excitement that week had centered on Red Sox pitcher George Herman Ruth. On the fourth of July, headlines on sports pages across the country declared that Ruth had jumped the Boston club to pitch for Chester. Boston management threatened injunctions, but teammates didn't believe the news and said they expected to see the Babe back any day. His Red Sox pals were right. Ruth had stormed home to Baltimore after an argument with Manager Ed Barrow, but returned once tempers cooled.

LIBRARY OF CONGRESS BAIN COLLECTION

Chester Manager Frank Miller later conceded that he had received a wire from Ruth, but said the pitcher had asked only to play for his team on the holiday, and hadn't inquired about a job in the shipyard.

"Ruth doesn't even know I am managing the Chester team," Miller insisted. "He probably thinks I am still running the Upland club, which was abandoned because of the war. The Chester Shipbuilding Company is not financing the ball club. It was simply organized by the employees and has to be self-supporting."[20]

Draft calls and enlistments continued depleting big-league rosters as the summer wore on. A government "work or fight" order covering male workers nationwide added to the woes. Shipyard teams naturally attracted many worried ballplayers. Hog Island Manager Johnny Castle, who'd had a cup of coffee with the Phillies in 1910, stoutly defended his team's ex-big leaguers.

"If any new men wish to enter this work they can start at about $35 a week and they will earn every cent they get," Castle said. "If they show any unusual ability they will receive more. Not one cent extra will be paid to ball players. Hans Lobert and Chief Bender are on the job from morning until night and play ball on their off days. That's how things are run at Hog Island. I don't know anything about the other yards."[21]

Shipyard workers and Philadelphia-area fans alike seemed to accept such arguments. The Delaware River league drew good crowds as the summer waned.

"Shipyard baseball is a very exciting branch of our great national outdoor sport," wrote Robert W. Maxwell, the *Public Ledger* sports editor. "It is beginning to cut a wide swath in the sporting world, and if the big leagues take the count these independent teams will step in and furnish the fans some real fun and amusement. It is a different kind of baseball, but the spectators are handed more thrills."

Maxwell described the rural Upland field, where 3,500 fans could watch Chester play Harlan, as "one of the most picturesque spots we have ever seen... On that field you can see more exciting baseball in one afternoon than you can witness in a modern park in a month."[22]

This was a hardscrabble shipyard league in wartime, however, and hardly a dreamy idyll. Several teams played their home games not in pastoral perfection, but within the confines of their own clanging shipyards. An exhibition game between Chester and

LIBRARY OF CONGRESS BAIN COLLECTION

George Mogridge defected in mid-May from the New York Yankees to the shipbuilding league, prompting a tirade from manager Miller Huggins against the aggressive recruiting. According to Huggins, one of his players "was offered more money... than his American League baseball contract called for."

Sun Ship at the latter's new athletic field on a raw, rainy Memorial Day provided a perfect example.

"On all four sides of the field are tents pitched for the shelter of a company of soldiers who are training and on guard duty at the plant," the *Chester Times* reported. "The sight was an attraction in itself and the boys went through their drills while the game was in progress. Another singular incident was the launching of a minesweeper by the Sun Company. The boat glided into the Delaware while the game was ending and no one knew anything of the launching."[23] (Later in the season, fans also saw the launching of a cargo ship during a game at the Harlan yard in Wilmington.)

Chester had the pennant nearly sewn up in late July. "Frank Miller and his crowd of Chester clouters have captured the championship of the Delaware River Ship League. They visited Bristol on Saturday and had a slugfest at the expense of Merchants," the *Public Ledger* reported—somewhat prematurely, as it turned out.[24]

Questions about player eligibility still beset the league. A week after the *Public Ledger* item appeared, Chester, Merchant, and Sun all were forced to forfeit a game apiece, with two more games still under protest. "The managers accepted the rulings gracefully, claiming they did so in ignorance, believing the men protested had fulfilled all the league qualifications,"

LIBRARY OF CONGRESS BAIN COLLECTION

Joe Jackson went to work as a painter at a subsidiary of Bethlehem Steel and suited up for his first game Harlan's Steel League on June 1.

the *Chester Times* explained.[25] The uncertainty persisted far into August. "DELAWARE RIVER SHIP TITLE STILL UP IN AIR ON PLAYERS' ELIGIBILITY," the *Public Ledger* headlined.

"The pennant in the Delaware River Shipyard Baseball League will not be awarded until the eligibility status of a number of players under question has been further investigated," said Edgar S. McKaig, league secretary and a member of the Emergency Fleet Corporation.[26] The season ended with Chester, Harlan, and Hog Island all even.

"TRIPLE TIE IN SHIPYARD LEAGUE WILL BE BROKEN BY END OF THE WEEK," the *Public Ledger* announced.[27]

The tie wasn't broken on the diamond, but rather in corporate meeting rooms. An eligibility committee issued a ruling on August 22, taking victories away from both Chester and Hog Island. As a result, the Chester club plummeted from atop the standings with a record of 12–2 to fourth place at 8–6. Harlan was suddenly tied with New York Ship, both with revised 11–3 records.

"CHESTER LOSES TO 'OFFICIALS,'" blared the *Chester Times*. "There is no denying but Chester has

the best team," the paper groused. "It is unfortunate that a league of this kind should have fielded such an incompetent set of officials who might do well in deciding a game of ceckers, [sic] but are way off in baseball."[28]

The league arranged a one-game Harlan-New York playoff, set for noon Wednesday, August 28. The Strawbridge & Clothier Athletic Field at 63rd and Walnut Streets in Philadelphia provided the neutral site.

Harlan's other baseball team meanwhile had finished third in the Steel League following a 19-game schedule. Joe Jackson, who had led the Bethlehem league with a .393 batting average, now at last joined Harlan's Delaware River lineup. Former Washington Nationals Patsy Gharrity and George Dumont also made the switch with him.

"Just what the eligibility rules of the Shipyard League are we do not know," wrote *Philadelphia Inquirer* sportswriter Edgar Wolfe (under the pseudonym Jim Nasium), "but Chester must have committed murder if they were found guilty enough to have their games thrown out, while the acts of Harlan in reinforcing its team with players from another league solely for the decisive championship contest can be considered innocent."[29]

Harlan easily won the playoff game, 5–0. Jackson played center field, went one for three at the plate, walked once, and scored a run. "With Joe Jackson the Wilmington Bunch Grabs Play-off," the *Chester Times* headlined.[30] Still resenting the technical ruling that had cost Chester the pennant, the newspaper said little else about Shoeless Joe's very belated league debut.

The playoff victory next sent Harlan into a best-of-five series for the championship of Atlantic Coast shipyards. The new opponent was Standard Shipbuilding of Staten Island, which had won the New York Shipyard League pennant. Jackson again was in the Wilmington lineup for the opener September 7 at the Phillies' ballpark, the Baker Bowl. Standard led the game 2–1 entering the ninth inning.

"The Harlans looked like a beaten team until Jackson, who is suffering with an injured right foot, took Dumont's place at bat in the ninth," the *New York Sun* reported.[31] Shoeless Joe "lammed out a hard drive down the first base line for a single," the *Inquirer* added. "Jackson could have easily made a two-bagger out of the hit if it had not been for his injured foot, as it was all he could do to reach first."[32] The single started a rally that brought Harlan a 3–2 victory.

The series shifted north to the Polo Grounds the following day. In a steady drizzle, and with Jackson out of the line-up, the old Chicago battery of Williams and Lynn held Standard scoreless before 4,000 fans. Two first-inning runs held up for Harlan's 2–0 victory.

The Wilmington team went for the sweep back in Philadelphia on September 14. Jackson returned to the Harlan lineup before 4,500 fans, doubled, and homered twice off former Cardinal and Dodger pitcher Dan Griner. "Shoeless Joe was a whole show in himself," the *Public Ledger* marveled.[33]

"When Jackson hit his second home run, which virtually clinched the game and series for Harlan, the Wilmington fans went money mad and showered him with greenbacks," the *New York Sun* added. "For more than five minutes he was kept busy walking to the boxes and pulling in bills. After he had his fist full he walked over to a box directly behind home plate and handed them to his wife."[34]

"Joe was not a bit backward about accepting the financial reward and he made a tour of the boxes collecting everything handed out," reported the *Philadelphia Inquirer*, which put the total windfall at $60.[35]

The 4–0, two-hit victory by Williams gave Harlan & Hollingsworth the Atlantic Coast Shipyard championship. With it came the Coxe Trophy, a 30-inch-high silver loving cup donated by William G. Coxe of the Emergency Fleet Corporation. This final, stirring game was also the brightest moment in the league's brief history.

The First World War ended with the armistice on November 11. Many shipyards downsized or closed by the following spring. The Delaware River Shipbuilding League briefly fielded six amateur teams before folding in 1919. Shoeless Joe Jackson and Lefty Williams both returned to Charles Comiskey's big-league club in Chicago, where their names would be forever tarred by the Black Sox scandal. ∎

Notes

1. "Poor Rules May Hamper Shipbuilders' Baseball," *Philadelphia Public Ledger*, May 13, 1918.
2. Ibid.
3. Ibid.
4. "Joe Jackson Must Resign in Two Weeks," *Washington Times*, May 13, 1918.
5. "Joe Jackson to Be Shipbuilder; Quits White Sox," *Indianapolis Star*, May 14, 1918.
6. "Caught on the Fly," *The Sporting News*, October 3, 1918.
7. "Major Kolnitz Former Player Defends Jackson," *New Castle* (Pennsylvania) *News*, February 6, 1919.
8. "Little League Furnish Lots of Excitement in Week-end Baseball Games," *Philadelphia Public Ledger*, May 20, 1918.
9. "Pusey & Jones Here Saturday," *Chester Times*, June 12, 1918.
10. Lewis Lee Arms, "Huggins Sounds Warning of 'Ship Building' Menace to Game," *New York Tribune*, May 15, 1918.
11. "Shipyard Players Do Not Camouflage," *The Sporting News*, August 8, 1918.
12. Ibid.
13. "Little League Leaders Suffer Severe Setbacks; Southampton Swamped," *Philadelphia Public Ledger*, June 17, 1918.
14. "Ship League Game Will Feature Schedule in Minor League Circuit," *Philadelphia Public Ledger*, June 22, 1918.
15. "Lansdowne Looms Strong as Winner of the First Half Main Line Pennant … Chester Chases 'Lefty' Williams," *Philadelphia Public Ledger*, June 24, 1918.
16. "Sun Ship Trims Chester Outfit … Bender Does the Trick," *Chester Times*, July 8, 1918.
17. "Hog Island Ball Nine Only Half Game From Lead in the Ship League," *Philadelphia Public Ledger*, July 8, 1918.
18. "Chester Wins Thrilling Game From Hog Island," *Chester Times*, July 15, 1918.
19. "Thirteenth Scheduled Contest on July 13 a Hoodoo for Lupton… Chester Looks Like a Winner in Ship League," *Philadelphia Public Ledger*, July 15, 1918.
20. "Ruth Is Peeved But Babe Will Pitch for Red Sox," *Auburn* (New York) *Citizen*, July 10, 1918.
21. Robert W. Maxwell, "Reprieve by President Until October 15 Only Can Save Major Leagues … Few Soft Jobs Left—Men Must Work Like the Others," *Philadelphia Public Ledger*, July 20, 1918.
22. Robert W. Maxwell, "Thrills of Old Days of Baseball Revived in Shipyard Circles," *Philadelphia Public Ledger*, July 15, 1918.
23. "Sun Wallops Chester Ship," *Chester Times*, May 31, 1918
24. "'Little League' Ball May Soon Prove the Center Attraction," *Philadelphia Public Ledger*, July 22, 1918.
25. "Chester Loses Protest Game," *Chester Times*, July 25, 1918.
26. "Delaware River Ship Title Still Up in Air on Players' Eligibility," *Philadelphia Public Ledger*, August 12, 1918.
27. Robert W. Maxwell, "Triple Tie in Shipyard League Will Be Broken by End of the Week," *Philadelphia Public Ledger*, August 16, 1918.
28. "Chester Loses to 'Officials,'" *Chester Times*, August 23, 1918.
29. "Harlan Team Is Ship Yard Champ," *Philadelphia Inquirer*, August 29, 1918.
30. "Harlan Trims New York Ship," *Chester Times*, August 29, 1918.
31. "Standard Shipyard Nine Is Defeated," *New York Sun*, September 8, 1918.
32. "Harlan Triumphs Over Standard," *Philadelphia Inquirer*, September 8, 1918.
33. "Harlan Wins Coxe Trophy," *Philadelphia Public Ledger*, September 16, 1918.
34. "Jackson's Homers Defeat Standards," *New York Sun*, September 15, 1918.
35. "Joe Jackson Bats Harlan to Title," *Philadelphia Inquirer*, September 15, 1918.

Harry Passon

Philadelphia Baseball Entrepreneur

Rebecca T. Alpert

Semi-professional baseball, black and white, flourished in Philadelphia in the first half of the twentieth century. Harry Passon (1897–1954), a Jewish owner of Philadelphia's leading sporting goods store, played a strategic role in organizing and promoting it. In his youth, Passon played first base for a variety of local baseball teams and was a well-respected basketball player for the renowned South Philadelphia Hebrew Association team (SPHAS). He also coached evening school basketball at the University of Pennsylvania as well as basketball, baseball, and football in the Army.[1] Newspaper reports described him as "the well-known local all-around athlete."[2] However, after World War I his interests turned to the business side of sports. Along with Ed Gottlieb, his childhood friend, teammate, and eventual business associate, Passon was responsible for making Philadelphia a leading center for semi-professional sports, especially baseball. This essay will examine Passon's experience in and contribution to the segregated world of black baseball in Philadelphia.

Passon's involvement in sports management began when he, Gottlieb, and Hughie Black, founders and stars of the basketball (and baseball) SPHAS, opened PGB Sporting Goods in 1920. They reported having done so because they wanted better uniforms for their teams than the sponsoring organization would provide.[3] Passon saw the financial and social benefits of supplying good-looking uniforms and high-quality equipment to local teams. Running and promoting the sporting goods store became his central focus. Before long Passon bought out Gottlieb and Black and brought his younger brothers in to help him run the business.[4] Passon's Sporting Goods, located at 507 Market Street, was the hub of the Philadelphia semi-professional sports world for decades. Gottlieb maintained offices for his own sports promotion enterprise in the building through the mid-1940s. Passon's Sporting Goods was the home base of the Passon Athletic Association, a member of the Amateur Athletic Union. The Union sponsored all the Passon Clubs (baseball, basketball, boxing, track and field, and soccer).[5] The store also housed a booking service and served as a place where managers, players, and umpires came to meet and find one another to talk sports, purchase equipment, make deals, and schedule contests. Passon was appointed State Commissioner of semi-professional baseball in 1936, organizing the tournament that selected the team that would represent Pennsylvania in Ray Dumont's National Baseball Congress Tournament in Wichita. Passon also maintained and rented out Passon Field at 48th and Spruce Streets. He was among the first baseball entrepreneurs to install lights for evening games, and he played a key role in challenging Pennsylvania's Blue Laws that were finally overturned in 1934. He also organized semi-pro leagues and owned several baseball teams, both white (Passon's Athletic Club) and black (the Bacharach Giants).

Passon had a complicated relationship with the black teams he owned, operated, and scheduled. Beginning in the 1920s, African Americans ran most black teams—it had become a mark of racial pride. White ownership became a point of contention between the newly-developing leadership of the Negro Leagues, Rube Foster and Ed Bolden. The best team in Philadelphia in that era, the Hilldale Daisies, was the project of Bolden, a middle-class black man who worked for the Post Office. Although Bolden also identified himself as a "race man," he understood that in order to finance his team, he would need the support of powerful whites who had access not only to capital but to playing fields and other teams to play. Foster also relied on white financing, but was less public about it. As organizer of the Eastern Colored League, Bolden had made peace while working with Nat Strong, the man who controlled black baseball in New York City. Passon became acquainted with Bolden through the world of semi-professional baseball in Philadelphia, and the Daisies were among Passon's first clients in the sporting goods store. When Bolden was having difficulties keeping Hilldale afloat he initially turned to Passon for help and support. But when Bolden's efforts did not make it off the ground, Passon started his own team, the Bacharach Giants.

Bolden then turned instead to Passon's friend and rival, Ed Gottlieb, who became Bolden's silent partner with his newly organized team, the Philadelphia Stars.

As early as 1923, when Passon was in his mid-twenties, he was identified in the black press as the manager of two local black baseball teams, the Texas Eagles and Philadelphia Giants.[6,7] As many athletes played baseball in the summer and basketball in the winter, most of Passon's connections derived from his experiences in the basketball world. Apart from his work with the SPHAS, he also coached the Panthers, a black basketball team that often practiced with the SPHAS.[8] A few years later, Passon was no longer associated with the SPHAS, but began to operate his own white team in the American Basketball League. Passon became the league's leading scorer in addition to managing the team.[9]

Passon's business acumen developed and he decided it would be a good investment to become the proprietor of a baseball field as well. By 1929, he had taken over the popular field at the northwest corner of 48th and Spruce Streets in West Philadelphia and renamed it Passon Field. Formerly called Lit Brothers Field and Elks Field, the grounds were in need of improvements. By May, Passon had added 1,500 new seats in hopes of making the location an even more popular attraction for black and white audiences. With good access to public transportation and in the midst of a middle-class white neighborhood with a very small African American population, this field had the potential to provide Passon with a regular source of income, although he only rented the land. Making sure the arena was popularly known as Passon Field also created another opportunity to advertise the brand that was becoming a household word in the Philadelphia sports community.

From the opening of the 1929 season Passon used the field as a location from which to challenge the Blue Laws, scheduling his (white) Passon Athletic Club for Sunday games. The Passon Club, managed by his associate Malcolm McGowan, was playing against a black team, the Broncos, managed by the well-known Negro League player Louis Santop. Both managers were arrested and, oddly, charged with disorderly conduct.[10] Passon testified in court to how peaceful the game was. Passon repeatedly challenged the blue laws in order to, as he said, "find out just where amateur baseball stands in Philadelphia." He resented the fact that other sports (like miniature golf) were not shut down, but only subject to "summons and fine."[11]

Before the 1930 season commenced Ed Bolden sought Passon's help. Bolden assumed that the collapse

COURTESY OF THE PASSON FAMILY VIA THE AUTHOR

Harry Passon, the Jewish owner of a sporting goods store, played a strategic role in promoting both black and white semi-pro baseball in Philadelphia.

of the American Negro League (a league organized in 1929 from teams that survived the collapse of Bolden's Eastern Colored League the year before), coupled with the stock market crash, meant the end of the Hilldale team. Planning to start a new club in Philadelphia, he did not renew the lease on the ballpark in Darby, the suburb where the team had played for many years, and shipped the team's equipment to Passon Field. It was rumored that Passon would be financing a new Hilldale team that Bolden would be organizing.[12] Three members of the old Hilldale Corporation blocked Bolden from dissolving the club and secured themselves a new lease to continue to operate the original club in Darby. Bolden's plan to develop a new team with Passon did not come to pass, although rumors continued to surface about Bolden organizing a new team, operated by former star John Henry "Pop" Lloyd and sponsored by "the Passon interests" in the winter of 1931.[13]

Instead, Passon went out on his own and began to organize an independent black team. Passon did not use his own name for the black team. Rather, he appropriated the name of the Bacharach Giants, an old Eastern Colored League team from Jacksonville, Florida, that had been playing in Atlantic City until the collapse of the American Negro League. The Giants had been a successful franchise but, like other teams, were undone by the Crash and played their last games in 1929 to meager attendance. Ironically, the Bacharachs were named after another white Jew, Atlantic City mayor Harry Bacharach. Bacharach himself was supportive of the team, but had no official affiliation with it. Passon's Bacharachs would be based in

Philadelphia, and play at Passon Field on Monday evenings, where Passon had installed lights to his refurbished field. The team planned to travel on Wednesdays and Saturdays. To assemble the Bacharach team, Passon drew on many players who had been successful with other teams, including Hilldale and the St. Louis Stars. Otto Briggs, who was close to Bolden, managed them. Former stars "Sleepy" Joe Lewis also signed on to play for the team, as did Turkey Stearns, Jesse "Nip" Winters, Pop Lloyd, and Obie Lackey.[14] The Bacharachs played well against highly-skilled opponents like the Pittsburgh Crawfords, Homestead Grays, New York Black Yankees, Hilldale, and the Lincoln Giants. Rumors circulated in the black press about the possibility of a new league forming, or at the very least a round-robin tournament to determine a champion, although in 1932 the teams continued to play independently.[15]

In 1933, as interest in the Bacharachs grew, Passon made improvements to the field, adding a grandstand, clubhouse, and a more sophisticated lighting system.[16] Ed Bolden, meanwhile, started a new independent black team, the Philadelphia Stars. Instead of working with Passon, Bolden's co-owner was Ed Gottlieb. Bolden and Gottlieb would own the Stars together, with Gottlieb remaining the financial power and silent partner, until Bolden's death in 1950 when Gottlieb took control. For the 1933 season, the Stars played at Passon Field. The Bacharachs and Stars, the top two black teams in the area, were billed as rivals.[17] In addition to games against each other, both teams played against Passon's own white team, on which at least one of the Passon brothers, probably Chickie, continued to play first base.[18] They also battled Gottlieb's Jewish team, the SPHAS, as well as popular traveling teams that Gottlieb booked, like the House of David.[19] The black press built up the rivalry, probably at Gottlieb's urging, to encourage fan interest.[20]

Although Passon's teams did well and received a fair amount of media attention, he was not sure that he wanted to continue running the Bacharachs. He told Rollo Wilson that independent co-plan baseball was causing problems and, if he were to continue with the Bacharachs, he would want to pay the players on salary and be part of a league. The problem was that some of the players were taking advantage of the access to goods in his store. He told a reporter:

> They came into my sports goods store, got radios, clothing and other articles and never paid for them. Not all of the men did this, understand, but some of them did, and I am stuck for plenty.

I have had my experience in that line and I am through.[21]

In 1934, however, things changed for the better on several counts. First, due to Passon's earlier efforts and the influence of Connie Mack, the Pennsylvania legislature opened the Sunday blue laws to the possibility of playing games on Sunday afternoons and charging admission without fear of arrest or having to pay bribes.[22] Second, a new league was being formed.

Passon was recruited by sportswriter and entrepreneur Cumberland Posey to join Gus Greenlee's newly established National Negro Association of Baseball Clubs (that would later become the Negro National League). The Bacharachs applied for league membership and Passon attended several organizational meetings during the winter. Nevertheless, the Bacharachs were denied membership because, as the *Pittsburgh Courier* reported, Stars owners Bolden and Gottlieb refused to join if the Bacharachs were included. Bolden said that he made this move against Passon because he did not believe that the city could support two teams. In response to the opposition from his rivals, Passon withdrew his request for full membership. To the press he expressed surprise, not anger. Randy Dixon reported that he was also shocked by Bolden's move and Passon's acquiescence, as Passon appeared to be prepared to post forfeits and assume obligations of membership. Cum Posey, who was both an owner and a columnist for the *Courier*, expressed his disappointment with the decision. In his column, he argued that as long as the clubs did not play in Philadelphia on the same date, the Bacharachs—who could draw on the road—would be an important attraction for the league.[23]

Passon, the black press, and other team owners like Cum Posey had difficulty understanding Bolden's opposition. They did not agree with the assessment that Philadelphia could not support two league teams. It is unlikely that Bolden worried about attracting fans, because he committed to having the Stars play at Passon Field, and convinced Passon to make more improvements to the field. Passon did so, adding another 4,000 seats. The Stars played their weekend home games there for the season as did the Bacharachs. Bolden's opposition may have stemmed from his anger at Passon for starting his own team rather than working with Bolden. Bolden would also have been unhappy had the Stars not been the top Philadelphia team, and having the Bacharachs in the league could have threatened the Stars' status. It is also possible that Gottlieb's rivalry with Passon contributed to the problem. Bolden chose Gottlieb, not Passon, as the white man he would work with. The relationship among the three was complex.[24] The Bacharachs were subsequently accepted to associate membership, which meant they would play games against league teams and would be protected against being raided for players (insofar as the league could control its members) in exchange for a 50 percent franchise fee.[25]

The Stars began their season in the new league at Passon Field against the Newark Dodgers. Articles about the event boasted about the refurbished stadium with the additional seating. An officer of the Pennsylvania State Athletic Commission threw out the first ball and the Octavio Catto Band entertained.[26] Coverage in the black press noted that fans were pleased by the new field arrangements and praised Passon for providing them.[27] The Bacharachs had a strong first-half season as associate members. Former Hilldale star Otto Briggs was managing and the team won 22 of its first 27 games. Sportswriters spread rumors that Passon was trying to obtain the services of Satchel Paige.[28] The "big hearted" Passon won the admiration of the black press for how he handled himself in the context of the business of black baseball. Rollo Wilson, who was both a sportswriter and the commissioner of the league, devoted an entire column to praising Passon's "sportsmanship" and "intestinal fortitude." Wilson appreciated how Passon handled his players who "overdrew accounts, went into his store and bought stuff and didn't pay and didn't deliver baseball of which they were capable." And many of them didn't play well and left at the end of the 1933 season, making it difficult for Passon to put together a team for the following season. Yet Passon paid salaries, met obligations, and vowed to put together a better club in 1934.[29] Based on their first-half performance, Passon's team, despite Bolden's objections, was awarded full membership in July 1934. At that league meeting, the team was represented by Harry's brother Chickie, Otto Briggs, and Malcolm McGowan, Passon's chief assistant and general manager.[30]

Unfortunately for Passon, these successes were short-lived. The Bacharachs did not do as well in the second half of the season, compiling a record of 3–11 by mid-August.[31] And several episodes of violence at Passon Field marred the rest of the season. In one case, a player assaulted an umpire.[32] Later that season a detective was injured arresting men accused of beating a park attendant. The newspaper noted complaints all season about a gang of alleged "hoodlums" who waited in left field and kept the balls knocked out of the park. Passon had retained a man named Henry Taylor to retrieve the balls. One night the detective caught the men as they were beating up Taylor.[33] The neighbors raised concerns about safety, and it was clear that Passon did not have the situation under control. In addition, visiting teams complained that Passon had set the admission price too low. He raised the fees when the league played some of the "World's Colored Championship Series" there in September.[34] But Bolden and the Stars would move their "home" games to the nearby Penmar Field at 44th and Parkside the following year. The park had a larger seating capacity and was under Gottlieb's control.

The following January when the league owners met, Passon was ready to rejoin. He and Malcolm McGowen, along with new manager Phil Cockrell, another former Hilldale player, represented the Bacharachs.[35] Although Passon was once again praised in the national black press for being among those owners who "caught the vision and pledged unstinted efforts toward making a permanent and abiding organization for Negro baseball," Passon had decided to quit.[36] He offered to sell the franchise for $400, which was the amount that he had advanced in player contracts. One of the owners suggested that it really wasn't necessary for the other owners to make good on those contracts and suggested that they "just go on and sign them up anyway." Passon went away disappointed with the way the league owners treated him and his players.[37] Passon continued to field the Bacharachs as an independent semi-pro team that still played against (and served as a source of young players for) the Stars and other league teams. Passon continued his association with the league in another way—his sporting goods store supplied equipment to the league and the Worth ball that he sold remained the official ball of the National Association in 1935 and 1936.[38]

Nineteen thirty-five was also a tumultuous year in Harry's personal life as his wife, Bessie Greenbaum, died at 34, leaving Harry alone with a young daughter. Nonetheless, he took on a new project, turning his attention to the white, semi-professional game as the Pennsylvania Commissioner in 1936. Under his leadership, Pennsylvania became the first state to organize championship games for entry into Ray Hap Dumont's national showcase for semi-pro teams, the National Baseball Congress in Wichita.[39] Passon also sponsored international soccer matches, welcoming the Maccabee Tel Aviv F.C. soccer team in 1936 from Palestine to play against his own Passon soccer team.[40]

Passon Field was at the center of another controversy in 1937 when Joe Louis brought his "Brown Bombers" softball team to play against a white Philly

NATIONAL BASEBALL HALL OF FAME LIBRARY, COOPERSTOWN, NY

Ed Bolden, whose Hilldale Daisies were among Passon's earliest customers, would later become a rival when Passon started the Bacharach Giants.

All-Star team that Passon organized. A crowd estimated at 30,000 wanted to see the contest—but the park only seated 4,000. As people were entering, the grandstand collapsed. Five people were hurt in the crush. The white press reported they were "all Negroes," although the crowd was integrated. The game was moved to another time and location.[41]

Passon continued to have his teams, the black Bacharachs and the white Passon team (often called the "storeboys"), play at Passon Field through the 1930s. He also sponsored football, soccer, and tennis at the location. By 1937 Tom Dixon, a former Negro Leagues player and Passon's employee in the sporting goods store, was managing the Bacharachs. Along with Malcolm McGowan, Dixon has been credited with bringing the young Roy Campanella into professional baseball. The Bacharachs would be the first team he played for, and they[42] continued to serve as a "feeder" team for other Negro League teams through the mid-1940s, although they no longer played at Passon Field.

Unfortunately, pressures in Harry's life continued to be difficult for him, and family members reported that Harry was depressed and had threatened suicide. In February 1954 he was found dead in the ammunition vault of his store, a gun at his feet from which one bullet had been fired.[43] Although he could not compete with Ed Bolden or Ed Gottlieb for prominence or power, Harry Passon was an important part of what made black baseball in Philadelphia strong and prosperous for many years—and his store and field left an important legacy in Philadelphia baseball history. ■

Notes

1. "Passon Coaching Evening School," *Philadelphia Inquirer*, January 29, 1918.
2. "Plenty of Activity on Independent Baseball Fields," *Philadelphia Inquirer*, August 11, 1918; "Harry Passon to Coach Camp Jackson Athletes," *Philadelphia Inquirer*, November 12, 1918, 12.
3. Rich Westcott, *The Mogul: Eddie Gottlieb, Philadelphia Sports Legend and Pro Basketball Pioneer* (Philadelphia: Temple University Press, 2008), 26.
4. According to Passon's niece's recollection, funding came from Passon's father-in-law, Benjamin Greenbaum. (He was also Passon's brother Sam's father-in-law). They brought their brothers Henry (Chickie), Morris, and Nat into the business. Posted at ancestry.com, 19 December 2010 http://boards.ancestry.com/surnames.passon/10.3/mb.ashx. Passon's sister Gertrude [Silverman] and her husband also worked in the store. Harry's other sister, Bertha, became a pharmacist, and other brother Morris later became an attorney. Sam left the sporting goods store in the 1950s and opened his own electronics business. The store moved from the Market Street location in 1953 when Philadelphia purchased the property to create a site for the Liberty Bell and relocated to 733 Arch Street, relocating to 1028 Arch in 1960 and remaining there through the 1970s. The brothers began a mail-order business that they subsequently sold. It remains in business to this day. (Bonnie Silverman, personal communication, September 30, 2012; Barbara Joyce-Jones, telephone conversation, October 6, 2012; "Building at 731 Arch is Sold to Stationers," *Evening Bulletin*, February 9, 1960.)
5. "Passon Club in A.A.U.," *Evening Bulletin*, March 4, 1932.
6. "Texas Eagles are Setting a Dizzy Pace," *Philadelphia Tribune*, August 2, 1924.
7. W. Rollo Wilson, "Eastern Snapshots," *Pittsburgh Courier*, June 27, 1925.
8. "Panther Five to be Formidable Foe This Season," *Pittsburgh Courier*, October 4, 1924.
9. "Borgeman Threatens Goal-Tossing Leader," Washington Post, March 10, 1927.
10. "Broncos Leading By One Run When Police Break Up Game," *Philadelphia Tribune*, September 5, 1929.
11. "Three Sentenced for Sunday Ball Game in Philly," *Syracuse Herald*, August 5, 1930; "3 Men Get 30 Days for Sunday Ball," *Evening Bulletin*, August 4, 1930.
12. Neil Lanctot, *Fair Dealing and Clean Playing: The Hilldale Club and the Development of Black Professional Baseball, 1910–1932* (Jefferson, NC, Mc Farland and Co., 1994), 203. See also *Pittsburgh Courier*, April 12, 1930; April 19, 1930.
13. Randy Dixon, "Money Man Aligns with Hilldale Team," *Philadelphia Tribune*, February 26, 1931.
14. *Evening Bulletin*, June 12, 1931; W. Rollo Wilson, "Sports Shots," *Pittsburgh Courier*, April 9, 1932; no author, "The Bacharach Giants" *Colored Baseball and Sports Monthly* in Art Carter Files, box 12, Moorland-Spingarn Research Center, Howard University.
15. Dick Sun, "Negro World Series Gets Underway," *Philadelphia Tribune*, September 10, 1931; W. Rollo Wilson, "Sports Shots," *Pittsburgh Courier*, August 1, 1931; September 12, 1931 and Randy Dixon, "Randy Says," *Philadelphia Tribune*, August 20, 1931.

16. "Quaker Team to Open Soon," *New York Amsterdam News*, April 5, 1933.

17. "Bolden's Stars and Bacharachs Start Five Game Series," *Philadelphia Tribune*, June 22, 1933.

18. "Negro Clubs to Oppose Passon '9'" *Philadelphia Tribune*, July 13, 1933.

19. "Bolden's Nine Trims Bearded Clan by 5 to 1," *Chicago Defender*, May 13, 1933; "Passon Outfit Set to Check Bolden's Stars," *Philadelphia Tribune*, July 6, 1933.

20. "Boldenmen at Passon's Wed." *Philadelphia Tribune*, August 17, 1933; "Bacharachs and Boldenmen Settle Dispute Saturday," *Philadelphia Tribune*, August 24, 1933; "Passon Nine to Meet Bacharachs and Boldenmen," *Philadelphia Tribune*, August 31, 1933.

21. Rollo Wilson, "Sports Shots," *Pittsburgh Courier*, December 9, 1933.

22. See David Jordan, "Another Quaker City Champion: The 1934 Philadelphia Stars" *Black Ball*, 5:1 (Spring 2012), 24–32.

23. "Baseball Owners En Route to Philly Pow Wow," *Pittsburgh Courier*, February 10, 1934; Randy Dixon, "Baseball Magnates Convene in Parlay Here," *Philadelphia Tribune*, February 15, 1934; "Blacksox, Grays Not Included," *Pittsburgh Courier*, February 17, 1934; Cum Posey, "Posey's Pointed Paragraphs," *Pittsburgh Courier*, March 3, 1934.

24. Although the newspapers attribute the concerns to Bolden, it is hard to imagine that Gottlieb was not somehow involved. The meetings began at Passon's Sporting Goods Store (and Gottlieb's office) but were moved to the Citizens Republican Club at 25th and Lombard. Gottlieb, not Passon, appears in the photo that was taken of the owners at the meetings. "Moguls 'Talk Shop' in Baseball Pow-Wow," *Pittsburgh Courier*, February 24, 1934.

25. "Bolden's Team to Play All Games at New Passon Field," *Chicago Defender*, March 24, 1934.

26. Advertisement, *Philadelphia Tribune*, May 10, 1934.

27. W. Rollo Wilson, "Sports Shots," *Pittsburgh Courier*, May 19, 1934.

28. "Otto Briggs Revamping Bacharachs," *Philadelphia Tribune*, June 14, 1934.

29. W. Rollo Wilson, "Sport Shots," *Pittsburgh Courier*, October 13, 1934.

30. "Bees and Black Sox Join National League," *Philadelphia Tribune*, July 5, 1934.

31. "Philly Drubs Yanks," *Chicago Defender*, August 11, 1934.

32. "Players Pay for Offenses," *Pittsburgh Courier*, August 4, 1934.

33. "Crack Detective is Hurt Nabbing Man," *Afro-American*, August 18, 1934.

34. "Display Ad," *Philadelphia Tribune*, September 20, 1934.

35. G. Fleming, "Men Admit Two New Members," *Afro-American*, January 19, 1935.

36. Chester Washington, "Sez Ches," *Pittsburgh Courier*, March 9, 1935.

37. William Jones, "Sidelights on League Meeting," *Afro-American*, March 16, 1935; "Oust Wilson as Baseball Czar," *Philadelphia Tribune*, March 14, 1935.

38. "League Will Open," *Philadelphia Tribune*, March 26 1936.

39. "National 1936 Championship," *The Sporting News*, April 23, 1936.

40. Display Ad, *Jewish Exponent*, October 30, 1936.

41. "14 Hurt in Crash of 2 Grandstands," *Evening Bulletin*, September 21, 1937; "Joe Louis in Game at Stadium Today," *Philadelphia Inquirer*, September 21, 1937; "Joe Louis Mobbed by Crowd of 30,000," *Pittsburgh Courier*, September 25, 1937.

42. See Neil Lanctot, *Campy: The Two Lives of Roy Campanella* (New York: Simon and Schuster, 2011).

43. "Harry Passon is Found Dead," *Philadelphia Inquirer*, February 17, 1954. The story of Passon's death was front page news in the daily paper. He was described as a former sports star, founder of the SPHAS, a leader in organizing sandlot sports, co-owner of Passon Sports Company, and as active in Jewish charities. An obituary that did not mention the suspicion of suicide appeared in the *Jewish Exponent*. Passon had become involved in the Jewish community, sponsoring the Maccabiah soccer team and becoming a leading contributor to the Jewish Theological Seminary and Germantown Jewish Center in Mt. Airy where he resided with his second wife, Tillie (he remarried in 1938) and their two daughters from prior marriages, Dorothy and Marcie. "Harry Passon," *Jewish Exponent*, February 26, 1954.

The Real Jimmie Foxx

Bill Jenkinson

"You just can't imagine how far he could hit a baseball." Ted Williams spoke those words to me in a 1986 interview in Winter Haven, Florida. He was talking about his former friend and teammate, Jimmie Foxx. Ted's reflection created an unforgettable image. Yet, it wasn't what Williams said that made it so. It was how he said it…almost like a prayer whispered in a church. Teddy Ballgame was a grounded man, not given to hyperbole or casual sentimentality. But on the topic of Jimmie Foxx, he was like a child recollecting the deeds of a beloved older brother.

Later in the same conversation, Williams became teary-eyed and unashamedly emotional as he remembered Foxx, the man. Pausing to compose himself, he settled on the only words he could utter in that difficult moment: "He was a real peach of a guy." Of course, the story of Jimmie Foxx is bitter-sweet, and that was on Ted's mind as he spoke. He was there when Jimmie was still in his prime as one of baseball's greatest sluggers. He was there when Foxx's career diminished prematurely as he battled injury and alcohol. And Williams was well aware of how Jimmie Foxx struggled with life after baseball, and ultimately died before his time. So, who was James Emory Foxx, and how should he be perceived by fans in the twenty-first century?

It began in 1907, when Jimmie was born in the rural setting of Maryland's Eastern Shore. It is a place which remains today much as it was then: rolling farmlands where folks live a simpler, unadorned way of life. By 1924, at age 16, Foxx's combination of good genes, strenuous farm work, and rigorous athletic competition had created a physical prodigy. Playing minor league ball that same year for iconic fellow Maryland native Frank "Home Run" Baker, Foxx's Herculean abilities were quickly recognized. Before that first professional season ended, Jimmie signed with the Philadelphia Athletics to begin life as a major leaguer. And, although he traveled far while earning fame and fortune over the next two decades, his persona never really changed.

Foxx started as a catcher, but his legendary manager, Connie Mack, acquired Mickey Cochrane the same year. Mickey was four-and-a half years older and more experienced than Jimmie, so "Black Mike" had the inside track on that position. Cochrane proved his worth behind the plate, ultimately earning his place in Cooperstown. Yet, this initial change, combined with Foxx's athletic virtuosity, caused young Jimmie to become somewhat of a defensive gypsy, moving from position to position throughout his career.

In his first few seasons, Jimmie Foxx mostly sat on the bench beside Mack, who, recognizing his potential as well as his vulnerability, groomed him cautiously. In 1928, believing his gifted protégé was ready, Mack allowed Foxx to play in 118 games (mostly at third base) for the fast-rising Athletics. In 1929, Connie turned him loose and Jimmie Foxx, age 21, became a star first baseman.

He was built like a Greek god with bulging biceps and sculpted physique. His rounded face was marked by handsome features set off by a full head of brown hair and bright blue eyes. His joy was infectious, hustling on the field with a spontaneous smile and boundless enthusiasm. He played the game with a combination of speed and power that a later generation would see in Mickey Mantle. Foxx ran like a cheetah, threw like an Olympic javelin champion, and hit the ball like Babe Ruth.

During the season in those early years, Jimmie often boarded with his Aunt Virginia, who lived in North Philadelphia, not far from Shibe Park. On other occasions, he rented rooms from homeowners who resided close to the ballpark. As a result, folks came to know him well. Local merchants, stadium personnel, and ordinary townspeople watched Jimmie Foxx grow up. They liked what they saw. Life was like a dream for young Jimmie Foxx. In 1928, when the Athletics nearly dethroned the lordly New York Yankees, led by Babe Ruth and Murderers' Row, he teamed with future Hall of Famers Mickey Cochrane, Al Simmons, and Lefty Grove, as well as aging legends Ty Cobb, Eddie Collins, and Tris Speaker. Then, in 1929, with Jimmie pounding 33 home runs, Philadelphia actually defeated the Yanks for the American League pennant and went on to win the World Series.

In 1930 the Athletics repeated as World Champions, while Foxx slammed 37 home runs. The following year, the A's barely missed their third straight championship when the St. Louis Cardinals prevailed in a hard-fought, seven-game fall classic. Jimmie added 30 more circuit shots that year, despite two serious leg injuries. Although the Yankees reclaimed the AL pennant in 1932, the personal ascendancy of Jimmie Foxx became complete. He batted .364, slugged .749, drove in 169 runs, scored 151 times, and slammed 58 homers to challenge Ruth's so-called "unbreakable" season record of 60. As a result, Jimmie earned the American League's Most Valuable Player Award.

Sadly, finances intervened, and the glory days of the Philadelphia Athletics came to an abrupt end. Largely due to Pennsylvania's so-called "blue laws," which prohibited Connie Mack from scheduling profitable Sabbath baseball in Philadelphia until 1934, he was forced to sell his best players. Al Simmons went first, sold to the Chicago White Sox immediately after the 1932 season. Lefty Grove and Mickey Cochrane followed after the 1933 campaign, respectively joining the Boston Red Sox and Detroit Tigers.

In the interim, despite the dwindling fortunes of his team, Jimmie Foxx enhanced his individual legacy. In 1933 he won the American League Triple Crown by recording a .356 batting average, along with 48 homers and 163 runs batted in. Jimmie also added his second straight Most Valuable Player Award. Even as the Athletics plummeted in the standings during 1934–35, Foxx kept pounding away. In those two otherwise gloomy seasons, he added 80 more home runs, batted a combined .340, and drove in 245 runs.

Yet, seemingly unknown at that moment, a malady of body and mind was growing inside Jimmie Foxx. The affliction would not destroy Foxx quickly. It would gradually erode his gifts to the point where he would never attain the supremacy for which he seemed to be destined. On October 8, 1934, while barnstorming in Winnipeg, Canada, Jimmie was struck violently on the left side of his head by a pitched ball. Batting helmets were not worn at that time. Although x-rays were negative, Foxx was diagnosed with a concussion.

He stayed in the local hospital for four days, but two days after leaving was too lethargic to play in an exhibition game in Spokane. Although this should have raised a red flag, Foxx resumed a prearranged tour to the Far East with other American League stars and sailed across the Pacific Ocean. There he played in every one of his team's international games, including 18 in Japan. Upon returning to Philadelphia on January 6, 1935, Jimmie confirmed that he would resume

NATIONAL BASEBALL HALL OF FAME LIBRARY, COOPERSTOWN, NY

Foxx started out as a catcher, but Connie Mack acquired Mickey Cochrane in the same year, and the future Hall-of-Fame catcher nabbed the position, pushing Foxx to the infield corners, mostly third in 1928 and first in 1929.

the grueling duties of catcher, a position that he had not manned in seven years.

But on January 24, before leaving for spring training in Florida, Foxx underwent a double surgical procedure in Philadelphia. Dr. Herb Goddard removed Jimmie's tonsils, along with a nasal obstruction. Hardly anyone took notice of that event, but it was a harbinger of the eventual downfall of Jimmie Foxx. The effects of his "beaning" a few months before in Canada were beginning to manifest.

As promised, Jimmie played catcher in every spring game, as Connie Mack saluted him as the best receiver in the American League. He stayed there until third baseman Pinky Higgins was injured, whereupon Foxx, the dutiful soldier, temporarily replaced him. He moved back to catcher before finally resuming his normal spot at first base on May 25. Through this period, Foxx and his teammates rarely enjoyed a scheduled off day, playing in-season exhibition games in Carlisle, Pennsylvania, Buffalo, Allentown, Pennsylvania, Bridgeton, New Jersey, and Hartford. When the season ended, Jimmie joined another troupe of barnstormers for an extended schedule of games in Mexico. These events directly preceded his sale (officially called a release) to Boston.

Coming from nearby Maryland and growing up on the A's roster, Jimmie was viewed as a hometown hero. After he married, Foxx purchased a home in the Philadelphia suburbs, further endearing him to the local populace. Connie Mack understood this, and desperately wanted to keep "Double X" as an Athletic. Foxx played like a superstar, and wanted to be paid like one, but Mack was on the brink of bankruptcy in those hard Depression times, and was powerless to keep him. The last star level player to leave, 28-year old Jimmie Foxx departed Philadelphia for the Boston Red Sox in 1936.

In truth, Foxx was elated with the opportunity to again play for a contender while earning an income commensurate with his skills. However, he immediately acknowledged how much he would miss the Philadelphia fans with whom he had grown into manhood. For their part, Philly fans were devastated. They feared that they would never again see such a talented player in an Athletics uniform, and they never did. Predictably, Jimmie Foxx became immensely popular in Boston.

When Jimmie returned to Shibe Park for the first time as a visiting player on April 19, 1936, he was greeted in typical Philadelphia fashion. He was wildly cheered on his first at-bat, but booed thereafter by some in attendance. Even then, that was a Philly tradition. But, in their hearts, the local fans would always have a special place for Jimmie Foxx. They demonstrated that on another visit to town later that same season.

In a custom typical of the times but unknown in the modern era, the Athletics scheduled pre-game field events on September 19, 1936, when the Red Sox returned to Philadelphia. The big attraction was a 75-yard sprint race by the fastest players from both squads. It featured the A's Lou Finney and Wally Moses against Boston's Foxx. Although Jimmie had been a Maryland state sprint champion in high school, by that time in his career, he was primarily viewed as a burly slugger. Moses was regarded as the fastest man in the American League (along with Ben Chapman) with Finney rated right behind them. Yet, when the race ended, there was a virtual dead heat between the three; all were timed at 7.75 seconds. After some deliberation, Finney was declared the winner although the *Boston Herald* insisted that Foxx had finished in front.

Despite his still blazing speed, fielding virtuosity, and titanic home runs, Jimmie Foxx was showing signs of physicality that were not so benign. Earlier in the month, Jimmie had complained about vision problems associated with a sinus condition. Since he was playing productively, little attention was given to the matter.

However, when Foxx suffered through a long bout with the flu during spring training the following year, he slowly became aware that something was amiss. The Red Sox were scheduled to open the 1937 season in Philadelphia on April 20. Still not feeling well, Foxx decided to see his personal physician a few days before that opener. Again suffering from vision issues and pain above both eyes, Jimmie was quickly admitted to Jewish Hospital, where he stayed for over a week. Despite the severity of the ailment, no long-term solutions were offered. There was no apparent linkage between Foxx's 1934 head trauma and his development of these alarming symptoms.

Consistent with the behavioral norms of his era, Jimmie Foxx rarely said anything about his almost constant battle against chronic, so-called sinus pain. But in 1939, Ted Williams joined the Red Sox, and immediately bonded with Foxx. The two men talked about their rare but mutual gift for power-hitting along with many other topics. So, when Jimmie sidetracked to Philadelphia for further treatment of his problem during a trip from Chicago to Washington on May 12, 1939, Williams knew all about it. For the record, Foxx was administered the new "radio beam treatment" without any apparent results. Within a few days of returning to Boston, he suffered a relapse. That prompted Boston team physician James Conway to assert that Foxx should have been in the hospital back in 1937 instead of playing baseball.

Later that season, Jimmie succumbed to the constant pain in his lower abdomen, and checked himself into St. Joseph's Hospital in Philadelphia on September 9, where an emergency appendectomy was performed. When questioned by his surgeon prior to the operation, Foxx admitted that he had experienced symptoms for the past one-and-a-half-years! He finally sought treatment only when the pain became unbearable. This cost Jimmie the remainder of the 1939 season.

That incident, although not directly related to the main issue of Foxx's "sinuses," is an indicator of how Jimmie Foxx approached his health care. First, he never complained. Despite high levels of pain, Jimmie would simply march on, doing his best despite his burdens. Second, there was a clear pattern of postponing treatment until he could see his familiar caregivers in his former home base of Philadelphia. Many folks have that tendency, but Foxx went to extremes. Boston boasted some of the best hospitals in the country, yet Jimmie followed his country-boy instincts, and insisted on being treated only by those he knew and trusted. From a medical perspective, it was reckless and ineffective.

During those years, despite his health issues, Jimmie Foxx was still one of America's most successful athletes. From 1936 through 1940, his first five seasons with the Red Sox, Jimmie averaged about 40 home runs per year. In 1938, when he won his third American League MVP Award, Foxx slugged 50 homers, batted .349, and drove in 175 runs (still a franchise record). But in 1941, at only age 33, Jimmie Foxx suddenly fell off the athletic cliff. Ted Williams was one of the few people who understood what was really happening.

In May of that year, Jimmie had again sought treatment for his recurring blurred vision and facial pain. This time, he was told to quit smoking, which he did. Yet there was no relief. Williams remembered those times well, and recounted some of the details in that 1986 interview. Foxx himself had been wondering if the whole pattern had begun as a result of his 1934 beaning. Prior to that time, he had no such issues.

Ted remembered Jimmie being only a "social drinker" when he (Williams) joined the Sox in 1939. He actually believed that Foxx did some of his partying because of his desire to emulate Babe Ruth. Yet, Ted did not recall any overt drunkenness on the part of Double X. Then, as Jimmie's pain increased, so did his drinking. Williams recalled a cross-country airplane flight at the conclusion of the '41 season when the altitude exacerbated Jimmie's condition. As a remedy for the pain, Foxx gulped down "about a dozen" miniature bottles of scotch.

It didn't help that Jimmie had unwisely invested in St. Petersburg's declining Jungle Club Golf Club in late 1939. Florida's Gulf Coast was experiencing a downward real estate spiral at the time, and Foxx had been duped into the ill-advised venture. Since Foxx loved playing golf in Florida, he had been an easy mark for business sharks trying to unload unprofitable properties. When the market failed to rebound, Jimmie's life savings were lost. According to Williams, all this converged on Foxx at about the same time, causing Jimmie to turn more frequently to the bottle.

When Jimmie belted his 500th career home run at the implausible age of only 32 on September 24, 1940, many observers, including Ted Williams, assumed that he would ultimately surpass Ruth's record total of 714. The next day, Williams was quoted in the *Philadelphia Evening Bulletin* as saying: "What a man. And I'll bet he does it, too!" Just two months before, on July 14, Foxx had badly sprained his left knee in a collision at first base, and did not return to full duty for five days. When he did, Jimmie volunteered to catch in order to help his team. Think about that: Foxx was an established super-star slugger with 15 years of major league seniority, returning to the lineup after a serious knee injury. And he came back as a volunteer catcher, staying there for nearly six weeks!

Within days, Sox manager Joe Cronin hailed Jimmie as the finest catcher in the American League, while adding accolades about his diverse skills. In the *Boston Evening Traveler* on August 2, 1940, Cronin was quoted: "He's a marvel, isn't he? Tell me: who was a better all-around ball player than Foxxie? Why right now I'd say he was the best catcher in the American League...They can talk all they want to about some of those old time ball players being able to play different positions. I'll take Foxxie. They don't come any better."

Accordingly, two future Hall of Fame legends (Cronin and Connie Mack) had labeled Foxx as the league's best catcher, though he played that demanding position only part time. Cronin's sentiments should not be dismissed as those of a manager hyping one of his own players. Back in 1933, when they were still adversaries, Joe had referred to Foxx as "the greatest all-around ball player in the game today." That quote appeared in the *Philadelphia Record* on October 13, 1933, with Cronin specifically citing Jimmie's fabulous power, superior throwing arm, and defensive versatility. That was the day after Foxx was voted AL MVP, just ahead of the second-place Joe Cronin. Jimmie has historically been regarded as an indifferent defender, but facts say otherwise. Surely, the testimony of Cronin and Mack means something.

On August 2, 1940, the *Washington Times-Herald* featured even more laudatory sentiments from writer Frank "Buck" O'Neill. He opined: "Some of these days when baseball historians meet to award the capital prize of the national game to its greatest player of all time, they are not going to give the title and plaque to Tyrus Raymond Cobb, nor to George Herman Ruth... The present day has its candidate for the greatest of all ballplayers, and his name is James Emory Foxx of the Boston Red Sox."

Jimmie was a victim of his superb athleticism, and was often obligated to change positions. As a result, he never acquired much standing in any particular spot. Williams watched all this unfold, and never forgot Foxx's team spirit and stalwart tenacity. It is no wonder that, in 1940, Ted thought that Jimmie would go on forever. But, almost a half-century after the fact, Teddy Ballgame felt that he knew why it didn't work out that way. The combination of physical pain along with family and financial pressure eventually became too much for Foxx to endure. Adding to his already

NATIONAL BASEBALL HALL OF FAME LIBRARY, COOPERSTOWN, NY

Foxx was struck in the head with a pitch during while barnstorming after the 1934 season. During spring training 1935, Foxx took up catching again for the Athletics but did not last long at the position, first replacing the injured Pinky Higgins at third, and then resuming his usual post at first on May 25.

toxic situation, Jimmie's wife had refused to move to Boston when he was traded there, staying in Philadelphia with their young son.

Jimmie Foxx hit only 19 home runs in 1941, and the Red Sox management hoped it was simply an off year. But when he struggled early in the 1942 season, they shipped him off to the Chicago Cubs, where his play did not improve. The disillusioned Foxx sat out the entire 1943 season, but returned to play part time in 1944 and 1945 when World War II depleted the major league talent pool. As late as 1944 Cubs manager Charlie Grimm acknowledged that Jimmie still possessed awesome power, but couldn't hit because he could no longer see the ball. Then, playing big league baseball for the final time with the Phillies in 1945, there were even more flashes of Foxx's once formidable athleticism.

On August 19 he was the starting pitcher for the Phils. Featuring a fastball and twisting screwball, Jimmie went six and two thirds strong innings, striking out five while recording the win. Three weeks later at Pittsburgh's Forbes Field, Foxx blasted his final two major league homers by launching a pair of 420-footers into Schenley Park. When it was all over, Jimmie Foxx had accumulated 534 home runs, an impressive total, but far from the 714 predicted just a few years earlier.

As Ted Williams told us, however, many of those 534 were hit so far that Jimmie's power now seems fictional. In every American League stadium of his era, as well as dozens of exhibition and barnstorming sites, the trail of Foxx's longest drives challenges credibility. Twenty-four times he cleared the 65-foot high left field grandstand roof in Philadelphia. At Comiskey Park in Chicago, where no one else reached the towering roof more than twice (until home plate was moved forward in the 1980s), "The Beast" did it six times. In St. Louis at Sportsman's Park, Jimmie powered seven tremendous drives over the left field bleachers. And so on. Everywhere Foxx logged more than just a few games, and in many places where he stopped only once, the man hit home runs that defied logical analysis.

How do we assess the career of Jimmie Foxx? Let's indulge in some revisionist speculation. What if Jimmie Foxx was wearing a batting helmet when struck on the head by that pitched ball? Although nobody can say, it is not hard to make the case that Jimmie Foxx could have recorded 700 home runs along with the associated acclaim. Sure, in today's world with even more substance abuse alternatives, he might have fallen just as far into temptation. So too with his financial hardship: We still see successful athletes lose their money. And, although Jimmie was self-absorbed on occasion, consider the counterpoints: Foxx had a proven history of honesty, likeability, perseverance, resilience, and intelligence. Given those attributes, negative outcomes seem unlikely.

Obviously, something did happen to Jimmie Foxx in 1941, which caused him to diminish rapidly as an athlete. There is no definitive medical proof that the 1934 event caused his subsequent problems. His medical records are now gone, but the available data strongly point in that direction. Interestingly, in February 1940, Boston teammate Fritz Ostermueller had suffered from the same symptoms as Foxx. In the case of "Ostie," physicians linked his problem to a head trauma similar to the one Jimmie experienced in '34. On May 25, 1935, while Fritz was pitching at Fenway Park, Hank Greenberg savagely lined a ball off the left side of his face. He soon recovered but, according to the *Boston Globe* (February 23, 1940), "At that time, it was also learned doctors told Fritz he might experience a reaction from the blow within 'three or four years.'" So, why is it that nobody has connected the dots, and given Jimmie the same understanding?

Also, in the latter years of his career, Foxx referred to his malady as "neuralgia" instead of "sinus problems." Jimmie wasn't a physician, so it seems logical that he learned the term from one. Neuralgia and sinusitis are not the same. Neuralgia is a generic name for nerve pain which is often linked with trauma. Sinusitis is generally attributed to infections. What does it all mean? It is hard to know. Yet, with the advantage of well-documented hindsight, it seems likely that 26-year-old Jimmie Foxx had his nasal passages knocked violently out of alignment by the errant pitch in the autumn of 1934. As a result, he suffered a chronic infirmity from which he never recovered.

This we do know for sure: at the conclusion of the 1940 season, Jimmie Foxx was regarded as a genuine baseball hero. He was viewed as an athletic dynamo and poster boy for behavioral excellence. It is virtually impossible to find anyone who had anything bad to say about Jimmie. That includes players, coaches, managers, umpires, administrators, writers, fans, clubhouse attendants, or anyone else associated with Major League Baseball. Foxx was admired for his gentlemanly disposition, abiding generosity, work ethic, sincere camaraderie, and physical toughness. Then a combination of chronic pain and financial ruin became too much for him. Sadly, his premature decline has become his most notable legacy.

In the twenty-first century, Jimmie Foxx is often caricatured as a drunken failure. That is wrong. Jimmie drank heavily toward the end of his career, but there is no evidence that he was anything more than a moderate drinker until around 1940, when extreme adversity pushed him in the wrong direction. It is also true that life was often unkind to Foxx after his playing days, but, until near the end of his career, he was one of baseball's greatest success stories. Jimmie always did his best, and did so with grace and charm. He should primarily be remembered for his joyful demeanor and Olympian talent.

How would we react if we turned on our televisions or computers at the end of a summer night, and watched a highlight of Double X blasting a 500-foot home run? Keep in mind that modern technology tells us that such blows are very rare phenomena: only two 500-footers have been hit by the combined rosters of all MLB teams since 2000. Then consider that Jimmie Foxx personally recorded at least ten such drives in his wondrous career. What would we do? In all probability, we would react just like Ted Williams. We would be in awe… and we would speak about Jimmie Foxx with respect and admiration. ∎

SOURCES

Books

Kashatus, William. *Connie Mack's '29 Triumph*, (Jefferson, NC, and London: McFarland and Company, Inc. 1999.)

Millikin, Mark R. *Jimmie Foxx: The Pride of Sudlersville*, (Lanham, MD, Toronto, Oxford: The Scarecrow Press, Inc. 1998.)

Newspapers

Baltimore Sun
Boston Evening Transcript
Boston Evening Traveler
Boston Globe
Boston Herald
Boston Post
Brooklyn Eagle
Chicago Daily News
Chicago Herald & Examiner
Chicago Tribune
Cincinnati Enquirer
Cleveland Plain Dealer
Cleveland Press
Detroit Free Press
Detroit News
Japan Times
Los Angeles Times
New York Daily News
New York Herald-Tribune
New York Times
New York World-Telegram
Philadelphia Daily News
Philadelphia Evening Bulletin
Philadelphia Inquirer
Philadelphia Public Ledger
Philadelphia Record
Pittsburgh Courier
Pittsburgh Press
Providence Journal
St. Louis Globe-Democrat
St. Louis Post-Dispatch
St. Petersburg Times
Washington Evening-Star
Washington Post
Washington Times-Herald
Winnipeg Free Press

The Day Ted Williams Became the Last .400 Hitter in Baseball

Bill Nowlin

September 28, 1941. Shibe Park, Philadelphia. The Red Sox split a Sunday doubleheader with Connie Mack's Athletics on the final day of the 1941 season. These were meaningless games in the standings; the Red Sox were in second place but 17½ games behind the Yankees and the Athletics were dead last, 37½ games out of first. But these were professionals and there was something else at stake.

Young Ted Williams, who had turned 23 less than a month earlier, woke up that morning hitting .39955 on the year, just .00045 below the hallowed .400 mark. Except for a stretch from July 11–24, when his batting average dipped as low as .393, he'd been hitting above .400 since May 25.

After closing out Boston's final home game at Fenway Park on September 21, Williams was batting .4055. There were six games left in the season; three in Washington and three in Philadelphia. Ted was 1-for-3 on the 23rd, and then in a doubleheader on the 24th, he was 0-for-3 and 1-for-4. He'd gone 2-for-10 and seen his average plunge to a perilous .4009. The weather was turning colder–not good for Williams. There was a lot on the line, and the team had two days off, the 25th and 26th. On the morning of September 27, the *Philadelphia Bulletin* headline noted what Williams faced: "Williams Risks Batting Mark" with a subhead showing his determination to play out the full season: "Boston Star Refuses to Protect his Season's Record of .401." This is when Ted could have sat out the final three games.

There's a longstanding legend that Sox manager Joe Cronin had gone to Ted on Saturday evening and told him he could sit out the game to preserve his average, and nobody would have blamed him. If this had occurred, it would have been Friday night, before the Saturday game. Indeed, the *Bulletin* reported, "There was a rumor that Manager Joe Cronin would let Ted spend the rest of the year on the bench to protect his batting mark." Williams took "a special session of batting practice at Shibe Park" during the day on Friday, after the Red Sox arrived in town, and Ted told the *Bulletin*'s Frank Yeutter, "I either make it or I don't."

Yeutter mentioned to readers a couple of obstacles Williams would face: "the lengthening shadows of autumn afternoons, and facing strange young pitchers getting the usual end-of-the-season tryouts." The advantage, he said, was in the pitcher's favor.

On Saturday the Athletics rookie pitcher Roger Wolff was pitching in only his second-ever major league game (he had lost a tight 1–0 game in Washington the previous Saturday, allowing just three hits). Williams drew a walk from Wolff his first time up and then doubled to right field. But then he flied out to Eddie Collins Jr. in right, fouled out to first baseman Bob Johnson, and struck out—the only man Wolff whiffed. It was Ted's last strikeout of the season, number 27.

By batting 1-for-4, Ted's batting average dropped to .39955. It could have been rounded up to .400 if he had sat out the two Sunday games. But .39955 was not .400.

Naturally, Williams wanted to hit .400. He had no way to know that he'd be the last .400 hitter in the twentieth century, but a .400 batting average in 1941 was still a major mark of distinction. Ty Cobb and Rogers Hornsby had each hit .400 three times. Hornsby could have done it a fourth time, if one applied rounding. Entering the last game of the 1921 season, he was hitting .39966. Hornsby played that game, failed to get a hit in four at-bats, and saw his final average fall to .397.

Ted said that his own teammate Jimmie Foxx had once lost a batting title to Buddy Myer by sitting out the last day of the season in 1935. It was not true, but Williams and biographer John Underwood apparently believed it was. Foxx finished third, batting .346 to Joe Vosmik's .348 and Myer's .349. In fact, Foxx did bat and was 3-for-4 on the final day. Myer had a 4-for-5 day.

In his autobiography, *My Turn At Bat*, Williams recalls Joe Cronin telling him, "You don't have to be put in if you don't want to. You're officially .400."[1] Ted reports his reaction: "Well, God, that hit me like a goddamn lightning bolt! What do you mean I don't have to play today?"[2]

At some point, the subject had been raised. The September 29 *Christian Science Monitor* reported, "A week

Contrary to legend, Red Sox manager Joe Cronin almost certainly never offered Ted the opportunity to sit out the final two games in Philadelphia.

ago it was suggested to the young outfielder that he might stay out of the game for the remainder of the season and thus assure his finishing in the select circle. But he chose rather to play the season out in his regular position, even though it jeopardized his standing."[3]

The Sporting News said Ted had declared, "I want to have more than my toenails on the line."

Williams didn't want to hit .400 by the rounding of a number, and truth be told, .39955 is not .400—as he would have been reminded by newspaper headlines he may have seen that Sunday morning. Williams was an inveterate newspaper reader, typically reading four or five a day. If he saw *The New York Times*, he would have seen WILLIAMS AT .3996 AS RED SOX WIN, 5–1; STAR BATTER SLIPS BELOW .400 GOAL. Had he seen the *Washington Post*, he would have read its headline: WILLIAMS DROPS BELOW .400 AS RED SOX DEFEAT A'S, 5–1. Whether the *Chicago Tribune* made it to Philadelphia before game time, we don't know; the *Tribune* headline read WILLIAMS DROPS UNDER .400. The *Boston Globe*'s game story headline? WILLIAMS GETS ONLY ONE HIT, with a subhead reading "Average Now is .399 as Red Sox Win, 5–1."

And Sunday morning's *Philadelphia Inquirer* was unambiguous: "SOX TOP A's; WILLIAMS FALLS TO .399."

Ted really didn't have a choice. He had to hit. Perhaps it took a little less personal courage, but his actual accomplishment was no less dramatic. Everyone knew what was on the line. He'd be facing Dick Fowler in the first game–a rookie like Wolff, pitching in only his fourth big-league game. Mr. Mack reportedly told the Athletics to play it straight, as Porter Vaughan—the second pitcher to face Williams in the first game—explained: "Connie Mack didn't talk to the pitchers but he talked to the catcher, Frank Hayes. Frank was a good catcher. When Ted came to bat, he told Ted that the pitchers had the word from Mr. Mack that they didn't ought to let up at all on Ted, and if they did, they'd have to pay the consequences."[4]

Joe Cronin had told the *Boston Globe* before the game: "If there's ever a ballplayer who deserved to hit .400, it's Ted. He's given up plenty of chances to bunt and protect his average in recent weeks. He wouldn't think of getting out of the lineup to keep his average intact. Moreover, most of the other stars who have bettered the mark before were helped by no foul strike rules or sacrifice fly regulations."[5] Indeed, had the rule been in effect which does not count a sacrifice fly as an at-bat, Ted would have entered the day hitting comfortably above .400, at .40498. But in 1941, a sacrifice fly—Ted had six of them—was counted as an at-bat and an out.

Ted himself kept it simple: "'Gee, I only hope I can hit .400,' was all he would say."[6]

The *Philadelphia Bulletin*'s Yeutter reported that "Before the two games started he was nervous and sat on the bench, biting his fingernails. His mammoth hands trembled. He condemned himself for getting only one hit for four times at bat Saturday. He wondered who was going to pitch for the Athletics. He asked Jimmie Foxx if the late afternoon autumn shadows ever bothered him when he was a kingpin hitting in Shibe Park. He asked if the Athletics had knuckleball pitchers, for knucklers had been his nemesis all year." Wolff, who had struck out Ted his last time up the day before, was a knuckleballer.

After Saturday's game, Ted was nervous. That evening, he said he walked the streets of Philadelphia for several hours with Red Sox clubhouse man Johnny Orlando, walking maybe ten miles talking about it.[7] John Holway quotes Williams: "I went to bed early, but I just couldn't sleep. I tossed and turned and finally went to sleep, still thinking about that .400 average."[8]

Williams was batting cleanup, and Fowler retired the side in the first, so Ted led off the top of the second. "Bill McGowan was the plate umpire, and I'll never forget it," Ted recalled. "Just as I stepped in, he

NATIONAL BASEBALL HALL OF FAME LIBRARY, COOPERSTOWN, NY

"The Kid" always said that if he had it all to do over again, he'd have taken more batting practice —and this from a guy who would routinely take batting practice after everyone else had gone home, if he'd been dissatisfied with his work at the plate that day.

called time and slowly walked around the plate, bent over and began dusting it off. Without looking up, he said, 'To hit .400 a batter has got to be loose. He has got to be loose.'"[9]

The first pitch was low and outside. The second was low and inside. On the 2–0 count, Ted was ready and he swung at Fowler's next pitch. He "singled sharply to right" according to the *Inquirer*'s Stan Baumgartner. In *My Turn At Bat*, Williams called it "a liner between first and second." Gerry Moore of the *Boston Globe* called it "a sizzling single past first baseman Bob Johnson's right."

After that first hit, Ted's average stood at .40089. If he'd made an out his second time up, he'd be hitting exactly .400. He had nothing to lose by taking that second at-bat. If he'd made an out, would he have allowed himself to be taken out of the game? We can't know. But the question became moot when he led off the fifth inning, still facing Fowler, and homered on a 1–0 pitch, driving the ball over the high right-center field wall, a shot of perhaps 440 feet. It was his 37th homer of the year; he led both leagues in homers. Now he was batting .40222 and could make outs each of the next two times up and still be hitting a little over .400 at .40044.

But he didn't. The Red Sox had taken a 3–2 lead in the top of the fifth, but the A's scored nine times in the bottom of the inning, building up an 11–3 lead.

Next time up, in the top of the seventh, Ted was facing reliever Porter Vaughan, who threw two straight curve balls, both of which missed the plate. Vaughn threw another curve, and Ted guessed correctly. He was waiting for it. "I hit a bullet right through the mid-dle–base hit."[10] It was a single, and the Red Sox scored six runs that inning, closing the gap to 11–10 (they'd scored once in the sixth, too), and he singled off Vaughan a second time.

Vaughan told the story:

He got two clean singles off me. On the first one, he hit off a curve ball. Our second baseman was Crash Davis. Crash and I had come up at the same time. He played Ted in the hole between second and first. Ted hit the ball to the right of the second baseman. The second one he hit was a fast ball. I threw him a fastball. Bob Johnson, who was a leftfielder, was playing first base. Dick Siebert, our regular first baseman, had gone back to Minnesota; he taught out there. Johnson didn't get to the ball; it was between him and the base. It was close to first base. Ted hit it right down the line. Obviously I didn't fool him at all. He had wonderful eyesight and very quick hands. It was almost impossible to fool him. He really studied pitchers and remembered everything they threw him."[11]

Williams was 4-for-5 in the first game with two RBIs and two runs scored. He might even have been 5-for-5 but for the official scorer. In his final at-bat against Newman Shirley, yet another rookie (the hardest pitchers for Ted to hit, since they were neither predictable nor necessarily accurate), he grounded to second base and reached base, but with an error charged to second baseman Crash Davis. The Associated Press said that "a very ponderous" scoring decision "robbed" Ted of his fifth consecutive hit, though in his book, *The Last .400 Hitter*, John Holway noted that none of the other writers argued the decision.[12]

And even though Boston scored twice in the top of the ninth and won the game, 12–11, the Philly fans were all for Ted all day long. "Each time he came to bat the crowd roared, and when he went back to left field each inning the bleacherites gave him added applause," wrote the *Evening Bulletin*.

By the end of the first game, Williams was batting .40397. He could have gone 0-for-4 in the second game and still been above .400 at .40044.

But he wasn't done. In the second game, he faced Fred Caligiuri, who remembered Mack telling him to bear down: "Don't give him anything! Pitch to him!" Caligiuri talked about pitching to Ted. "He could hit most fast balls, and the only way to get him out is to change speeds on him. We tried to change up on him, if I remember. I know one changeup I threw him he hit—in Shibe Park there was a kind of a megaphone that sits up on top of the wall, and that ball went on a line right into that megaphone and fell back into the park for a double. I suppose that megaphone was at least maybe two feet across, just a speaker up there. He hit it pretty good. It kept it in the ballpark. If it had been a few feet left or right, it would have gone out of the ballpark."[13] Indeed, only the ground rules kept the ball from being a homer, since the loudspeaker was deemed in fair territory. That ground-rule double was Ted's second hit of the second game; he'd singled between first and second his first time up.

Finally, in his eighth time to the plate that day, with darkness encroaching, the Athletics got Ted Williams out, when he flied out to right field. He was officially 6-for-8, hitting .40570, or, when rounded up: .406.

"There was not a questionable hit among the group," wrote the *Inquirer*. "All were slashing drives that whistled through the infield or fell far out of reach of the outfielders."

After the game, Ted said he'd never felt nervous in baseball before. Now, he said, "I was shaking like a leaf when I went to bat the first time. Then when I got that first hit, I was all set. I felt good. Gee, there's a lot of luck making that many hits." He turned to Jimmie Foxx and exclaimed, "Just think–hitting .400. What do you think of that, Slug? Just a kid like me hitting that high."

The September 29 *Philadelphia Evening Bulletin* wound up its story:

Although the second game was called in the eighth inning by Umpire John Quinn on account of darkness, at least 2,000 persons waited around the Boston dressing room and on 21st Street, to see Williams leave. He was surrounded by a mob that pinned him against the wall and made

him autograph every conceivable kind of paper, book or scorecard. A couple of cops rescued him so he could make a train from North Philadelphia. But he enjoyed the ordeal and left only when he was shoved in a taxicab.

By virtue of reaching base six of the eight times up (not counting reaching on the error), Ted Williams had achieved a season on-base percentage of .553. More than half the times he came to bat in 1941, he got on base, and he struck out only 27 times all season.

In 2012 Miguel Cabrera of the Detroit Tigers won the Triple Crown for the first time since Carl Yastrzemski did it for the Boston Red Sox in 1967. Will someone hit .400 again? That's the gist for another story, but a good place to start would be pages 77–132 in Stephen Jay Gould's *Full House: The Spread of Excellence from Plato to Darwin* (New York: Harmony Books, 1996), an expansion of his essay "Entropic homogeneity isn't why no one hits .400 any more," which appeared in the August 1986 issue of *Discover*. ∎

Acknowledgments
Thanks to Rock Hoffman for providing photocopies of the Philadelphia newspapers of the day.

Notes
1. Ted Williams with David Pietrusza, *My Life in Pictures* (Kingston NY: Total Sports Illustrated, 2001), 43.
2. Ibid.
3. *Christian Science Monitor*, September 29, 1941.
4. Porter Vaughan interview with author, July 30, 1997. Williams says Hayes told him, "Ted, Mr. Mack told us if we let up on you he'll run us out of baseball, I wish you all the luck in the world, but we're not giving you a damn thing." Ted Williams, *My Turn At Bat* (New York: Fireside Books, 1969), 90.
5. *Boston Globe*, September 29, 1941.
6. *Boston Globe*, September 29, 1941.
7. *My Turn At Bat*, 87.
8. John Holway, *The Last .400 Hitter* (Dubuque: William C. Brown, 1992), 282.
9. *My Turn At Bat*, 90.
10. Holway, 285.
11. Porter Vaughan interview with author, July 30, 1997.
12. Holway, 287.
13. Fred Caligiuri interview with author, July 7, 1997.

The Philadelphia Phillies' 1943 Spring Training

James D. Szalontai

By 1942 World War II was already impacting the Philadelphia Phillies' spring training activities as they prepared for the regular season in the soft sands of Miami Beach, Florida. Air corps stunts were observed above Flamingo Park; the players inspected fighters and bombers at a nearby base; and manager Hans Lobert, who had run the US Military Academy baseball team from 1918–25, persuaded Army officers to lead the squad in military drills preparing them for a patriotic display as they marched with bats on their shoulders before a Grapefruit League game against the Boston Braves.

In 1943 major league teams were forced to abandon the salubrious conditions of the South. They adhered to Commissioner Kenesaw Mountain Landis's edict, which allowed baseball to meet government travel restrictions and promote a positive image in the public mind. Teams had to scramble to find northern training camps and were often burdened by harsh weather, fewer exhibition games, inferior training facilities, second-rate playing equipment, depleted rosters, and uncertainty regarding continuation of the game as the ballplayers departing for military service were replaced with 4-Fs, teenagers, old-timers, and career minor leaguers. Dan Daniel of the *New York World-Telegram* penned these eloquent words in March 1943:

> There is no Florida sun. There are no bathing beauties. There are fewer steaks and it is tougher to get up a perspiration. There are more aches and muscles that never hurt before, squawks against calisthenics. There are dull hours. But there are good beds and long nights in which to rest in them. And God is with us![1]

Finding a spring training site north of the Ohio and Potomac Rivers was difficult for stable major league franchises. But the Phillies were in a precarious situation, concluding the last five seasons in the basement (with at least 103 losses per year) and their financially strapped owner, Gerald Nugent, heavily in debt to the National League. Chester Smith of the *Pittsburgh Press*

insisted that the Phillies "didn't have enough talent to put up more than a fair battle in a class B league."[2]

Naturally, Nugent's predicament had a deleterious effect on the Phillies as they prepared for spring training. To raise funds, he traded his only decent players—Rube Melton, Nick Etten—for bodies and cash. He sent out no contracts.

It was believed that the Phillies would train near their home ballpark, possibly at the University of Pennsylvania's Franklin Field. However, Nugent had his eye on Swarthmore College, which had a large field house with a dirt floor that could be transformed into a baseball diamond. The Phillies were courted by several towns and cities. Hershey, Pennsylvania, made an attractive bid, but it was initially believed that travel restrictions would make it difficult for the Phils to accept. By mid-January, the college town of Princeton, New Jersey, had made its bid, as did the seashore resort city of Wildwood and the eventual spring training home of the New York Giants, Lakewood. Phillipsburg, New Jersey, and Lancaster, Pennsylvania, came calling by early February.

Nugent's fate was decided at the National League meeting on February 9, as the National League took control of the beleaguered franchise, and on February 18 sold it to a syndicate headed by William D. Cox, a wealthy lumber broker. Meanwhile, Swarthmore College informed the Phillies that they were unable to allow them to conduct spring training activities on their campus. The offer was rescinded because a unit of Navy engineers would possibly be assigned to the college. Cox insisted that he would allow the new manager to pick the camp site and mentioned Lancaster, Milford, and Newtown, Pennsylvania as possible destinations. Ultimately and perhaps reluctantly they settled on Hershey, a community founded by chocolate king Milton S. Hershey, as their spring training headquarters.

COMMANDO TRAINING

William D. Cox was an enthusiastic 33-year-old, who had played baseball and ran cross-country on the track team as a freshman at New York University before

NATIONAL BASEBALL HALL OF FAME LIBRARY, COOPERSTOWN, NY

Former collegiate track athlete William D. Cox became owner of the Phillies at age 33 and immediately demanded changes in player conditioning, stating, "I want the team to run morning and afternoon."

transferring to Yale and leaving during his senior year to take a job in New York. The former president of the New York Yankees football team had reportedly thrown batting practice for the 1928 Boston Braves, managed by Rogers Hornsby, and written a book titled *Boxing in Art and Literature*.[3]

Cox quickly gained a reputation as an iconoclast, insisting that he would not force his ideas on new manager Bucky Harris, but also maintaining that the Phillies would endure "commando-type" training and incessantly run. He developed his devotion to running from his freshman track coach, Emil von Elling, and said, "I want the team to run morning and afternoon, and to come down to the start of the season ready to go top speed."[4]

To execute his running philosophy, Cox hired Harold Anson Bruce to be the physical education director. The team's baseball activities would be augmented by two hours of rigorous calisthenics each day. Bruce was a widely respected physical education specialist who coached the track teams at Lafayette and then at Union College, was named American Olympic manager in 1932, and coached the long-distance runners at the Los Angeles Summer Olympics. From 1935–38 he was the head coach of the Austrian National Track and Field Forces, leading them in the 1936 Berlin Olympics.

Bruce quickly developed a few ideas on how the team could improve their performance; sore-armed pitchers, for example, would exercise their arms the day after pitching to work the stiffness out, and sprained ankles would be treated with hot and cold applications. Bucky Harris, an old-school skipper who disapproved of Bruce's presence, facetiously suggested

he focus on speeding up the Phillies' catchers—with their incessant squatting, they would grow slower as the season progressed. Stan Baumgartner, a Philadelphia sportswriter and former Phillies pitcher, reported that after the first week of training Bruce was given an "unqualified stamp of approval."[5] Instead of watching from the sidelines, Cox would often participate in workouts with the club, running around the field, practicing quick starts, going through calisthenic drills, and playing catch with the players. The sportswriters developed colorful headlines, such as the one in *The Sporting News* on March 25: "Chilly Phillies Warm Up to Commando Conditioning."

Bruce's unusual conditioning program included several enervating exercises with names like the "pinwheel twist," "jingle jangle," "gorilla hedgehop," and the "elephant walk," for which a player lay down on his back, with his stomach towards the sky, and walked by using his arms as legs. Baumgartner observed, "The players tried. They fell down, they collapsed in the middle. They laughed at their own awkwardness and not more than three were able to go ten feet."[6]

The players grew tired of some of Bruce's controversial tactics, such as forcing them to drink hot water before, during and after practice. He made sure that the players ate fruit, improving their diet. Meanwhile, Bruce was amazed that his individual physical examinations were considered unique, and not ubiquitously employed by other major league teams.

Danny Litwhiler said Bruce "was a good man, our ball club was well conditioned. We were probably in as good a shape as any team as far as conditioning is concerned. The main thing was run, run, run."[7]

Harris was looking for a reason to be rid of Bruce, and finally had his chance when the trainer fell asleep on the bench, surrounded by sliced oranges. His dismissal perturbed Cox and served as a harbinger of things to come. Harris was fired after 92 games (39–53) as Cox claimed he called the players "jerks" and failed to motivate them.[8] Harris said, "He's a fine guy to fire me—when he gambles on games his club plays." The gambling allegations were true and on November 23 Cox was banned from baseball by Judge Landis.[9]

THE ROSTER

Bill Cox was not expected to be a miracle man. The Phillies, after all, had just completed a season in which they garnered only 42 wins and finished 62½ games behind the pennant-winning Cardinals. He possessed enthusiasm and confidence, but also a roster that was perilously thin because of wartime departures. Hugh Mulcahy, the Phils' best pitcher, had a low draft number and was the first major leaguer inducted by Uncle Sam on March 8, 1941. Seven more Phillies joined the fight in 1942 and 11 entered the military in 1943.

Baumgartner believed that it was possible that the Phillies might win fewer than 40 games in 1943, writing, "If the Phillies suffer losses through injuries, sore arms or further calls to the service, the team is going to look like the cat that was machine-gunned on the back fence."[10]

At the National League meeting it was suggested that each club sell the Phillies one player at a bargain price. Branch Rickey, the Dodgers president, was apoplectic, shouting, "To Hell with that!" when asked if the league would help the Phillies solve their manpower problem. "If a club gets down, the others kick it around. To climb requires gameness, initiative, working capital, love for baseball, management, and a willingness to lose around $125,000 a year for a few seasons." He also insisted, "Baseball is no place for charity."[11]

The key cogs for the 1943 Phillies included position players Mickey Livingston, Buster Adams, Babe Dahlgren, Pinky May, Danny Murtaugh, Ron Northey, Glen Stewart, Coaker Triplett, and Jimmy Wasdell. On the hilltop there was Al Gerheauser, Jack Kraus, Schoolboy Rowe, Dick Barrett, Si Johnson, and Newt Kimball.

Before spring training began, the situation was so bleak for the Phillies that they held an open tryout on March 1 and the only three players to show up were "a minor leaguer, a local sandlotter who lacked the qualifications and a one-eyed youngster from Hartford, Conn."[12]

As the Phillies prepared for the regular season, the war was putting their roster into turmoil with players coming and going and uncertain situations. Their spring training roster was replete with career minor leaguers, 4-Fs, old-timers, and unproven youngsters. Additionally, the Phillies were very active in the trade market during early 1943, acquiring players like Rowe, Kraus, Stewart, and Dahlgren in deals. It was widely believed that the Phillies had improved their roster dramatically during the spring through trades and acquisitions and Baumgartner even wrote that with a little luck "Harris and the Phillies can be a real drawing card."[13]

A close examination of the Phillies' spring training roster shows how desperate they were to fill their uniforms with warm bodies and how the war was impacting their roster. In January, they signed 23-year-old Bill Anske, who had played in the low minors in

Manager Bucky Harris (left) was not enamored of the "commando" training. The acquisition of players like Babe Dahlgren (right) was much more crucial to the team's ability to win. Dahlgren had been classified 4-F because of migraine headaches that occasionally caused blackouts.

1940 and 1941 before catching for Narberth in the Philadelphia Main Line League in 1942, where his season was cut short because of an injury. He was also the bullpen catcher for the Phils during that 1942 campaign. His primary occupation was as a fireman for the Philadelphia and Reading Railroad. Anske's big league debut never materialized as he went into the Army before spring training ended.

To bolster the infield, Harris recruited Penn freshman baseball coach, Red Kellett. Kellett failed to record a hit in nine at-bats while playing for the 1934 Boston Red Sox, managed by Harris. Like Anske, he did not play in a regular season game in 1943.

The Phillies were hoping that first baseman Eddie Murphy, who had played for their Trenton Inter-State League farm team in 1942 and had a 13-game cup of coffee, could step up into the big tent. Instead, he decided to continue working at his war job in Joliet, Illinois, and asked to be placed on the voluntary retired list. Meanwhile, fly chaser Paul Busby asked to be removed from the voluntary retired list, and batted .250 in 40 at-bats for the 1943 Phillies.

Catcher Joe Holden was forced to leave spring training and return to his war defense job with the

NATIONAL BASEBALL HALL OF FAME LIBRARY, COOPERSTOWN, NY

Bethlehem Steel Company because his leave of absence had expired.

George Hennessey had yielded eight runs in seven innings for the 1937 St. Louis Browns and performed much better for the 1942 Phillies, going 1–1 with a 2.65 ERA over 17 innings. "Three Star" Hennessey had paid his dues in the bushes, playing for 11 minor league teams since he started his career as a semi-pro in 1928. The former prize fighter was hoping to be a part-time player for the Phillies in 1943. The United States, however, needed his services as a vital war worker as a skilled mechanic at the Eastern Aircraft plant in Trenton, New Jersey. He worked the night shift from 11 PM to 7 AM. Hennessey, who had intended to skip spring training, did not play in 1943, but made it back to the big leagues in 1945, pitching in two games for the Chicago Cubs.

A headline in *The Sporting News* on April 8 declared, "Del Savio Fills Out Infield Of Phillies." Garton Del Savio had played independent ball in 1942 and had been training with the Reds in Bloomington, Indiana, before being released. Baumgartner insisted that the Phillies were "fortunate" to obtain Del Savio and this career minor leaguer was expected to fill the Phillies shortstop hole.[14] Del Savio appeared in four regular season games, getting only one hit in 11 major league at-bats.

Pitcher Johnny "Specs" Podgajny was nearsighted and classified 4-F. He went 4–4 with a 4.22 ERA before being traded to Pittsburgh during the season. Babe Dahlgren batted .287 with a .354 on-base percentage for the 1943 Phils and made his only All-Star team. Dahlgren was also classified 4-F: When he was 12 years old, he was hit in the face with a ball, and he suffered migraine headaches into adulthood, carrying a box of aspirin wherever he went, and even occasionally blacking out during a game, unable to see a ball farther than five feet away.

SPRING TRAINING

The Phillies began spring training on March 15 in Hershey with fewer than a dozen players signed to contracts and only 20 men on the roster.

During the first day of practice, Harris had to choose between a frozen field and an indoor gymnasium. The weather created problems during the first week and there were "mingled feelings" about the Northern spring training experiment.[15] *The Sporting News* insisted that long underwear would become ubiquitous during spring training and that the players had gone from the "Citrus Belt" to the "Sinus Belt." Censorship restrictions prevented reporters from giving

certain information on the conditions in which the players were training, but if it was reported that teams trained inside a gymnasium or fieldhouse, then it can be assumed that the conditions were poor.[16]

Harris incessantly urged his men to "forget this defeatist idea" and act as if they belonged in the majors. He treated his players like men, refusing to use a detective to see if the players complied with the midnight curfew, and insisted that they abide by the honor system. As a result the players generally trusted and respected Harris.[17] Hershey was isolated, but "Chocolatetown, USA" had good food and plenty of amusement.

Because it took so long to fill holes in the roster through trades and acquisitions, Harris was not able to play an intra-camp game before the Phils took on the Philadelphia Athletics in Wilmington, Delaware, on April 4. There were fewer exhibition games in 1943, and they were generally played only against teams in the immediate vicinity of the camps. The four-game city series against Connie Mack's woeful Athletics was going to be the highlight of the exhibition season.

The Athletics took the opener, 5–3, as Si Johnson yielded all five runs in the third inning before 5,000 fans. Frank Skaff hit a two-run homer to lead the Athletics attack. Earl Naylor went yard for the Phillies, Danny Litwhiler smacked two hits and drove in a run, while Garton Del Savio and young pitcher Bill Webb also made good impressions. Johnny Podgajny and Webb pitched scoreless ball for Harris's aggregation. The starting infield consisted of Dahlgren at first, Murtaugh at second, Del Savio at short, and May at third. In the outfield from left to right there was Litwhiler, Naylor, and Busby. Livingston was behind the plate and Johnson on the hill.

On a chilly afternoon, 1,581 fans paid their way into Shibe Park on April 10, and watched Philadelphia's American League aggregation take the second game, 5–2. Johnny Podgajny authored four scoreless frames before the Mackmen posted a three-run fifth. Former Villanova collegian Frank Skaff hit a double in the big inning, while a walk and two more doubles by Jo-Jo White and Eddie Mayo did the damage. Si Johnson yielded the other two runs in the seventh stanza. In the eighth, the Phillies scored their two runs on an error, doubles by Mickey Livingston and Ron Northey and a Danny Litwhiler single. Murtaugh had two hits, plated a run, and stole a base out of the leadoff spot, while Northey, Litwhiler, Naylor, and Livingston had a hit apiece.

The Shibe Park crowd numbered 5,000 on the following day as Charlie Fuchs and Jack Kraus combined

NATIONAL BASEBALL HALL OF FAME LIBRARY, COOPERSTOWN, NY

Ron Northey was another key cog for the 1942 Phillies, who had so few men in spring training camp they held an open tryout.

Burleigh Grimes's Toronto Maple Leafs of the International League trained in Lancaster, Pennsylvania, and did not encounter the warm weather which they anticipated, instead dealing with snow and low temperatures. They were forced to cancel three games with the Phillies.

The foul Northeastern weather also forced the Phillies to endure an unpleasant road trip to Hagerstown, Maryland, on April 13. The Phils boarded the 6AM train out of Harrisburg, traveled to Hagerstown, and had the game with the Buffalo Bisons halted by rain in the bottom of the second inning.

Besides the city series the only other game against major league competition took place on April 15 in Trenton, New Jersey, against the Washington Nationals before 300 freezing fans. Podgajny and Al Gerheauser held the Nationals to one run and four hits in nine innings as the two teams fought to a 1–1 tie. Ron Northey garnered a triple off Dutch Leonard in the fourth inning and scored on a sacrifice fly. Mickey Haefner followed Leonard to the bump and held the Phillies to two singles in four scoreless innings.

Perhaps the most famous exhibition game played by the Phillies in 1943 took place in New Haven, Connecticut, against Yale University. The Phillies battery in the first inning consisted of owner Bill Cox as catcher and Yale athletic director Ogden Miller as the pitcher. At the plate, Cox walked and Miller struck out. Red Rolfe, a former Yankee who was coaching the Yale team, played third base for the collegians. Gerheauser and Padden took over "the battery duties from the two tired businessmen" and the Phillies won, 7–0.[18]

The Phillies played well during the abbreviated exhibition schedule, which included two impressive wins against local Army teams. The first game took place on a cold, blustery day, in New Cumberland, Pennsylvania, on April 7, as they defeated the 1301st

on a three-hit shutout, giving the Phillies their first victory in the city series. Pinky May drove in both runs for the Phils, singling in the second to score Naylor and hitting a sacrifice fly in the fourth. The Phillies had seven hits as Litwhiler led the way with two. Fuchs started, giving up one hit in five innings, baffling the A's with a sneaky fastball and good curve. Kraus, a left-handed pitcher with a smooth overhand delivery, worked the final four innings and was equally effective, handcuffing the A's with a live fastball.

On April 18, the Phillies received superb pitching from Kraus and Schoolboy Rowe as they defeated the Athletics, 4–1, to conclude the city series in a 2–2 tie. The A's mustered only one run and five hits against Kraus in five innings and then watched helplessly as Rowe pitched four perfect frames. Earl Naylor hit a two-run bomb in the three-run sixth off John Burrows. The 3,500 Shibe Park fans watched the Phillies collect nine hits, including two by Litwhiler and May.

The Philadelphia Phillies 1943 Spring Training Schedule

Date	Opponent	Location	Result	Pitcher of Record
April 4	Philadelphia Athletics	Wilmington, DE	L, 5–3	Si Johnson
April 7	1301st Service Unit team	New Cumberland, PA	W, 5–3[1]	Jack Kraus
April 8	Indiantown Gap Army Service team	Lebanon, PA	W, 14–0[2]	Schoolboy Rowe
April 10	Philadelphia Athletics	Philadelphia, PA	L, 5–2	Johnny Podgajny
April 11	Philadelphia Athletics	Philadelphia, PA	W, 2–0	Charlie Fuchs
April 13	Buffalo Bisons	Hagerstown, MD	T, 0–0[3]	
April 15	Washington Senators	Trenton, NJ	T, 1–1	
April 18	Philadelphia Athletics	Philadelphia, PA	W, 4–1	Schoolboy Rowe
April 20	Yale University	New Haven, CT	W, 7–0	Al Gerheauser

1. Six-inning game
2. Seven-inning game
3. One-and-a-half-inning game

Service Unit team, 5–3, in a six-inning game. Manager Joe Lawler's Army team consisted of several former major and minor leaguers, including former Phillies pitcher Tommy Hughes, catcher Bill Peterman, and second baseman Harry Marnie. Hank Simmons of the *Philadelphia Inquirer* insisted that the "game had its points, despite a slight snowfall and the unpleasant wind," as Kraus and Fuchs impressed their manager while firing bullets. Murtaugh and Northey set the table, batting first and second in the Phillies lineup, collecting four of their six hits and scoring three runs.[19]

The second game was a rout, as the Phillies faced little resistance from a group of youngsters playing for the Indiantown Gap Army Service team, on April 8 in Lebanon, Pennsylvania. Harris's aggregation prevailed 14–0 as Rowe, Gerheauser, and Andy Lapihuska combined to pitch a no-hitter in the seven-inning contest. The offensive eruption was spearheaded by Northey, Litwhiler, May, and Padden, who each hammered out two hits.

The Phillies drastically improved their roster during spring training, played well during the exhibition season, and then won 22 more games than they had in 1942. They avoided the cellar, finishing in seventh place with a 64–90 record. All the running they did in Hershey did not make them any faster, as they finished last in the major leagues in steals, pilfering an abysmal 29 bases. It had been a memorable spring training with a colorful new owner, an old-fashioned skipper and an innovative physical education director who brought the best conditioned team to the starting line. ◼

Notes

1. *The Sporting News*, March 25, 1943.
2. Finoli, *For the Good of the Country*, 55.
3. *The Sporting News*, February 25, 1943.
4. *The Sporting News*, March 4, 1943.
5. *The Sporting News*, March 25, 1943.
6. Ibid.
7. Goldstein, *Spartan Seasons*, 103.
8. Mead, *Baseball Goes to War*, 108.
9. Roberts and Rogers, *The Whiz Kids and the 1950 Pennant*, 27.
10. *The Sporting News*, March 18. 1943.
11. *The Sporting News*, February 18. 1943.
12. *The Sporting News*, March 11, 1943.
13. *The Sporting News*, April 22, 1943.
14. *The Sporting News*, April 8, 1943.
15. *The Sporting News*, March 25 1943.
16. *The Sporting News*, March 11, 1943.
17. *The Sporting News*, March 25, 1943.
18. *The Sporting News*, April 29, 943.
19. *Philadelphia Inquirer*, April 8, 1943.

Newspapers

Philadelphia Inquirer
The Sporting News

Books and Articles

Dickson, Paul. *The New Dickson Baseball Dictionary*. San Diego: Harcourt Brace, 1999.

Finoli, David. *For the Good of the Country: World War II Baseball in the Major and Minor Leagues*. Jefferson, N.C.: McFarland, 2002.

Goldstein, Richard. *Spartan Seasons: How Baseball Survived the Second World War*. New York: Macmillan, 1980.

Graham, Frank, Jr. "When Baseball Went To War." *Sports Illustrated*, April 17, 1967.

Jordan, David M., Larry R. Gerlach, and John P. Rossi. "A Baseball Myth Exploded: Bill Veeck and the 1943 sale of the Phillies." *The National Pastime: A Review of Baseball History 18*, 1998.

Mead, William B. *Baseball Goes to War*. 1978. Washington, D.C.: Broadcast Interview Source, 1998.

Palmer, Pete, and Gary Gillette, eds. *The 2006 ESPN Baseball Encyclopedia*. New York: Sterling, 2006.

Roberts, Robin, and C. Paul Rogers III. *The Whiz Kids and the 1950 Pennant*. Philadelphia: Temple University Press, 1996.

Internet Sources

www.baseball-almanac.com
www.baseball-reference.com
www.sabr.org

Eddie Waitkus and *The Natural*

What Is Assumption? What Is Fact?

Rob Edelman

Eddie Waitkus, the Fightin' Phillies first-sacker, is best remembered not for his 182 hits and .284 average on the 1950 National League pennant-winners and not for any other on-field accomplishment. Instead, his name is inexorably linked to the plight and fate of the central character in an all-time classic baseball novel.

One might imagine that *The Natural*—written by Bernard Malamud and published in 1952—is unadulterated fiction, while the 1984 screen adaptation is a baseball fantasy with a literary origin. However, a question that has long intrigued aficionados and scholars involves how much of Malamud's story has been culled from real life. To what extent was he influenced by baseball history and baseball lore? Even more specifically, what was Malamud's inspiration for one of the novel's crucial episodes: the near-fatal shooting in a Chicago hotel room of Roy Hobbs, the story's principal character, by a black-garbed mystery woman? Was it in fact a direct reference to the blast from a rifle wielded by an overwrought fan which almost snuffed out the life of Waitkus, also in a Chicago hotel room, on the night of June 14, 1949?

Malamud (1914–86) was loath to discuss his literary sources. As reported in an editor's note in *Talking Horse: Bernard Malamud on Life and Work*, "...during his lifetime as an artist and writer, [Malamud] said little in private about his own work. In public he said even less." So determining the genesis of the Hobbs shooting, not to mention other actual baseball influences in *The Natural*, is purely speculative, the equivalent of piecing together a giant puzzle that keeps changing shape.

In relation to the real-life Eddie Waitkus and the fictional Roy Hobbs, the two on the surface have little in common. Edward Stephen Waitkus was born in Cambridge, Massachusetts, on September 4, 1919. After debuting with the Chicago Cubs in 1941, he earned four Bronze Stars while serving with the U.S. Army in the Pacific during World War II. He returned to the Cubs in 1946 and, with Hank Borowy, was traded to the Phillies for Dutch Leonard and Monk

Dubiel after the 1948 campaign. "During his early career," explained Waitkus biographer John Theodore in *A Natural Gunned Down: The Stalking of Eddie Waitkus*, a documentary extra found on the Director's Cut DVD release of the movie version of the novel, "[Eddie] was called 'The Natural' by a few sportswriters. The writers back then also called him the 'Fred Astaire of first basemen.' At the plate, he had a wonderfully natural swing. Ted Williams called it one of the best swings he had ever seen." Off the field, according to Theodore, Waitkus "was very urbane. He spoke four languages. He was a Civil War historian. He loved ballroom dancing. [He was] not your typical blue-collar baseball player."

A two-time National League All-Star (in 1948–49), the 29-year-old Waitkus was hitting .306 when he was shot on June 14, 1949; his assailant, Ruth Ann Steinhagen, a stenographer, was a decade his junior. He did not don a Phillies uniform for the remainder of the 1949 season. However, on August 19, the ballclub sponsored "Eddie Waitkus Night," during which the ballplayer was deluged with gifts. He rejoined the team the following season, playing in all 154 games for the World Series-bound Whiz Kids—and the Associated Press cited him as the Comeback Player of the Year. Prior to the 1954 campaign, the Baltimore Orioles purchased him. He was released by the Orioles during the 1955 season and returned to Philadelphia before retiring at year's end. All in all, Waitkus enjoyed an eleven-year big league career, hitting .285 with 1,214 hits.

Hobbs, meanwhile, is neither big-city sophisticate, weathered war veteran, nor veteran major leaguer. He is a true innocent: a 19-year-old hot prospect, a product of rural America, and a pitcher with untold potential. Harriet Bird, the woman in black, is older than Steinhagen, and she exploits Hobbs's youthful ardor before shooting him and then committing suicide. Her motives—and whether she indeed is acting on her own or is in cahoots with others—remain unclear. But Hobbs's career is sidetracked, and he spends the next decade and a half languishing in obscurity with his promise an unfulfilled dream. Then, as a

NATIONAL BASEBALL HALL OF FAME LIBRARY, COOPERSTOWN, NY

Eddie Waitkus, Fightin' Phils first-sacker: Is he the inspiration—or merely one of a number of inspirations—for the Roy Hobbs character in Bernard Malamud's *The Natural*?

middle-aged rookie, he returns to baseball as a hitter and leads the last-place New York Knights up in the standings. Hobbs rises from the ashes when he is 34: an age when Waitkus was inauspiciously winding down his big league career. And there was nothing mysterious about Steinhagen. When she shot and wounded the unmarried big leaguer in room 1297A of Chicago's Edgewater Beach Hotel, the Phillies were in town to play the Cubs—and Steinhagen had been obsessed with Waitkus for several years, dating from his time in Chicago. According to John Theodore, the 19-year-old had constructed a shrine to the ballplayer, consisting of hundreds of photos and clippings, which she would stare at for hours. Her mother reported that she even would set a place for him at the family dinner table. After his trade to the Phillies, she felt abandoned—and her infatuation became deadly.

The story of Steinhagen was extensively covered in the media. As reported in several accounts published in *The New York Times* and elsewhere, a note from the teenager awaited Waitkus's arrival at the hotel that evening. It was signed "Ruth Anne Burns" and, in it, Steinhagen wrote:

It is extremely important that I see you as soon as possible. We're not acquainted, but I have something of importance to speak to you about. I think it would be to your advantage to let me explain this to you as I am leaving the hotel the day after tomorrow. I realize this is out of the ordinary, but as I say, it is extremely important.

Steinhagen originally was planning to stab Waitkus and then shoot herself. Accounts vary as to what exactly happened when Waitkus entered her room. But what is clear is that, in an instant, Steinhagen changed her plans and shot the ballplayer but lost her nerve and failed to harm herself.

After the incident, Waitkus told reporters, "I went up to my room and called her because I thought it might be someone I knew—someone from downstate or a friend of a friend. When she opened the door, she took a look and said, 'come in for a minute.' She was very abrupt and businesslike. I asked what she wanted and walked through the little entrance hall over to the window. When I turned around there she was with the .22 caliber rifle. She said, 'You're not going to bother me anymore.' Before I could say anything else, whammy!" He added, "She had the coldest looking face I ever saw. No expression at all. She wasn't happy—she wasn't anything." Waitkus noted that he had never met Steinhagen, and was unsure if he ever had received correspondence from her. "We ballplayers get a lot of letters from girls and don't pay any attention to them. We call them 'baseball Annies.'"

Waitkus was rushed to Illinois Masonic Hospital, where he was reported to be in critical condition with a rifle slug lodged in muscles near his spine. The bullet first pierced and collapsed his right lung, and he received two blood transfusions as well as oxygen. The bullet was surgically removed and, on June 18, another operation was performed to remove blood from his lung cavity. All in all, Waitkus underwent four procedures, and doctors described his quick improvement as "little short of miraculous." The ballplayer also told reporters, "I haven't got over the whole surprise. It's just like a bad dream. I would just like to know what got into that silly honey picking on a nice guy like me. She must be crazy, charging around with a rifle. It was safer for me on New Guinea, wasn't it?"

For her part, Steinhagen was booked by the police and charged with "assault with intent to murder." She told the authorities that she "just had to shoot somebody," adding that she liked Waitkus "best of anybody in the world" and had been dreaming about him—and praying for him. According to the *Times*, the police "attributed Miss Steinhagen's action to a twisted fascination for the ball player and a desire to be in the limelight." She was committed to Illinois' Kankakee State Hospital, where she was given shock treatments. Steinhagen never went on trial for shooting Waitkus. Instead, she remained at Kankakee until 1952, when she was declared cured and released. She then faded into obscurity, and resided for decades in Chicago. In March 2013, the *Chicago Tribune* reported that she had died in Chicago three months earlier at age 83, after a fall in her home.

While Waitkus, unlike Hobbs, did not have to wait a decade and a half to resume his baseball career, one can only speculate on the overall impact of the shooting on the quality of his play. Sure, he was one of the stars of the 1950 Whiz Kids, but would he have enjoyed additional all-star seasons with the Phillies? What numbers might he have put up? Might he even have been worthy of consideration for the Baseball Hall of Fame? We will never know. However, the shooting clearly affected the ballplayer's private life. For one thing, in the late 1980s, *New York Times* sports columnist Ira Berkow heard from Waitkus's son, Edward (Ted) Waitkus Jr., a Boulder, Colorado, lawyer. The junior Waitkus reported that his father had met his mother while recovering from the shooting in Clearwater Beach, Florida. "Had it not been for this horrible event in his life, my sister and I would probably not be here," he noted. "Life is very ironic. I think sometimes that all horror that comes to us has reason...."

Given that *The Natural* was published in 1952, Bernard Malamud could not have known what the future would hold for Eddie Waitkus. Yet certain aspects of Waitkus's later life did indeed reflect on the plight of Roy Hobbs as envisioned by the writer. According to Ted Waitkus, his father "had always told me he understood the four years of his career lost to World War II. 'Everyone went,' he would say. He, however, never quite accepted being shot, that is, the time lost because of the shooting." He also noted, "My dad was an easy-going, trusting guy at the time, and kind of flippant with women.... The shooting changed my father a great deal, as you might imagine. Before, he was a very outgoing person. Then he became almost paranoid about meeting new people, and pretty much even stopped going out drinking with his teammates, which is what I guess they did in those days." And he added, "When [Steinhagen] was about to be released from the mental hospital after only a few years—they said she had fully recovered—my father and my family fought to keep her in. My father feared for his life."

After his retirement from baseball, Waitkus faded from the limelight. In 1961 he split from his wife and suffered a nervous breakdown. "In my research talking

to doctors," reported John Theodore, "they concluded that he was suffering from post-traumatic stress disorder because his symptoms were classic. He avoided people. He had anxiety. He self-medicated his depression with alcohol." A partial return to baseball came in 1966, when he hired on as a hitting instructor at Ted Williams's baseball camp. However, in 1972, at the all-too-young age of 53, Waitkus died of esophageal cancer. At the time, he was living in a Jamaica Plain, Massachusetts, boardinghouse. "Different doctors through the years have expressed the theory that the stress of the shooting, combined with the four operations, allowed the cancer to take hold," explained Ted Waitkus. "Cancer of the lung or esophagus can take up to 20 years or more to be fatal. My dad was never diagnosed as having cancer. It wasn't until after the autopsy that this came out. So I think Ruth Steinhagen was more successful than she thought."

Conjecture regarding the connection between fiction and reality in *The Natural* dates from its publication. In his review of the book in the August 24, 1952, *New York Times*, Harry Sylvester observed that Malamud "draws heavily on baseball legend and history, almost interchangeably." Since then, writers, reviewers, and historians have speculated about the players, personalities, and events that may (or may not) have influenced Malamud during the writing process.

Countless observers have assumed—and casually reported—that the entire premise of *The Natural* is directly linked to the Waitkus shooting. Here are some representative examples:

> "The shooting of Eddie Waitkus inspired Bernard Malamud to write *The Natural*, first published in 1952." (Charles DeMotte, in "Baseball Heroes and Femme Fatales," The Cooperstown Symposium on Baseball and American Culture: 2002)

> "What happened to Waitkus provided the inspiration for Bernard Malamud's *The Natural*." (Wil A. Linkugel and Edward J. Pappas, *They Tasted Glory: Among the Missing at the Baseball Hall of Fame*)

> "The incident inspired Bernard Malamud to write his 1952 novel *The Natural*." (Joshua Prager, *The Echoing Green: The Untold Story of Bobby Thomson, Ralph Branca and the Shot Heard Round the World*)

"...the attack [on Waitkus] was the seed from which Malamud's story had grown." (G. Richard McKelvey, *Lost in the Sun: The Comebacks and Comedowns of Major League Ballplayers*)

"[Waitkus'] story was the inspiration for the Roy Hobbs character in Bernard Malamud's *The Natural*." (Steve Johnson, *Chicago Cubs Yesterday & Today*)

"[The Waitkus case] inspired Bernard Malamud to write *The Natural...*" (Gordon Edes, writing in the *South Florida Sun Sentinel*)

"[The book was] inspired by the 1949 shooting of Philadelphia Phillies first baseman Eddie Waitkus..." (Carolyn Kellogg, writing in the *Los Angeles Times*)

"[The Waitkus shooting] inspired Bernard Malamud to write his 1952 classic novel, *The Natural*." (Bob Minzesheimer, writing in *USA Today*)

"[The book's] immediate inspiration was the real-life case of one Eddie Waitkus, a first baseman for the Philadelphia Phillies who was also shot by a deranged woman in a hotel room." (Kevin Baker, in the introduction to a 2003 reprint of *The Natural*)

Nonetheless, it is flat-out incorrect to declare that the murder attempt on Eddie Waitkus was the singular inspiration for *The Natural*. For one thing, might the shooting of Roy Hobbs have been an outgrowth of an altogether different incident: the July 1932 shooting of Chicago Cubs shortstop Billy Jurges by Violet Valli, a showgirl with whom he was romantically connected? To expand this further, might Malamud have been aware of a certain piece supposedly penned by *New York Times* columnist Arthur Daley—the existence of which has taken on a life of its own? In the novel (as opposed to the screen adaptation), Roy Hobbs's ego allows him to be fatally corrupted—and it is noted in "A Talk With B. Malamud," published in the *Times* in 1961, that *The Natural* "was suggested by a column written by Arthur Daley for this newspaper—why does a talented man sell out?" Even though there are no direct quotations from Malamud in this piece, in *After Alienation: American Novels in Mid-Century*, published in 1964, Marcus Klein reported that the book "was suggested, Malamud has said, by one of Arthur Daley's columns in *The New York Times*, which raised

NATIONAL BASEBALL HALL OF FAME LIBRARY, COOPERSTOWN, NY

Might the shooting of Roy Hobbs in *The Natural* been inspired by the 1932 shooting of Chicago Cubs shortstop Billy Jurges—pictured above—by showgirl Violet Valli, with whom he was romantically involved?

the question, why does a talented man sell out?" In a Daley obituary published in *Dictionary of American Biography*, Kevin J. O'Keefe noted that "one of Arthur Daley's columns concerned a talented baseball player's betrayal of his principles and was turned into a book, *The Natural*, by Bernard Malamud." In a paper titled "Daley's Diamond: The Baseball Writing of Arthur J. Daley," Jim Harper observed, "Daley's treatment of gambling and fixing in sport inspired novelist Bernard Malamud to explore the theme of a talented athlete gone wrong in *The Natural*."

On the rare occasion in which he discussed the genesis of the book, Malamud in fact stressed that he had Brooklyn—and the Dodgers—in mind when conjuring up *The Natural*, rather than any one event or any team in Philadelphia or Chicago. In *Conversations with Bernard Malamud*, the author observed that the book "was the experience of being a kid in Brooklyn. I lived somewhere near Ebbets Field. The old Brooklyn Dodgers were our heroes, our stars, like out of myths. Since the stadium was that near, it had to concern you." Malamud continued, "I didn't play much baseball as a kid but I went to Ebbets Field and Yankee Stadium, I saw Babe Ruth, Dazzy Vance, and enjoyed the Brooklyn Dodgers in action." He added that ballplayers "were the 'heroes' of my American childhood. I wrote *The Natural* as a tale of a mythological hero... [I] tried to use [mythology] to symbolize and explicate an ethical dilemma of American life."

On another occasion, Malamud told *Paris Review* interviewer Daniel Stern, "As a kid, for entertainment I turned to the movies and dime novels. Maybe *The Natural* derives from Frank Merriwell as well as the adventures of the Brooklyn Dodgers in Ebbets Field." (In this interview, he also declared, without citing Waitkus or any other baseball figure, "Events from life may creep into the narrative..." and "When I start I have a pretty well-developed idea what the book is about and how it ought to go, because generally I've been thinking about it and making notes for months, if not years.") In a talk given at Bennington College in 1984, two years before his death, Malamud noted, "Baseball had interested me... but I wasn't able to write about the game until I transformed game into myth, via Jesse Weston's Percival legend with an assist from T. S. Eliot's 'The Wasteland' plus the lives of several ballplayers I had read, in particular Babe Ruth's and Bobby Feller's. The myth enriched the baseball lore as feats of magic transformed the game." In all these discussions, Malamud clearly does not cite Eddie Waitkus.

During the summer of 1949, the writer and his family moved from New York City to Corvallis, Oregon, where he began teaching at Oregon State University. It was here where the bulk of *The Natural* was written. In a detailed, superbly researched article, "'Them Dodgers is My Gallant Knights': Fiction as History in The Natural," Harley Henry offers what is perhaps the definitive connection between Waitkus and Hobbs: "We can assume that before leaving New York he had a baseball story in mind, though perhaps only a short story inspired by the shooting of the player Eddie Waitkus in June 1949, an event around which the first short section of *The Natural* is composed."

In shaping *The Natural*, Malamud admittedly incorporated the public personas of Feller and Ruth and his youthful remembrances of the Brooklyn Dodgers. But Henry reported that he also "began to shape an 'exile and return' plot imitating current events, for which he fleshed out his conception of Roy—based on Feller and Ruth—with allusions to three other players, two of them active at the time: Joe Jackson, Ted Williams, and Sal Maglie." He added that "Roy Hobbs is an amalgam of Feller's youthful innocence, Ruth's hungry prowess, Williams's hostility and pride, and Jackson's natural but corruptible talent."

Roy Hobbs starts out as a teen pitching phenom who travels by train for a tryout. His experiences on board mirror that of the young Bob Feller as he journeyed to join Cleveland in 1936. They are described in *Strikeout*

Story, Feller's 1947 autobiography, a copy of which, according to Henry, Malamud brought with him to Corvallis. Additionally, another episode in the book—Hobbs's strikeout of Walter "The Whammer" Wambold, clearly a Babe Ruth clone—mirrors the untested Feller's whiffing of eight St. Louis Cardinals in an exhibition game. And Hobbs's transition from potentially great pitcher to fence-busting slugger reflects the career of the Bambino. "Ruth's legend, and its retellings after his death in 1948," noted Henry, "were matters Malamud could not possibly ignore when he began conceiving a baseball hero that very same year."

Hobbs's desire to be acclaimed the best damned ballplayer ever is pure Ted Williams—and, like Teddy Ballgame, he wears number 9 in the movie. The inspiration for "Wonderboy," Hobbs's hand-carved bat, could be Shoeless Joe Jackson's lumber, which he called "Black Betsy." (In his review of *The Natural*, Harry Sylvester described "Wonderboy" as a "trick bat—not unlike that used by Heinie Groh of the Cincinnati Reds back in the Twenties...") Hobbs's coming to the majors and his heroics for the New York Knights parallel the plight of Sal Maglie, who debuted with the New York Giants in 1945 and summarily was banned from professional baseball by Commissioner Happy Chandler after joining the Mexican League. Maglie, like Hobbs, was in his thirties when he resurrected his career, returning to the Giants in 1950 and sparking the team with an 18–4 won-lost record. At the novel's finale, a newsboy's query of "Say it ain't true, Roy?" (in response to allegations that Hobbs threw a ballgame) echoes the legendary "Say it ain't so, Joe?" question put to Shoeless Joe Jackson regarding his participation in the 1919 Black Sox scandal. And Hobbs's banishment from the game mirrors the expulsion of Jackson and his White Sox cohorts.

Hobbs's smashing a homer that breaks the face of a clock, resulting in a shower of broken glass, may embody the flight of a ball hit by the Boston Braves' Bama Rowell in the second inning of the second game of a doubleheader at Ebbets Field on May 30, 1946. The ball smashed into the face of the Bulova clock that adorned the top of the scoreboard, spraying Dodgers right fielder Dixie Walker with falling glass. Furthermore, it may be said that the pre-Hobbs New York Knights are a version of the inept Brooklyn Dodgers of the 1930s. The Knights' owner, Judge Goodwill Banner, shares similar characteristics with Dodgers general manager Branch Rickey, starting with a propensity for cheapness.

Clearly, as he shaped *The Natural*, Bernard Malamud had in mind a range of baseball facts and folklore.

The near-murder of Eddie Waitkus, the Fightin' Phillie and Whiz Kid, was just one of them.

THE PHILLIES AND THE NATURAL: A CAMEO APPEARANCE

If Rocky Balboa slugged home runs in Connie Mack Stadium instead of opponents in a boxing ring, one might boast of Philadelphia being the locale of at least one beloved baseball film. But such is not the case. Regrettably, the Phillies and A's—unlike the teams in New York, Chicago, or Brooklyn—rarely have been represented in any baseball film, good or bad. However, the Phillies do make a cameo appearance in the screen version of *The Natural*, as well as the novel upon which it is based.

The New York Knights may be a fictional team, but their opponents are real-life National League nines. The Knights' ineptitude is summarized in a pair of onscreen newspaper headlines: "Phils Blank Knights" and "Knights Lose—Philly Wins Four to Three." The Knights and Phillies also match up in Roy Hobbs's big league debut. It's the bottom of the seventh inning, and the Philadelphia nine lead the New Yorkers by a 4–3 score. The Knights are at bat, a runner leads off first, and Hobbs is called on to pinch hit. Pop Fisher, the Knights manager, cheers him on by yelling, "Alright Hobbs, knock the cover off the ball." But no one expects that this literally is what the rookie will do once he swings and bat meets horsehide. (In the novel, Fisher's line is, "Knock the cover off of it." After Hobbs does just that, Bernard Malamud writes, "Attempting to retrieve and throw, the Philly fielder got tangled in thread.") ∎

SOURCES
Books

Alan Cheuse and Nicholas Delbanco, editors, *Talking Horse: Bernard Malamud on Life and Work* (New York: Columbia University Press, 1996).

Philip Davis, *Bernard Malamud: A Writer's Life* (Oxford: Oxford University Press, 2007).

Charles DeMotte, "Baseball Heroes and Femme Fatales," The Cooperstown Symposium on Baseball and American Culture: 2002 (Jefferson, North Carolina, McFarland & Company, 2002).

Rob Edelman, *Great Baseball Films* (New York: Citadel Press, 1994).

Kenneth T. Jackson, editor, *Dictionary of American Biography, Supplement 9: 1971–1975* (New York: Charles Scribner's Sons, 1994).

Steve Johnson, *Chicago Cubs Yesterday & Today* (Minneapolis: Voyageur Press, 2008).

Marcus Klein, *After Alienation: American Novels in Mid-Century* (Cleveland: World Publishing Company, 1964).

Bruce Kuklick, *To Every Thing a Season: Shibe Park and Urban Philadelphia 1909–1976* (Princeton: Princeton University Press, 1991).

Lawrence M. Lasher, editor, *Conversations with Bernard Malamud* (Jackson and London: University Press of Mississippi, 1991).

Wil A. Linkugel and Edward J. Pappas, *They Tasted Glory: Among the Missing at the Baseball Hall of Fame* (Jefferson, North Carolina: McFarland & Company, 1998).

Bernard Malamud, *The Natural* (New York: Farrar, Strauss and Giroux, 2003).

G. Richard McKelvey, *Lost in the Sun: The Comebacks and Comedowns of Major League Ballplayers* (Jefferson, North Carolina: McFarland & Company, 2008).

Alyssa Milano, *Safe at Home: Confessions of a Baseball Fanatic* (New York: William Morrow, 2009).

Joshua Prager, *The Echoing Green: The Untold Story of Bobby Thomson, Ralph Branca and the Shot Heard Round the World* (New York: Pantheon Books, 2006).

Richard Scheinin, *Field of Screams: The Dark Underside of America's National Pastime* (New York: W.W. Norton & Company, 1994).

John Theodore, *Baseball's Natural: The Story of Eddie Waitkus* (Carbondale: Southern Illinois University Press, 2002).

John Thorn, Pete Palmer, Michael Gershman, and David Pietrusza, *Total Baseball*, Fifth Edition (New York: Viking, 1997).

Newspaper and Magazine Articles/Papers

Ira Berkow, "Sports of the Times: The Shooting of a Baseball Idol," *The New York Times*, August 12, 1988.

Peter Carino, "History as Myth in Bernard Malamud's The Natural," *NINE: A Journal of Baseball History and Culture*, Fall 2005.

Gordon Edes, "Ballplayers Are at the Mercy Of Twisted Fans," *South Florida Sun Sentinel*, July 9, 1995.

Ron Fimrite, "A Star With Real Clout," *Sports Illustrated*, May 7, 1984.

Jim Harper, "Daley's Diamond: The Baseball Writing of Arthur J. Daley," *American Society for Sport History*, 1989.

Harley Henry, "'Them Dodgers is My Gallant Knights': Fiction as History in The Natural," *Journal of Sport History*, Summer 1992.

Louther S. Horne, "Baseball Star Shot By Girl Fan Rallies," *The New York Times*, June 16, 1949.

------. "Gain by Waitkus 'Near Miraculous'; Operation on Ball Player Succeeds," *The New York Times*, June 81, 1949.

Carolyn Kellogg, "Batter up! 9 baseball books to kick off the season," *Los Angeles Times*, March 31, 2011.

Bob Minzesheimer, "John Grisham tosses out a baseball morality tale," *USA Today*, April 9, 2012.

Mervyn Rothstein, "Bernard Malamud Dies at 71," *The New York Times*, March 19, 1986.

Daniel Stern, "Interviews: Bernard Malamud, The Art of Fiction No. 52," *The Paris Review*, Spring 1975.

Harry Sylvester, "With Greatest of Ease," *The New York Times*, August 24, 1952.

"A Talk With B. Malamud," *The New York Times*, October 8, 1961.

"Arraigned, Indicted, Held Insane in 3 Hours, Girl Who Shot Waitkus Is Sent to Asylum," *The New York Times*, July 1, 1949.

"Girl Who Shot Waitkus Gains," *The New York Times*, September 14, 1950.

"Waitkus Assailant May Go Free," *The New York Times*, August 8, 1950.

DVD

"A Natural Gunned Down: The Stalking of Eddie Waitkus," documentary extra on the Director's Cut DVD release of *The Natural*.

Websites

(The Glory of Baseball) http://thegloryofbaseball.blogspot.com/2005/06/real-life-roy-hobbs.html.

Phillies Bonus Babies, 1953–57

Sam Zygner

Beginning in 1947 and ending in 1965, Major League Baseball instituted what became known as the "Bonus Rule." Major league owners, many slow to react to changes in the landscape of the game, were coming to the realization that in order to build a winning team, it was necessary to build a strong farm system. The strategy centered on signing highly touted prospects with the hope that these players would develop and produce winning results.

The "Bonus Rule" was an initiative by Major League Baseball to restore some semblance of competitive balance and counteract teams like the St. Louis Cardinals, Brooklyn Dodgers, and New York Yankees who were stockpiling and burying players in their vast minor league systems. Under the rule, any team was allowed to sign a prospect—many of whom were just out of high school—to a bonus of $4,000 or more under the stipulation that they spend two years on a major league roster. Failure to follow the guidelines exposed the player to waivers, allowing him to be claimed by another team. Bonuses generally far exceeded the $4,000 minimum. Scouts vied for the services of these "Bonus Babies" by offering them lucrative contracts. The rule was temporarily rescinded in 1950 after several owners expressed dissatisfaction, but was re-instituted in December 1952 by a committee chaired by Branch Rickey, swinging open the door to what would become the rule's most infamous years.[1]

During this period, one of baseball's most prominent owners, Robert Carpenter Jr., although quite critical of the Bonus Rule, was quick to jump into the scrum by signing three of the most high profile talents available: Thomas Francis Qualters, Frederick William Van Dusen, and Mack Edwin Burk.[2] Like most of these signees, they would find little gold at the end of their baseball rainbows. Nevertheless, each has a story to tell. Although major league dreams were fleeting, their experiences enriched their lives and forever changed them as individuals.

TOM QUALTERS: "THEY CAN BEAT YA, BUT THEY CAN'T EAT YA"

There were two areas where young Tommy Qualters took like a duck to water: the outdoors and athletics. Growing up in the friendly hamlet of McKeesport in western Pennsylvania, practically a stone's throw away from Forbes Field, he joyfully engaged in both endeavors. On the athletic side of the coin, young Qualters excelled in baseball, basketball, and football.

Although more focused on the gridiron than the baseball diamond, he had a change of heart after an encounter with a friend and member of the Pittsburgh Steelers, Ray Mathews. Though Qualters was only a sophomore in high school, Mathews engaged him in a conversation that changed the young lad's life.

> I had contacts from Division I schools, and things like that…So, I said, "how much money are you making Ray?" and he says $6,000. I went to bed that night thinking why would I go to college and get the heck kicked out of me for four years and if I'm any good I'll go to the pros and get the heck kicked out of me. And so I made a sudden turn and I went to the high school football coach the next morning and I quit playing football and decide to concentrate on baseball.[3]

At 6'0" and 175 pounds, the strapping teenager dominated his high school team, accruing a 27–5 record while leading his squad to the WPIAL finals his junior year and winning the championship his senior season.[4] In addition, Qualters honed his talents during the summer, hurling for the East End Merchants in the Greater Pittsburgh League and barnstorming with former major leaguer Frank Gustine's traveling club.[5] Reportedly, 15 of the 16 major league's team scouts were pursuing the baby-faced phenomenon who was commanding their attention with his crackling fastball. The Phillies made an offer of $50,000 (to be spread over an eight-year period), and upon graduating high school, Qualters was quick to sign on the dotted line.[6] Some sources quote the actual amount to be $40,000. "The Phillies pursued me harder than anyone," recalled Qualters. He added, "Come to find out, what I heard later on, I was the number one guy in the country."[7] Soon after signing he acquired the nickname "Money Bags" which followed him his entire baseball career.

The future appeared rosy for the 18-year-old, but his introduction to the major leagues would prove to be a rude awakening. To say his reception was cold would be an understatement. He remembered many of his teammates resenting his taking a roster spot from established veteran Jackie Mayo, which brought not only the ire of several players, but disdain from a clubhouse attendant nicknamed "Unk" who outfitted him in a too-small uniform for his first workout with the club. When Qualters approached the petulant attendant about receiving better-fitting togs, he was told in so many words, "If you don't wanna wear the God damned thing, you can leave."[8]

For two seasons, Qualters rode the bench and occasionally pitched batting practice. Admittedly, he knew he didn't belong there, but he was caught between a rock and a hard place. "It was very frustrating. The players and manager (Steve O'Neill) were from the old school and didn't accept me. You can imagine the resentment. …As a result I was off by myself most of the time."[9] However, a few of his teammates did their best to make the untried rookie feel at home, for which Qualters was grateful. "They treated me like one of the boys and were always giving me advice. I spent a lot of time with Jim Konstanty in the bullpen and he went out of his way to be nice, Robin Roberts, too."[10]

Finally on September 13, 1953, during a lopsided contest against the St. Louis Cardinals, Qualters made his major league debut. With the Phillies trailing 11–1 in the bottom of the eighth inning, preparing to face Steve Bilko, the nervous rookie took his warm-up tosses. Bilko had already collected a pair of doubles and a single. It was an inauspicious beginning for Qualters when Bilko drove the ball deep over the fence for a home run. The misery continued as he allowed six runs on four hits, walked a batter, threw a wild pitch, and hit a batter, retiring only one man before being mercifully relieved by Konstanty.[11]

With the two-year obligation coming to an end, the Phillies decided to assign the 20-year-old to their Class-B affiliate in Reidsville, North Carolina. On June 14, 1955, he made his first start and tossed a five-hitter against High Point-Thomasville, earning a 6–3 win. His next start against Fayetteville did not go quite as well; he allowed 12 hits and seven walks, but earned his second straight win in the 11–7 victory.[12] It wasn't what Qualters had envisioned, but at least he had his chance to pitch every fourth day.

Under the watchful eye of manager and former major league chucker Charlie Gassaway, Qualters regained his sea legs. "It was hard getting back into competition. I had doubts about myself," Qualters recounted.[13] Although he had lost some zip on his fastball he developed a sinker that he thought would help him get back to the majors. He finished the season leading his team in games started (23) while compiling a respectable record (8–9, 4.90 ERA).[14]

The next year, Qualters impressed the Phillies brain trust enough to earn an assignment with Triple-A Miami of the International League. Under the tutelage of skipper Don Osborn, his role would change from starting rotation to swingman. His two years in Miami left him with some of the happiest memories of his career.

Qualters laughs when remembering his introduction to Miami and a lifelong friendship he made with a baseball icon.

> So, I'll tell you an interesting story about that…The club was run by Bill Veeck…So it was a longshot, in my mind, for me to make that ballclub. I had only played a half a year of class B ball…and so I go down there and I'm really working my tail off and there were many ex-major league players on the ballclub. Then they start cutting guys…Finally it comes—Opening Day—and I am there, I'm still there, and I'm absolutely amazed I made the ballclub.

> Well, before the game started, a big crowd and everything, and all of the sudden here comes a helicopter in. It lands beside the mound and who comes out but Satchel Paige. And I thought, you old son-of-a-gun, you just took my job you…And it had turned out that they had cut another guy: it wasn't me. So, in the aftermath of that, Satch and I became very, very close.[15]

To this day Qualters still works with kids, helping them with their pitching and hitting skills. Among the many fond memories he has of his baseball career, are sharing those seasons in Miami with the great Satchel Paige and enjoying fishing expeditions, shooting the breeze in the bullpen and playing "Skidoodle" with the baseball legend who he still recalls as a friend.

There are moments in life when something or someone changes your course forever. Qualters remembers some sage advice from Paige that he credits with saving his career.

> We're in a game and it's very early in the season…But this was my first shot, here I am in AAA

baseball, and it felt to me like I had made it to the majors. From the time I was a little kid I was never afraid of anything or anybody as long as I had a couple of rocks in my pocket which I carried all of the time, or a baseball in my hand. I had absolutely no fear of anything. And I come in the game and I get out there on the mound, most of these guys I'm playing against are ex-major league players…All of the sudden I'm on the mound and I'm taking my warm up tosses and I get the shakes. I mean I became petrified. I know I haven't felt anything like that in my life. And you can't bullshit another ballplayer, you know. Ballplayers can sense that, they can see it where nobody else can. Somehow or another I got them out. I threw the ball up there and they hit it at somebody or whatever. I got out of the inning. And I went home that night and I'm trying to figure how I can quit and go home. Not because of the fans or anything like that, just that I couldn't stand the thought of players on the team thinking that I was a coward. I mean that was something that I had never gone through before. I was just totally lost.

So, we were in the bullpen the next night. Of course I'm sitting beside Satch and a couple of innings go along. Finally he comes and hits me on the leg and he said, "What's the matter son?" I didn't know what to do so I just told him the truth and I told him what happened. And he started laughing. He said, "I'm going to tell you son," he said, "Those sons-of-a-bitches can beat ya, but they can't eat ya." Geez, they called down there and it's me again. So I get back up there and I take my warm up tosses like right on the mound and I'm standing there and I start getting the shakes again, you know, and I just thought that's it, the sons-a-bitches can beat me, but you can't eat me and I got them out. From that day on I could hardly wait to get out there. But Satch, without question, saved my career.

With newfound confidence, Qualters put together two successful seasons in Miami in preparation for his return to Philadelphia. In 1956, he finished with a 5–5 record and an impressive 3.38 ERA working 80 innings. His second season was even better, again splitting time between the bullpen and starting rotation; he crafted an 11–12 record, started sixteen games, and collected three shutouts, improving his ERA to 3.29 while working 186 innings. He earned a late season call-up to the Phillies and appeared in 6 games, hurling 7⅓ innings, with an ERA of 7.36.[16]

Qualters made the Phillies roster in 1958, but appeared in only one game before he was purchased by the Chicago White Sox and handed the role of reliever. Qualters proclaimed, "Al Lopez, without a doubt, was the greatest manager."[17] Although the Sox staff was well-stocked with quality relievers like Turk Lown, Bob Shaw, and Gerry Staley, Lopez found a spot for Qualters who appeared in 26 games (43 innings, 4.19 ERA).[18]

Buoyed by the confidence Lopez had in him, Qualters reported to White Sox spring training in 1959 with high hopes of breaking into the starting rotation; he was slated as a fifth starter. However, for the first time in his career, Qualters developed a sore arm, which he blamed on the pitching coach, Ray Berres, who tried to change his mechanics. "I'm trying to be pleasant and listen to him, but when I'd get out to the mound I would throw the way I always threw it, which was nothing wrong with it…my mechanics were fine, but he wanted me to throw like something out of a book."[19]

Hoping that he would work through the injury, the White Sox assigned Qualters to Triple-A Indianapolis of the American Association. After pitching a few starts, he began to experience numbness in his fingers and his arm grew worse. Qualters recounted, "I was hurting all of the time and by the time I got to someone who knew a little bit about arms in those days…he gave me a shot of cortisone and he said don't pitch for seven to 10 days." He added, "Well I went back and told the manager [Walker Cooper] I wasn't supposed to throw for seven to 10 days and a few days later I'm throwing again."[20]

Qualters then began the nomad stage of his career, bouncing from Indianapolis to Houston and then San Diego in 1960 (7–9, 4.47 combined), and in 1961 to Indianapolis, Dallas Fort-Worth, and Williamsport (a combined record of 5–1, 4.90). By 1962, and pitching in constant pain, Qualters made a last stop in Dallas-Fort Worth (0–4, 10.80) before hanging up his cleats for good.[21]

Qualters made the transition to private life by working for the Atlantic Refinery Company managing service stations, before finding his true calling. After passing his civil service exam, he became a Conservation Officer and proudly served for 30 years before retiring. Tom and his wife raised five children and have 10 grandchildren.[22] One grandson, Shawn Stiffler, is a pitching coach and recruiting coordinator for Virginia Commonwealth University.[23]

FRED VAN DUSEN: FROM BAGGING GROCERIES TO THE BIG LEAGUES

During the summers of 1954 and 1955, Fred Van Dusen received his fill of the elixir and drew attention from scouts from every major league team. The brash and boyishly handsome kid out of Bryant High School in Jackson Heights, New York, was exhibiting all the necessary tools: hitting for power and average, speed in the field and on the base paths, and a rocket arm. Representing the Astoria Cubs (Kiwanis) team from Queens, in the Hearst Sandlot Classic (HSC) held in the Polo Grounds, the 6'3", 180-pound high school junior was turning heads. The HSC was one of premier tournaments in the country for young talent, featuring the likes of Whitey Ford, Billy Loes, Gene Conley, Al Kaline, and Moose Skowron, just to name a few. Hall of Famer Al Simmons, serving as a manager for the J-A All-Stars, cited the youngster from Queens PSAL as the top performer of the tournament.[24]

By graduation, the 18-year-old "phenom" was prepared to sign on the dotted line. The Van Dusen family was impressed by Phillies owner Robert Carpenter Jr. and they chose the Philadelphia Phillies and their generous bonus.[25]

Van Dusen would later refuse his bonus choosing instead to play in the minor leagues, but in 1955, like other Bonus Babies, Van Dusen was unfairly ostracized by most of his teammates.[26] Rarely able to even appear in the batting cage, he waited impatiently to contribute. Finally, on September 11, 1955 at Milwaukee's County Stadium, manager Mayo Smith signaled Van Dusen to step into the on-deck circle and prepare to hit. In the bottom of the ninth inning, with the Phils trailing the Braves 9–1, lanky right-hander Humberto Robinson stood on the mound ready to deliver the pitch. "I was numb, but I told myself to get up there and go down swinging," said Van Dusen.[27] On an 0–2 count Robinson delivered a bending curveball that nicked Van Dusen on the left knee, sending him to first base. The next batter, Stan Lopata, struck out, and Richie Ashburn popped out to right field to end the game. It would turn out to be Van Dusen's only major league appearance, giving him the distinction to be the only major league player hit by a pitch while never making an appearance on the field.

Even though his major league career was short-lived, Van Dusen recounted with great pride, "Wow, you know, even to be on the field with those fellas was something."[28]

After reporting to the Phillies spring training camp in 1956, Van Dusen was farmed out to the Wilson Tobs of the Class-B Carolina League.[29] It was a struggle for the 18-year-old, and he blamed his own immaturity for his lack of success. "It happens to a lot of young players back in those days. I don't think it happens today as much because they're more mature." He added, "But to come out of high school, go to the big leagues and sign, it was quite an emotional situation for a kid because you went from delivering groceries to being a big leaguer."[30]

Van Dusen rebounded strongly in 1957 at Class-B High Point-Thomasville, finding his stroke and batting .310 in 119 games while bashing 25 home runs. He was named the Carolina League "Player of the Year" and appeared to be back on track.[31] Brimming with confidence, Van Dusen was sure he would return to the Phillies in 1958, but instead was assigned to Triple-A Miami of the International League. As a 20-year-old brash youngster, he said with a smile, "They don't know what they're doing" and added "Chuck Essegian and I are the only .300 hitters on the roster. Don't worry, though, I'll be back. I'll have such a great season; the Phils will have to get me back."[32]

Van Dusen's stay in Miami was brief; he appeared in 22 games while batting a paltry .167 with one home run and 5 RBIs. "I really stunk up the joint down there to be honest with you," Van Dusen said.[33] Not used to being platooned, he was especially frustrated and found himself demoted to Class-A Williamsport of the Eastern League for the rest of the season. Van Dusen returned to the Grays in 1959 and finished the season batting .272 in 106 games, with 14 homers and 65 RBIs. Most impressive was Van Dusen's OBP of .437.[34]

Van Dusen stayed in the Phillies organization his whole career. He spent 1960 with Asheville of the Sally League and Indianapolis of the American Association and in 1961 with Chattanooga of the Southern Association.[35] By then he could see the handwriting on the wall. "You go from prospect to suspect," explained Van Dusen. He added, "You see younger guys pass you by and you know it's time to pack it in."[36]

Following his baseball career, Van Dusen found his niche in insurance and built his own lucrative business. He found love with his wife of 38 years and raised a happy family.

Now retired and living in Tennessee, Van Dusen received national attention when he threw out the first pitch on October 2, 2012, before a late season contest at Marlins Stadium. Van Dusen had been invited to this game to honor Adam Greenberg, who had become the second player to be hit by a pitch and never appear in the field. In his one-day comeback to the major leagues, Greenberg realized his dream of an official at-bat when he struck out on three pitches facing R.A. Dickey. Greenberg's ceremonial at-bat returned Van Dusen to his solitary spot as the only player to be hit by a pitch and never appear in the field.[37]

Van Dusen summed up his life experience:

> You know they say youth is wasted on the young. Because by the time you figure it out…I look at it as an experience. What I did learn was how to take defeat and get through it. I wish I could have learned that a little sooner, but that's how the game is. Because you don't always learn by doing it the hard way, but I learned by doing it the hard way.[38]

MACK BURK: "I THOUGHT I DIED AND WENT TO HEAVEN"

Mack Burk has a soothing southern drawl that naturally draws people to him like a Texas barbeque draws a crowd. The tall, lanky youngster grew up in Nacogdoches, Texas, and found out early that he was a natural athlete. He started out playing softball on the hard dirt fields in the neighborhood before moving to baseball.

Burk caught the eye of several scouts while playing shortstop at Stephen Austin High School and competing against adults as a member of the Mechanics Uniform Supply amateur team which won the American Baseball Congress national championship in 1955.[39] He was especially impressive during the tournament, batting a glossy .420 with a couple of home runs.[40]

After graduating high school, Burk at 6'4", 175 pounds accepted a scholarship to the University of Texas in basketball. "The only reason I took the basketball scholarship was because they offered it to me early and I felt I could play baseball, too," said Burk.[41] Texas head coach Bibb Falk was ecstatic to have an athlete of such caliber and happily accepted Burk on the squad. However, fate stepped in and, after breaking his collarbone during his sophomore season at UT, Burk decided to focus on the diamond instead.[42] On September 29, 1955, Burk sat down with his family and Hap Morse. After a bit of dickering he signed for a $45,000 bonus.[43] The deal stipulated a $10,000 advance, the balance to be paid in three annual installments. One benefit was that Burk, a college junior, was able to purchase an 800-acre Texas ranch in partnership with his father Edwin.[44]

Burk reported to his first spring training in Clearwater, Florida, in 1956 unsure how much playing time he would receive. Upon arriving, Burk exclaimed, "I thought I died and went to heaven."[45] Surrounding him were players who, up to that point, he had only read about in the newspapers. "And I mean, here I am a 20-year-old kid, you know, and you got guys like Robin Roberts, and Curt Simmons, and Andy Seminick, and Stan Lopata, and Granny Hamner, and Willie 'Puddin Head' Jones, Del Ennis and Richie Ashburn; these were all guys I had been watching for years. Here I am riding the bus with them and training with them."

Unlike many Bonus Babies, Burk had a very different experience with his baptism in the big leagues, as he fondly reminisced:

> Robin Roberts was probably the nicest guy in the world. He kinda took me under his wing and told me not to do anything without consulting him because he didn't want somebody taking advantage of me…he knew I was young. In fact all of them—Willie "Puddin Head" Jones and I were real good friends—the whole group, they accepted me and I didn't have any problems at all.[46]

On May 25 he made his first major league appearance pinch-running for Andy Seminick in the eighth inning of a Phillies 8–5 loss to Pittsburgh. His first big league at-bat came on June 5 at Crosley Field in Cincinnati. Pinch-hitting for Curt Simmons in the fifth inning, Burk singled sharply to center field off Reds starter Joe Nuxhall and later scored on a Lopata sacrifice fly. Although it was a special moment for Burk, the Phils fell short in the run column, 9–4.[47]

He saw limited action his inaugural season and was used almost exclusively as a pinch-runner. His manager, Mayo Smith, used him several times, mostly running for second baseman Solly Hemus late in games. "I was kinda his designated pinch-runner whenever it would get late in the ball games," said Burk. Although he received little playing time with the Phillies, Burk gained much experience working in the bullpen in addition to receiving advice from a hall-of-fame receiver. Burk recounted, "Of course I worked the bullpen. Benny Bengough was the bullpen coach. We were going north one year and playing the Yankees and Bill Dickey was still with the Yankees. And Benny took me over to him and the three of us sat down and talked for a long time about catching and everything."[48]

The 1957 season found Burk wearing olive drab instead of Phillies flannel while serving on active duty in the reserves. He missed that entire season. The Phillies had planned for Burk to play in the Panama League for winter ball, but because of his late release he was unable to participate. With his Bonus Rule obligation fulfilled, the Phillies assigned Burk to Class-AA Tulsa (Oilers) in April 1958.[49]

After appearing in only eight games, and batting .182 in Tulsa, Burk was transferred to Williamsport

Class-A of the Eastern League where he finished the year batting .236 in 94 games. That same season he returned to Philadelphia for his last major league at-bat and unceremoniously struck out. He closed his major league ledger with a .500 batting average.[50]

In 1959, Burk split time between Triple-A Buffalo of the International League and Williamsport again. Burk also served as Jimmie Coker's backup for the pennant-winning Bisons, batting only .200 in 35 at-bats. Contemplating retirement from the game he loved during the offseason, Burk decided to give it one more go on his father's prompting.

> So one Sunday afternoon I'm sitting in my den with my mother and my dad. And my dad looked at me and said, "Son, you don't have a job so you might as well go out there and get on that airplane and go to Florida to spring training." I hadn't even signed a contract. I go to Florida for spring training and give it one more shot. So I did and I ended up going to Asheville, North Carolina. They had some young pitchers there they wanted me to handle and so that was the last year that I played.[51]

Although it proved to be a fairly successful season behind the dish—with Burk hitting a solid .281 and driving in 46 runs in 114 games—he decided to hang up the tools of ignorance and move on. He was clear on his goals and stated, "I said I'm going to give it a few years and I'm not going to be a baseball bum and play in the minors for years…I just wanted to get established in life." He added, "If I wasn't going to make it, I wasn't going to make it and I was going to quit."[52]

After working many years in the electrical supply business, Burk retired in 1997 and now enjoys time off with his wife in the area of Houston, Texas. They enjoy traveling in their motor home and have been known to visit friends in Vero Beach, Florida now and again. He has no regrets from his baseball career and cherishes the friendships he made along the way. ■

Acknowledgments

I would like to thank Tom Qualters, Fred Van Dusen, and Mack Burk for their contributions to this article. I am especially grateful to them for sharing their experiences and recollections of playing professional baseball and their personal lives, as well.

Notes

1. Steve Treder, "Cash in the Cradle: The Bonus Babies," November 1, 2004, hardballtimes.com.
2. Joe Reichler, "Phillies Boss Raps Bonus Rule," *The Norwalk Hour*, October 20, 1949, 28.
3. Tom Qualters, telephone interview, March 5, 2010.
4. Oscar Ruhl, "From the Ruhl Book," *The Sporting News*, February 16, 1955, 14.
5. Ralph Katanik, "Tom Qualters: Phillies' Bonus Baby," *Pittsburgh Post-Gazette*, March 5, 1987, 7.
6. Les Biederman, "Bonus Baby Qualters Has No Regrets Over Bench-Warmer Role," *The Sporting News*, February 17, 1954, 8.
7. Brent Kelley, *Baseball's Biggest Blunder: The Bonus Rule of 1953–1957* (Lanham, Maryland, Scarecrow Press, 1997) 26.
8. Ibid.
9. Tom Qualters, telephone interview, March 5, 2010.
10. Les Biederman, "Bonus Baby Qualters Has No Regrets Over Bench-Warmer Role," *The Sporting News*, February 17, 1954, 8.
11. Baseball-reference.com.
12. "Tommy Qualters Making For Lost Time With Phillies," *The Sporting News*, 38.
13. Tom Qualters, telephone interview, March 5, 2010.
14. Baseball-reference.com.
15. Tom Qualters, telephone interview, March 5, 2010.
16. Baseball-reference.com.
17. Tom Qualters, telephone interview, March 5, 2010.
18. Baseball-reference.com.
19. Tom Qualters, telephone interview, March 5, 2010.
20. Ibid.
21. Baseball-reference.com.
22. Tom Qualters, telephone interview, March 5.
23. VCUathletics.com.
24. Morrey Rokeach, "New York All-Stars Power-Packed in Sandlot Classic," *The Sporting News*, August 11, 1954, 21.
25. *The Sporting News*, August 31, 1955, 4.
26. Art Morrow, "Phillies Line Up 44 Phenoms for Force-Feed Diet," *The Sporting News*, February 8, 1956, 20.
27. William Weinbaum, "Van Dusen Feels Greenberg's Pain," ESPN.com, March 16, 2007.
28. Fred Van Dusen telephone interview, April 6, 2010.
29. Baseball-reference.com.
30. Fred Van Dusen telephone interview, April 6, 2010.
31. *The Sporting News*, November 6, 1957, 26.
32. George Metzger, "Rookie, Farmed by Phillies, Says, 'Family Still Likes Me'," *The Sporting News*, April 2, 1958, 33.
33. Fred Van Dusen telephone interview, April 6, 2010.
34. Baseball-reference.com.
35. Ibid.
36. Fred Van Dusen telephone interview, April 6, 2010.
37. Joe Frisaro, "Like Greenberg, Van Dusen's career short-lived," MLB.com, October 2, 2012.
38. Fred Van Dusen telephone interview, April 6, 2010.
39. Baseball-reference.com/bullpen/Mack.
40. Art Morrow, Burk, "Latest Flash Phil Find, Flashes Dash of Dickey Behind the Dish," *The Sporting News*, March 7, 1956, 15.
41. Mack Burk telephone interview, October 19, 2012.
42. Art Morrow, Burk, "Latest Flash Phil Find, Flashes Dash of Dickey Behind the Dish," *The Sporting News*, March 7, 1956, 15.
43. Baseball-reference.com/bullpen/Mack.
44. Art Morrow, Burk,"Latest Flash Phil Find, Flashes Dash of Dickey Behind the Dish," *The Sporting News*, March 7, 1956, 15.
45. Mack Burk telephone interview, October 19, 2012.
46. Ibid.
47. Baseball-reference.com.
48. Mack Burk telephone interview, October 19, 2012.
49. Lee Schwartz, "Phillies' Bonus Player 1.000 Hitter When Sent to Minors," *The Sporting News*, April 30, 1958, 4.
50. Baseball-reference.com.
51. Mack Burk telephone interview, October 19, 2012.
52. Ibid.

Tom Qualters's Amazing 1954 Season for the Philadelphia Phillies

Stephen D. Boren MD, FACEP

Thomas Francis Qualters was a bonus baby whom the Philadelphia Phillies signed on June 16, 1953, for an estimated $40,000. He was a star pitcher at McKeesport, Pennsylvania and once struck out 21 batters in a seven-inning high school game and 24 in an eight-inning high school game, allowing only one hit in each contest.[1] When he joined the Phillies, he felt that most of the players were pleasant to him. However, manager Steve O'Neill and the coaches did not believe he should be on the team. Thus, they pretty much ignored him.[2] On September 13, 1953, O'Neill finally put Tom into a major league game when he relieved Tommy Glaviano in the bottom of the eighth inning, with the Phillies losing 11–1 to the Cardinals in St. Louis. Unfortunately, Steve Bilko greeted him with a home run and Peanuts Lowrey walked. After throwing a wild pitch, he hit Rip Repulski with a pitch. Harvey Haddix and then Solly Hemus singled, Red Schoendienst forced Hemus, Stan Musial doubled, and then Jim Konstanty replaced Qualters. A single by Enos Slaughter resulted in Qualters having faced seven batters and given up six runs on four hits, one walk, and one hit batter in the one-third of an inning he pitched (plus the one wild pitch).[3] Qualters would not play in a major league game again until September 7, 1957, despite the fact that he was on the 1954 Phillies' roster for the entire season.

According to the *Sports Encyclopedia Baseball*, only four players have been on a major league roster all season without entering a game: Dick Rudolph in 1921 (Boston, NL), Joe Heving in 1935 (Chicago, AL), Grover Hartley in 1928 (Cleveland) and Qualters in 1954.[4] All four have a designation in that volume after their names of "DP" for did not play. However, Rudolph had hurt his arm and was a coach, not a player in 1921.[5,6] Heving had been sent to the minors after the 1934 season, and Hartley, like Rudolph in 1921, was officially a coach in 1928.[7,8] Qualters was the only one to truly perform this odd feat of being on a major league roster all season, but never actually being in an official game.

A number of circumstances caused Qualters's unique 1954 season. Starting with the Detroit Tigers signing Dick Wakefield on June 21, 1941, teams were signing high school and college players for huge bonuses.[9] This escalated after World War II and team owners felt that this spending of huge bonuses on unproven young players was out of control. A number of these bonus players did have outstanding careers such as Hall of Famer Robin Roberts, and others such as Johnny Antonelli, Curt Simmons, Dick Groat, and Herb Score also had significant success. Unfortunately, there were many players such as Frank House (Detroit Tigers), J.W. Porter (Chicago White Sox), Paul Pettit (Pittsburgh Pirates), Marty Keough (Boston Red Sox), Eddie Urness (Boston Red Sox), Jerry Zimmerman (Boston Red Sox), Tom Casagrande (Philadelphia Phillies) and Billy Joe Davidson (Cleveland) who were either complete busts or at best just journeyman players. In December 1952, the owners created a new rule to protect themselves from themselves.[10] Any player who signed for more than a $4,000 bonus had to stay on the major league roster for two full seasons, or be released. They figured that no team would be foolish enough to spend all that money on untested players who had to use up precious spots on the 25-man roster. However, all 16 teams did sign such players. This rule was in effect from 1953 through 1957. Finally, after the 1957 season, the bonus rule was rescinded.[11]

Thus Qualters had to stay on the Phillies major league roster from June 16, 1953, through June 16, 1955. After 77 games in 1954, Phillies' manager Steve O'Neill was fired and Terry Moore replaced him.[12] Unfortunately, Moore felt the same way about Qualters as did O'Neill.[13] Many people have forgotten, but the Phillies from 1950 through 1955 were not bad teams. They had won the 1950 National League pennant but fallen to fifth place in 1951. However, they still had their nucleus of the 1950 Whiz Kids team including Robin Roberts, Curt Simmons, Jim Konstanty, Granny Hamner, Willie Jones, Del Ennis, and Richie Ashburn. They finished fourth in 1952 (only one game out of third place), were tied for third in 1953, and finished fourth in both 1954 and 1955. The fact that the team was very decent actually hurt Qualters's opportunity to pitch.

Starting in 1918, baseball divided up the World Series profit with all of the first-division teams.[14] The amount of money could be quite significant. The 1953 Phillies had 30 full shares of $810 each (and six other cash awards).[15,16] In 1954, while it was apparent before the season was half over that they would not win the pennant, they were always in the fight for first-division money. On August 1 they were tied in the loss column with the St. Louis Cardinals for fourth place.[17] By September 1 they were in fifth, behind the Cincinnati Reds but ahead of the Cardinals. As September progressed, the Phillies inched ahead of the Reds. Going into the last game of the season, they were only one game ahead of the Cincinnati Reds for fourth-place money. If the Reds won and the Phillies lost, they would be tied for fourth and have to split the money. Therefore the Phillies could not afford to pitch an inexperienced rookie such as Qualters with so much money at stake. Of note, both the Reds and the Phillies lost their September 26 game and thus the Phillies collected the fourth-place money.[18] There eventually were 33 full shares at $648.36 each and four other cash awards.[19] The average National League salary has been calculated to have been $13,772 in 1954.[20] Thus, the fourth-place money was a significant enticement for the Phillies to win games and finish fourth. Other teams such as the Pittsburgh Pirates, who were long doomed to eighth place (and would eventually lose 101 games that year), could easily use bonus pitcher Laurin Pepper, and thus started him in eight games and used him in relief in six more. Of note, the buying power of a dollar in 1953 compared to 2012 was $8.39 and thus the fourth-place money was worth $5,439.74 today.[21] Thus for many Phillies—the coaching staff as well as the players—this would be a significant windfall.

Also, the Phillies were not in any long, extra-inning games during the season.[22] Typically, extra-inning games involve many pinch hitters and thus multiple pitchers. In fact, in some long games, non-pitchers have been forced to pitch. For the 1954 Phillies the longest game was 15 innings on June 17, but Robin Roberts pitched a complete game, which was typical of him. There was a 13-inning game on July 23 that Bob Miller and Robin Roberts pitched. However, there were not any long games that required multiple pitchers.

Finally, there were no real "blow out" losses for the Phillies in 1954. On May 17, there was an 8–0 loss, but the game was only 5–0 going into the 8th.[23] In the June 20 15–6 loss to Cincinnati, the Phillies used Herm Wehmeier, Jim Konstanty, Murry Dickson, Ron Mrozin-

NATIONAL BASEBALL HALL OF FAME LIBRARY, COOPERSTOWN, NY

TOM QUALTERS *pitcher PHILADELPHIA PHILLIES*

Qualters signed with the Phillies on June 16, 1953 but made only a single appearance in September and rode the bench the entire 1954 season.

ski, and Bob Greenwood.[24] That possibly could have been a chance for Qualters. There was a 10–0 loss on July 5 that was 10–0 after four innings that Wehmeier, Konstanty, and Greenwood pitched.[25] Again, Qualters could have pitched. On July 30 in a 12–3 loss to the St. Louis Cardinals, the score was only 4–3 going into the seventh. Bob Miller, Wehmeier, Konstanty, and Mrozinski pitched.[26] On September 18, the Phils lost 9–1 to the Giants; Dickson, Miller, Steve Ridzik, and Ron Mrozinski pitched.[27] While there were no double-digit losses except for the July 5 game, there were a few games where Qualters felt he could have had a chance at major league pitching experience.[28]

Qualters went to the ballpark every day. He often pitched batting practice. Since they did not use any protective screen, this was a potential problem. Granny Hamner once lined a pitch that hit the bill of Qualters's cap. All pitchers, including Tom, had to have batting practice before the position players did. However, it was the batboy who pitched batting practice, not a pitcher or even a coach. After that, Qualters mainly went to the bullpen to watch the game, although he occasionally sat on the bench. He never was told by the managers or the coaches if or when he would pitch. He did not receive any pitching instructions from the coaches or managers until he was finally sold to the Chicago White Sox in 1958. There he was managed by Al Lopez and coached by legendary pitching coach Ray Berres.[29]

Qualters did pitch in an exhibition game on May 3, 1954, when the Phillies played their Terre Haute farm team (Class B, Three I League). He relieved Johnny Lindell in this 10–2 victory.[30] Qualters did start a game in 1954 against a major league team but not a regular-season NL contest. The Phillies and the Philadelphia

Athletics used to play an annual charity game and Qualters was selected for the seventh annual game. Thus on June 28, Tom Qualters started for the Phillies in this exhibition game.[31] He unfortunately beaned Vic Power in the first inning, knocking him unconscious. Qualters gave up four hits, and struck out one batter in only three innings, but was declared the winning pitcher. On July 12 during the All-Star Game break, the Phillies played an exhibition game against the Schenectady team. However, the Phillies tried to use as many former Schenectady players as possible and thus Qualters did not play, nor did he play the following day against Syracuse.[32] On August 23 the Phillies played the Fort Wayne American Van Lines. However, this was a semi-pro team, not a professional team. Behind Qualters's five-hitter, the Phillies won 6–4.[33]

Qualters was a fast runner.[34] In the minors he later did pinch running. However, despite slow players on the 1954 Phillies such as Del Ennis and Smoky Burgess, Qualters was never used as a pinch runner.

Pitcher Jim Brady of the 1955 Detroit Tigers almost was in the identical situation as Tom Qualters. He was signed to a large bonus on June 9, 1955, and did not play in any games that year.[35] However, the Tigers had played 52 games already and Brady was not with them all season.[36] In addition, it has been suggested that Brady was injured in 1955, but there is no evidence of his being on the disabled list.[37,38]

Perhaps Qualters, O'Neill, and Moore were the forerunners of Roy Hobbs and his manager Pop Fisher in the Robert Redford movie The Natural. When Roy Hobbs first came to the New York Knights, Fisher was very unhappy about his team signing Hobbs to a major league contract without his knowledge. Fisher said, "I ain't gonna play him," and for a long time he did not.[39] That was how O'Neill and Moore deep down felt about Qualters. As he said recently, "I'd been better off taking less money and signing with another team. But I was just a young, dumb kid then."[40] ■

Acknowledgments

The author wishes to acknowledge the help of Robert Gorman and Thomas F. Qualters Sr. for their help with this article.

Notes

1. Brent Kelley, Baseball's Bonus Babies: Conversations with 24 High-Priced Ballplayers (Jefferson NC: McFarland Press, 2006) 10.
2. Thomas F. Qualters. Personal phone interview. January 15, 2013.
3. www.retrosheet.org/boxesetc/1953/B09130SLN1953.htm.
4. David S. Neft, Richard M. Cohen, and Michael L. Neft, The Sports Encyclopedia: Baseball, 20th edition (New York, NY: St. Martin's Press, 2000).
5. www.retrosheet.org/boxesetc/R/Prudod101.htm.
6. Dick Leyden, "Dick Rudolph" http://sabr.org/bioproj/person/c7bc764a.
7. Bill Nowlin, "Joe Heving" http://sabr.org/bioproj/person/a4e4afdb.
8. Mike Cooney. "Grover Hartley" http://sabr.org/bioproj/person/ba3f05b5
9. The Sporting News Baseball Register (St. Louis, MO: Charles C. Spink and Son, 1944), 179.
10. The Sporting News Baseball Guide and Record Book (St. Louis, MO: Charles C. Spink and Son, 1953), 97.
11. The Sporting News Baseball Guide and Record Book (St. Louis, MO: Charles C. Spink and Son, 1958), 110.
12. www.retrosheet.org/boxesetc/1954/TPHI01954.htm.
13. Qualters interview.
14. Reach Official American League Baseball Guide For 1919 (Philadelphia: A.J. Reach Company), 195–196.
15. www.retrosheet.org/boxesetc/1954/09261954.htm.
16. The Sporting News Baseball Guide and Record Book (St. Louis, MO: Charles C. Spink and Son, 1954), 106.
17. www.retrosheet.org/boxesetc/1954/08011954.htm.
18. www.retrosheet.org/boxesetc/1954/09261954.htm.
19. The Sporting News Baseball Guide and Record Book (St. Louis, MO: Charles C. Spink and Son, 1955), 28.
20. Doug Pappas, Business of Baseball, http://roadsidephotos.sabr.org/baseball/1957-63sals.htm
21. www.dollartimes.com/calculators/inflation.htm.
22. www.retrosheet.org/boxesetc/1954/VPHI01954.htm.
23. www.retrosheet.org/boxesetc/1954/B05170PHI1954.htm.
24. www.retrosheet.org/boxesetc/1954/B06202PHI1954.htm.
25. www.retrosheet.org/boxesetc/1954/B07051NY11954.htm.
26. www.retrosheet.org/boxesetc/1954/B07300PHI1954.htm.
27. www.retrosheet.org/boxesetc/1954/B09180NY11954.htm.
28. Qualters interview.
29. Ibid.
30. Waterloo Iowa Daily Courier, May 4, 1954.
31. Art Morrow, The Sporting News, July 7, 1954, 15.
32. Schenectady Gazette, July 13, 1954, 21.
33. Valparaiso Vidette, August 24, 1954, 7.
34. Qualters interview.
35. www.retrosheet.org/boxesetc/B/Pbradj102.htm.
36. www.retrosheet.org/boxesetc/1956/VDET01956.htm.
37. Alan Roth, ed., Who's Who In Baseball (New York: Baseball Magazine, 1957), 77.
38. The Sporting News Baseball Register (St. Louis, MO: Charles C. Spink and Son, 1956).
39. www.script-o-rama.com/movie_scripts/n/natural-script-transcript-robert-redford.htm.
40. Qualters interview.

1964 Phillies, Fans, and Media

Andrew Milner

The 1964 Phillies enjoyed a six-and-a-half game lead in the National League with 12 games left in the season, proceeded to lose 10 in a row, and surrendered the pennant to the St. Louis Cardinals. The closing two weeks of the 1964 regular season inflicted psychic baseball wounds which began to heal after the Phillies' 1980 world championship and have faded with the passing decades and recent string of Phillies successes, (which began with the 2007 Phillies overcoming a seven-game deficit late in the season).

This article looks at the minds of Phillies fans in the weeks leading up to the 1964 collapse. In the manner of G.H. Fleming's *The Unforgettable Season* and Jean-Pierre Caillault's *A Tale of Four Cities*, this story is told through contemporary newspaper accounts.

SEPTEMBER 1

When you think of a baseball fan, the stereotype comes to mind: A noisy, pot-bellied guy, chest hair curling over a loud sports shirt, a torpedo-sized cigar in one hand and a six-pack in the other. He'll roost on a taproom stool all night, telling you how Jimmy Foxx belted 'em out of Shibe Park, or arguing whether Tris Speaker, Joe DiMaggio or Willie Mays could go get the deep ball with more class.

That's the old breed. It still flourishes, and Mr. R. R. M. Carpenter's accountants are grateful. The Phils, however, are luring a New Breed which comes in more ornamental designs than the old model.

The new fan wears toreador pants, a "Go, Phils, Go" button attached to a frilly shirt, and smells of Arpege rather than Corona-Corona. Pennant fever has destroyed the reason of most of Philadelphia's cupcake population. Chicks of all sizes and vintages are becoming wildly romantic about the Phils, of all people.

It is a little astonishing, as if Woody Allen suddenly began playing the hero in James Bond movies. Once the Phils were the objects of scorn, laughter and pity. Now they are cuddly, lovable, neat, fantastic and fab.

Nope, Connie Mack Stadium does not yet look like a run-down sorority house. If the Toreador Set is still in the minority, they are among the most intense loyalists in town. A word against John Callison will draw outraged screeches as fast—almost—as criticism of those furry cats from Liverpool, whatever their names are.

— *Bulletin*[1]

SEPTEMBER 2

You could look it up. Bunning is now 9–0 vs. the Mets and [Houston] Colts. He is 6–4 vs. the rest of the National League. That adds up to 15–4.

What that could add up to can only be guessed at, but Bernard Baruch might be needed to break it down to dollars and cents. It already includes a one-hitter—vs. the Colts—and a perfect game—vs. the Mets. It could add up to 20 wins. It could add up to a pennant. It could add up to the Cy Young Award. It could add up to the Most Valuable Player Award.

Before you know it, Jim Bunning will be able to write a check that can make a bank bounce.

— *Daily News*[2]

SEPTEMBER 4

The Phillies have reached the stage in their National League pennant quest where they win even when they lose.

That's because the mathematics are all on the side of a front-runner when a flag race goes into its final stages. The league leader can lose games and still gain time unless the other contenders begin to move at a fast clip—which is exactly what the Phillies have been doing for the last week.

A week ago, a .500 pace by the Phillies in their remaining games meant that the Reds would have to play .622 baseball to take the pennant and the Giants would have to play .778 ball to do so. In this last week the Phillies have played .500 ball—worsening the position of both chief contenders because the Reds must now play .724 ball to win and the Giants .808 ball if the Phillies simply maintain that .500 gait.

— *Daily News*[3]

SEPTEMBER 5

Sure, I love the Beatles. But do you want to know something? I love the Phillies even better. Yeah! Yeah! Yeah!

— *Daily News* letter to editor[4]

SEPTEMBER 8

Probably the only Philly fan in Philadelphia who doesn't show signs of pennant fever is manager Gene Mauch.

"He never mentions the pennant," said his brunette wife, Nina Lee. "He only talks about today's ballgame, and winning that."

Her comments come as no surprise to sportswriters, who have wondered privately if Mauch knew how to pronounce "pennant"—they've never heard him mention it, either.

But baseball fans who crowd into Connie Mack Stadium not only know the word, they know the chances of calling it theirs—they know that the Phillies have won 60 percent of their games so far this season, and that if they win half the remaining games, the nearest challenger will have little hope of copping the National League flag.

And they know if that happens, fans can plan on seeing the World Series open here Oct. 7.

Right before he leaves for the ballpark, Gene Mauch has his favorite food, hamburger, and then makes sure that jingling in his pocket with his change is a silver medal, his good luck piece ever since a Catholic friend presented him with it years ago.

"Of course we're not superstitious," said his friendly wife, smiling as she knocked on the wooden porch post enroute to seeing her visitor to the car.

"But wouldn't it be terrific if we did win the Pennant?"

— *Bulletin*[5]

I think the *Daily News* 'Go Phillies Go' banners on the opening day of the season had a lot to do with giving our team the spark to go out and win the pennant.

— *Daily News* letter to editor[6]

To the editor of *The Inquirer*:

I just came out of the desert to read in an Egyptian newspaper that the Phillies are leading the National League!

To a life-long Phillies fan this was so impossible that I had the French translated for me by an expert and he said, "In first place by seven games."

I still believe this is a trick, but even so it pleases me so much that I am going right out to the temples to

"Probably the only Philly fan in Philadelphia who doesn't show signs of pennant fever is manager Gene Mauch," reported the *Philadelphia Bulletin*.

NATIONAL BASEBALL HALL OF FAME LIBRARY, COOPERSTOWN, NY

pray to Isis, Ptha (sic), Hathor and Horus that this dream may continue through at least early October.

— *Inquirer* letter to the editor from James Michener[7]

SEPTEMBER 9

It would be a wonderful thing for baseball if the Phillies win the pennant because it took a phenomenon like the Mets to replace them in this land as a symbol of baseball's culturally deprived.

It would be no less wonderful if they won it by six games— their present margin over the Giants, Reds and Cards—or by eight or 10 games, but it might be more wonderful if they won it by one or two. The Phillies are a team that has gotten to where it is by somehow getting one more run than the other guy, and that is how the race should go. The 1950 Phillies, to their everlasting credit, blew a bigger lead than the 1964 Phillies now have, prolonging the agony until the 10th inning of the last day of the season. In retrospect, that was their greatest triumph. THAT took talent.

— *Daily News*[8]

Collectively and individually, the amazing Phillies are rewriting a lot of pages in the baseball record book this year as they make a valiant run for their first pennant in 14 years. In the process, they also are setting a new all-time attendance record—having exceeded, this week, the old mark of 1,217,205 which had stood since the 1950 season of those unforgettable "Whiz Kids."

This satisfying statistic indicates popular support for the Phillies unprecedented in their long history. In

NATIONAL BASEBALL HALL OF FAME LIBRARY, COOPERSTOWN, NY

"WHICH OF THESE THREE FAMOUS PHILLIES MADE THE BIGGEST HIT?" asked a 1964 newspaper advertisement. "Is it Jim Bunning, who hurled a perfect game?"

underscores, also, the need for a new and larger stadium to accommodate the growing throngs who would like to see their favorite baseball players in action on the home diamond.

If there ever was any question about Delaware Valley sports fans backing enthusiastically a winning baseball team, the doubts have now been effectively dispelled. The new attendance record provides an additional argument for expediting a spacious new stadium for Philadelphia, with plenty of parking space and convenient to public transportation.

— *Inquirer* editorial[9]

SEPTEMBER 10

I have been real nervous lately. Sharp-tongued, short-tempered. My old lady has been very nice about it, though. Oh, I haven't escaped entirely unmarked. She hasn't been that nice. A lump here, a lump there: about par for a married man.

I know what's bugging me, but can't do anything about it. You see, I'm a Phillies' fan, yet I dread the thought of them winning the pennant—if they have to meet the Yankees in the World Series.

Too well do I remember the fiasco of 1950. I can still see those Yankees dashing around the bases and scoring runs like they were playing the Rover Boys. A traumatic experience, the head-shrinkers would call it.

And, let's face it, the same thing will happen again this year if the Phils and the Yanks meet in the Series.

No wonder people are starting to call me Shaky.

—Joe Martin

Forget it, Shaky, and think of how the Dodgers clobbered the Yanks in four last year. —Ed.

— *Daily News* letter to editor[10]

Don't tell Gene Mauch the Cardinals are coming. Don't remind him St. Louis is five games back and rumbling through the final two months like a buffalo stampede.

"The only club in the National League that can beat us is the Phillies," Mauch said. "We did that tonight, and it ain't gonna happen any more."

The Cardinals got 20 hits and beat the Phillies, 10–5, last night in 11 weird innings, to snarl to within five games of the lead. It was a big game because the Giants had lost in the afternoon, and the Reds had lost at night, and a Phillies' victory would have meant a seven-game lead over the world.

"They might be peeking back at us," Cardinal third baseman Ken Boyer suggested, after getting three hits and driving in three runs, including the tying run with two out in the ninth inning.

"If they win it, they break it open. A seven-game pad would have been tough. Especially the way the schedule is."

Mauch sneered at Boyer's suggestion. "If I'm peeking back," he said, after a closed-door clubhouse meeting, "and we get one more out in the ninth inning, then I'm looking back seven games in front.

"Anyway, I'd rather be peeking back, than peeking ahead."

— *Daily News*[11]

Mayor James H.J. Tate more or less put the fate of the proposed stadium up to the Phillies Wednesday, stating if they did not win the pennant it would "seriously jeopardize" the sports bowl loan proposal.

"It will be a sad blow," the Mayor said commenting on the possible double tragedy.

Barring the Phillies dropping from first place the Mayor said he expects the $25 million loan proposal to pass along with three other loans on the November ballot.

— *Inquirer*[12]

The St. Louis Cardinals are in second place and they are coming. It is hard to see the Phillies blowing the pennant to the Reds or Giants, because the Reds and Giants don't seem interested enough, but it is not hard to imagine them blowing it to the Cardinals. The Cardinals are interested: they have won 13 of their last 16 games.

Down the stretch, the Cardinals have a few important things going for them, if a team five games out of first place on September 9 can have anything going.

They have their boss, Augie Busch. Busch recently fired general manager Bing Devine because the Cardinals weren't high enough in the standings for him. In other words, he didn't think Devine had done a good job of building a contender. No group of athletes has ever had a better chance to embarrass their boss, an incentive that's almost unfair to the Phillies.

They have this penchant for late-season heroics. A year ago the Cardinals won 19 out of 20 to project themselves into the big picture.

They have the Phillies. The Cardinals beat the Phillies. They have beaten them 10 out of 14 already. Three of the four remaining games are in St. Louis.

And they have Ken Boyer. He's nice, too.

— *Daily News*[13]

SEPTEMBER 11

Nobody knew the advantage of Chris Short's victory over the Cardinals yesterday more than Big Magic.

Big Magic now says that the Phillies have a 92 percent chance of winning the National League pennant.

Big Magic said the Phillies probably will face the White Sox in the World Series.

If you are wondering about Big Magic it is a huge hunk of metal. It can't go to its left. It couldn't reach the right field wall at Connie Mack Stadium if it tried until 1984.

Big Magic is a computer, a Honeywell 1400 computer if you please. It is housed at the Franklin Institute.

"This is the first time we've ever had the computer attempt to figure the pennant winner," said Al Polaneczky who feeds the computer with data cards once a day and gets the probabilities for the National and American League pennant races.

Big Magic's daily diet consists of the remaining schedules of each club against every other club. It digests the data, then gives its daily probabilities.

"The method we are using is much the same as we follow in computing sales," Polaneczky added. "We call it the Monte Carlo technique because we are actually gambling with data. The operation is well proven. It has a solid basis in mathematics."

Gene Mauch hopes so.

— *Daily News*[14]

LAS VEGAS, Nev. (UPI).—The Phillies were such prohibitive favorites in the legal bookmaking establishments here that no bets were being taken today on their chances of winning the National League pennant.

With the Phillies listed as "out," so far as wagering was concerned, the odds-makers in their day-to-day line posted the St. Louis Cardinals at 10–1 and the Cincinnati Reds and San Francisco Giants at 20–1.

— *Daily News*[15]

NEW YORK (UPI).—An old-fashioned "quickie" World Series—the first since 1956 when New York and Brooklyn played their last subway series—will be in the offing this year if the Phillies face either the New York Yankees or the Baltimore Orioles.

The elimination of the travel days between games two and three and five and six should the series opponents represent cities 300 miles or less apart was announced yesterday by baseball commissioner Ford Frick. The travel days would remain part of the series schedule in the event of a series between the Phillies and the Chicago White Sox.

— *Daily News*[16]

SEPTEMBER 13

It is a cinch who will be the hero, the darling of the masses, as the Phils whip down the stretch drive. Names such as Allen and Callison and Short and Bunning pale into triviality, compared to the true idol of World Series time.

The Most Valuable Player around Connie Mack Stadium is sure to be Frank (Everybody's Friend) Powell.

Powell cannot throw, run or hit. He has a graying thatch, thick specs and a comfortable girth. For the next three weeks, however, he will be the most popular Phillie in captivity—his fan mail will make the Beatles look like anonymous nonentities.

Powell is in charge of World Series tickets. His old title was Director of Sales. His new title is Big Chief With Heap Big Headache And Not Enough Pasteboards.

"Our first thought is to make sure the real Phillie fans, the ones who supported the club all year, get a chance at World Series tickets," said Everybody's Friend. "With a park this small (roughly, 34,000 seats), it's going to be a real problem. We could probably sell it out five times."

Letters asking to reserve Series tickets have hit Powell's desk at a 20–30-a-day clip since early in the year. A form letter goes back to each fan. The Phils will give the green light for customers Wednesday to shoot in Series orders. Prices, as last year's, will be $12 tops.

— *Bulletin*[17]

SEPTEMBER 14

WHAT COULD MAKE YOU HAPPIER THAN SEEING THE PHILLIES WIN THE PENNANT?

(Watching them take the Series on RCA Victor Color TV!)

Phillies fans, this is your year. Callison won the All-Star Game. The Phils must win the pennant. And who can argue that they'll win the Series in a climax? Your only problem is: how do you get to see the Series? Connie Mack stadium [sic] seats only 33,608 and maybe 2 million of us want "in." The answer is: at least see it in living color. And that means RCA Victor Color TV, the finest color available. It's the finest because RCA Victor has spent 10 years in pioneering and perfecting it. Your dealer can put you in front of a set for only $399.95.

It's worth the price just to see the whole Series in color—but, as a bonus, you can figure that there are 51 other weeks in the year of other great color TV shows as well.

P.S.: If the Phils don't win the pennant ... (bite your tongue!) color TV will not become obsolete. In fact, seeing the World Series, the NCAA football games and your favorite programs in color may help make life almost bearable.

— *Bulletin* full-page advertisement

NATIONAL BASEBALL HALL OF FAME LIBRARY, COOPERSTOWN, NY

Johnny Callison hit the game-winning homer in the All-Star Game and was named All-Star MVP, and was in the running for NL MVP honors, though he did not win.

SAN FRANCISCO, SEPT. 14— There are 20 sports writers in the United States who must decide whether Jim Bunning, John Callison or Rich (Don't call me Richie) Allen is the National League's Most Valuable player [sic] and Bunning, Callison and Allen won't cooperate.

All three keep behaving like MVPs, making it impossible to separate their contributions to the pennant that is growing in Philadelphia.

Yesterday, for instance, the Phillies moved a win and a day closer to the World Series and it was Bunning and Callison and Allen who did most of the moving in a wind-aided 4–1 victory over the Giants.

Bunning muzzled the Giants for ten innings, the best performance in a hurricane since Humphrey Bogart made *Key Largo*. Callison broke open the shivering tie with his single in the tenth. Allen's two-run homer followed—just in time to prevent 35,305 cases of windburn.

It was no way to help a sports writer make up his mind.

Somebody asked Gene Mauch what he would do if he was a sports writer and—before they carried the guy out—Mauch said:

"To tell you the truth, I couldn't cast a vote. I'd have to pass..."

— *Bulletin*[18]

Alvin Dark knows what made the Phillies tick like a time bomb.

Tick: Jim Bunning. Tick: Johnny Callison. Tick: Richie Allen. Boom.

Dark surveyed the wreckage of his battered pennant hopes yesterday after the Phillies whipped the Giants 4–1 in 10 innings.

Tick: Bunning pitched a gritty seven-hitter. Tick: Callison drove in the winning run with a single off lefthander Dick Estelle. Tick: Allen lashed a two-run homer off reliever Ron Herbel. Boom went the Giants, fluttering seven games back of the Phillies while the Cardinals stuck six games back.

"The Phillies couldn't have won it without Bunning," Dark said. "They couldn't have won it without Callison, or without Allen."

Not that Dark was running up the white flag. "The Phillies still have to win nine out of 19 to get to 95 games," he said, and people wrote it down out of politeness.

— *Daily News*[19]

SEPTEMBER 16

DEAR PHILLIES, 'UNCLE'

YOURS TRULY, GIANTS

— San Francisco theater marquee in photograph, captioned, "BY DAY IN 'FRISCO— Theater owner in Giants home town concedes National League flag to Phils"(above a photo of marquee at Gimbel's at 9th and Market in Philadelphia reading GO PHILLIES/WE'RE FOR YOU), *Bulletin*[20]

The Phillies' Magic Number is down to 12, which should mean things are getting better.

Big Magic, the Honeywell 1400 computer, sees it differently. It says the Phillies now have an 89 percent chance to win the pennant. The other 11 percent went to the St. Louis Cardinals in tests run this morning at the Computing Center of the Franklin Institute.

— *Bulletin*[21]

HOUSTON, Sept. 15.—The Phillies announced plans to accept World Series ticket applications Tuesday, then played like future champions as they took another stride closer to the National League pennant in their 1–0 night-game victory over the Houston Colts.

The second-place St. Louis Cardinals swept a twilight-night doubleheader with the Milwaukee Braves, reducing the Phillies' league lead to six games. Nevertheless, this—their third win in a row—was an important triumph for the Phils.

It's beginning to sound like a broken record, but it's a fact—John Callison batted in the winning run. The star right fielder, making a strong bid for the Most Valuable Player Award, singled home Richie Allen, who had led off the sixth inning with a double, and that was all the scoring.

It was the third straight game in which Callison knocked in the winning run.

— *Inquirer*[22]

WHO'S EXCITED?

Let's be Phillies-sophical about it all...

How would this look at the Victory Ball?

Thirty days hath September but we need only four in October.

I'm the guy that picked them in spring training.

So what if it did take 14 years—it was worth it.

I can see it waving now.

They make me feel young all over.

— Captions of fan photos in a Ballantine Beer ad, *Inquirer*[23]

SEPTEMBER 17

"This club," (Vic) Power said, "we're relaxed. When I was in Minneapolis, everybody was tense. Everybody was afraid of something, somebody. I don't know who. Maybe the owner. I know it wasn't the manager because he was a nice guy.

"This club is so relaxed—they're always jumping around, they play the radio real loud, they make jokes.

"When I was in San Francisco last week, I was almost going crazy—the radio was going real loud, they were making jokes, everybody was ribbing everybody.

"This club don't care about nothin'."

— *Bulletin*[24]

This is the year for The Phillies. This is the time when the most thrilling sound in the air is the crack of a bat. This is the time when every baseball fan salaams his favorite star, rubs his rabbit's foot and puts the double hex on every challenger. This is the time when you will want to decorate your den, office or club room with pictures of the 1964 Phillies players...

— *Bulletin* display ad

SEPTEMBER 18

Through most of the 1934 season, the world champion Giants were virtually unopposed. On Sept. 7th, with three weeks to go, the Cardinals trailed by seven games. This was the old St. Louis Gas House Gang of Frisch, and Pepper Martin and Joe Medwick and Leo Durocher, with the Dean brothers, Dizzy and Paul, winning 49 games between them.

This was also the year Bill Terry, the Giants' manager, asked at the wrong time and in the wrong tone: "Is Brooklyn still in the league?" On closing day the Cardinals led by one game, but in the ninth inning the Reds filled the bases against Dizzy with none out. Then the St. Louis scoreboard flashed the news: "Dodgers, 8; Giants, 5."

Diz grinned and fired the high hard one. Two batters struck out. The third popped up. Dean had his 30th victory and the Cardinals had the pennant.

Is Gene Mauch, of the Phillies, listening? About three weeks ago the teams his club had to beat were Cincinnati and San Francisco. The Cardinals were fourth, 11 games off the pace.

A week ago Philadelphia's lead was only five games, but it wasn't the Reds or Giants who had closed the gap. The Cardinals were second, having made up six games in a fortnight.

They had almost a month to go. If they could pick up six more games in that space...

NATIONAL BASEBALL HALL OF FAME LIBRARY, COOPERSTOWN, NY

Vic Power described the Phillies' winning attitude: "This club? We're relaxed. When I was in Minneapolis, everybody was tense. Everybody was afraid of something, somebody. I don't know who. Maybe the owner. I know it wasn't the manager because he was a nice guy. This club is so relaxed."

So far they haven't done it. They were idle Thursday, six games back before the Phillies' night game at Los Angeles. At that point each had 16 games to play. The Cardinals have five with the Mets, the Phils none with New York, Houston or Chicago.

Philadelphia starts the last week of the season with three night games in St. Louis, then finishes with a pair in third-place Cincinnati. After the confrontation with the Phillies, the Cards wrap it up at home with three shots against the Mets.

No, sorry. No forecasts, predictions, prophecies, prognosis or auguries.

— *Inquirer*[25]

WHICH OF THESE THREE FAMOUS PHILLIES MADE THE BIGGEST HIT?

Is it Jim Bunning, who hurled a perfect game?

Or Johnny Callison, who slashed the crucial homer in the all-star fracas?

Or is it the new Phillies Tip?

Phillies Tips, like the Phillies team, is on everybody's lips.

— Display ad, *Bulletin*[26]

SEPTEMBER 20

The city, stricken with pennant fever these past few weeks, has now come down with a delightful new ailment—the World Series virus.

Nearly everybody, or so it seems, has been infected by the bug as the Phillies, with only two weeks of the season left, drive for their first National League pennant since 1950.

"Go Phillies Go!" is the battlecry in every neighborhood, in every nook and corner of the metropolitan area—and even beyond.

The slogan, or some variation thereof, shines forth from bedsheet banners, flags and pennants, and from billboards.

Fans shout it. Signs in store after store proclaim it.

Pretty girls stroll about wearing five-inch buttons emblazoned with:

"Go Phillies Go."

On a billboard on the eastbound side on the Vine St. extension of the Schuylkill Expressway near the 22nd st. off-ramp, the regular Strawbridge and Clothier advertisement has been replaced with:

"All the way! PHILLIES"

And there's a story behind a huge Phillies banner outside the rail division of the Transport Workers Union, 1630 Arch St.

A union spokesman said John Mellon, president, and his staff were half an hour late for a meeting with management. They apologized, saying something important had come up.

They didn't explain, the spokesman said, that hanging the Phils' banner was the "important business."

Official Philadelphia is also getting ready to honor the Phillies and take care of the World Series crowds that will flock here, if the Phillies take the pennant.

Mayor Tate is forming a "host committee" to make Philadelphia's hospitality available to visitors to the fullest extent.

The members, to be announced tomorrow, include persons from the business, sporting and entertainment world as well as civic groups.

Some kind of big rally or demonstration is planned for after the Series—if the Phillies get into it—win or lose, a spokesman for the mayor said yesterday.

"We're highly gratified," he said, "about the number of organizations which have called in wanting to cooperate. It's an outpouring of enthusiasm for the Phillies."

A similar tale was told by a spokesman for the Chamber of Commerce of Greater Philadelphia.

"A lot of people are talking about doing something

spectacular," he said, "but nothing definite has been decided yet."

Another source indicated that the Phillies' management would like the players to concentrate entirely on winning ball games from here on in, instead of taking part in celebrations.

But the fans' enthusiasm is unbounded.

Three empty three-story buildings at 11th st. and Ridge av. are decorated from top to bottom with Phillies' slogans.

"Swing and stay all the way with the Phillies" and "You did it before; you can do it again" are a couple of them.

The bedecked structures are just opposite the Mummers Bar at 1105 Ridge av., sponsors of the Phillies' display.

The bar people plan to stretch a sign across Ridge av. from the bar to the buildings reading: "Go, Phillies, Go. 1964 World Champions."

A slightly more staid but just as enthusiastic salute to the home team are the 30 flags stretched along Chestnut st. saying: "Fight, Phillies, Fight."

"We're going to keep them up until the Phils win the pennant," said Jack Pearson, president of the Chestnut Street Association.

— *Bulletin*, front page[27]

Bucky Hoffman has been waiting for 14 years to get his right arm tattooed to match his left arm.

It looks as if this might be the year.

In 1950, Bucky had "Fighting Phillies 1950" tattooed on his arm.

"I got that done about two hours after Roberts beat Newcombe," he told me, when I found him tending bar, as he usually is, at the Mummers Bar at 11th st. and Ridge av. "I went right from Brooklyn into Manhattan and had it done."

Bucky has the design for his other arm drawn on cardboard and tucked behind the bar. It confidently says, "Phillies World Champs 1964."

It will also have Pike's name on it. Pike is a regular customer and buddy, and he made the design.

"That's the way he wants it on," Bucky said, "and that's what he's gonna get."

(...)

"We got about 300 more feet of flags to put up," Willy Kramer, Bucky's co-fanatic, told me. "We gotta paint the street some more. We've invited the Phillies team to have a party here. We'll get permission to close off the street and have string bands."

Bobby Searles and his wife came in, and he rolled up his sleeve to show me a tattoo which says, "Fighting Phillies."

"I got mine in 1943," he said. "I'm a rabid fan."

"If they blow the pennant," Bucky said in a moment of sober reflection, "I got my suitcase right here. I'm blowing town."

"If they don't win," one patron warned sternly, "this is gonna be a parking lot here, bud."

— *Bulletin*[28]

SEPTEMBER 21

Neither the prospect of catching early morning school buses, trains after a few hours shuteyes, the chill weather nor the fickleness of chartered airline schedules dampened the crowd of 2000 Phillies fans who swarmed to International Airport early Monday morning to welcome their heroes home.

School children, collegians, and elderly fans, who have been hanging on every pitch for months, were darned if they were going to miss the chance to give their pennant-bound team a fitting welcome.

And as Mayor James H. J. Tate strode out to meet the team's chartered American Airlines Boeing 707 Astro-Jet as it touched down at 12:30 AM, bedlam broke out in the airport's second-floor concourse.

The packed crowd, which had been waiting since late Saturday night, feverously wiped the fogged-up plate-glass windows with handkerchiefs and coat-sleeves to better see their "boys."

Schoolchildren who had been industriously working on their homework threw their books down and cheered lustily as Manager Gene Mauch led the team off the ramp.

Although pennants and signs were not in abundance the noise emanating from the concourse left little doubt as to where allegiances lay.

— *Inquirer*[29]

The throng let out a lusty welcome at 12:30 AM. when the Phils, led by manager Gene Mauch, came own the ramp of the jet that had brought them from Los Angeles.

But the cheers quickly died as the Phils headed for the nearest exit.

(...)

Some fans, obviously "sign-stealers," stationed themselves at exits where they could get a close up look at Rich Allen, Chris Short, Jim Bunning and others.

"Oh, they're wonderful," said Evelyn William, 35, a housewife, of 1724 N. Taney st.

"They're marvelous," commented Dorothy Falkenstein, of 234 Margate rd., Upper Darby.

Margie Connally, 19, of 235 Westmoreland ave., Hatboro, was breathless with joy.

But Mrs. Emma Bravo, 36, of 2308 Chestnut ave., Ardmore, wanted to know "Why they didn't com[e] up that ramp where we all waited." She came carrying a "Go Phillies Go" sign but left chanting "Down with the Phillies."

Bruce Kesler, 13, of 1803 Glenifer st, had two "Go Phillies Go" buttons on his sweatshirt. Close to tears he said, "I haven't missed a home game since July 28. I buy Phillies helmets, buttons, banners, everything with Phillies on it.

"But I didn't get to see hardly any of them. And, now I don't think I'll go to any games any more—even the World Series."

Even Bill Campbell, the radio announcer, caught a bit of the fans' wrath. One guy yelled as Campbell walked by, "There's another long ball that ain't going nowhere."

— *Daily News*[30]

Although the scent of World Series was in the air, some of the Phils are keeping their fingers crossed. Bunning was one.

"Don't forget," he warned, "we still have 12 games to play."

(...)

"I wanted to come here tonight," (Mayor) Tate said. "I wanted to extend my congratulations to the team and I'm hoping the pennant will be safe in Philadelphia by the weekend."

Mrs. Cookie Rojas was happy but calm.

"Yes, Sir," she said, "the way I see it we'll have it clinched by Thursday night."

— *Bulletin*[31] ■

Notes

1. Sandy Grady, "Yes, Dear, the Phillies Are Cute and Cuddly," *Philadelphia Bulletin*, September 1, 1964, 51.
2. Larry Merchant, "Banking on Bunning," *Philadelphia Daily News*, September 2, 1964, 47.
3. "Phils Have Calendar on Their Side," *Philadelphia Daily News*, September 4, 1964, 50.
4. Eileen, letter to the editor, *Philadelphia Daily News*, September 5, 1964, 7.
5. Eileen Foley, "Asks Wife of Phillies' Manager: Pennant Fever...What's That?" *Philadelphia Bulletin*, September 8, 1964, 60.
6. Leo O'Rourke, letter to the editor, *Philadelphia Daily News*, September 8, 1964, 35.
7. James A. Michener, Luxor, Egypt, letter to the editor, "Dazed Author Seeks Aid for Phils," *Philadelphia Inquirer*, September 8, 1964, 10.
8. Larry Merchant, "Two Big Lumps—One is Sugar," *Philadelphia Daily News*, September 9, 1964, 57.
9. "Another Record for Those Phillies" (editorial), *Philadelphia Inquirer*, September 9, 1964, 34.
10. "Shaky Phils Fan Dreads the Yanks"(letter to the editor), *Philadelphia Bulletin*, September 10, 1964, 10.
11. Stan Hochman, "Mauch Says Phils' Only Foe is Phillies," *Philadelphia Daily News*, September 10, 1964, 52.
12. "Phillies Handed Stadium 'Ball,'" *Philadelphia Inquirer*, September 10, 1964, 7.
13. Larry Merchant, "RBI: Runs Boyered In," *Philadelphia Daily News*, September 10, 1964, 53.
14. Frank Bilovsky, "Computer Figures It'll Be Phillies vs. White Sox," *Philadelphia Daily News*, September 11, 1964,. 35.
15. "Las Vegas Takes Phils Off Boards," *Philadelphia Daily News*, September 11, 1964, 53.
16. "'Quickie' World Series Likely," *Philadelphia Daily News*, September 11, 1964, 55.
17. Sandy Grady, "The Phils' World Series Ticket Nabob: He Doesn't Have an Enemy in the World... Yet!" *Philadelphia Bulletin*, September 13, 1964, 2 (sports section).
18. George Kiseda, "MVP Election: Candidates Run a Hard Bargain," *Philadelphia Bulletin*, September 14, 1964, 39.
19. Stan Hochman, "Phils Time Bomb Ticks... Ticks... Ticks," *Philadelphia Daily News*, September 14, 1964, 47.
20. *Philadelphia Bulletin*, September 16, 1964, 69.
21. "Phils Flag Chances Rated at 89 Per Cent," *Philadelphia Bulletin*, September 16, 1964, 69.
22. Allen Lewis, "Phils Score 1–0 Shutout At Houston," *Philadelphia Inquirer*, September 16, 1964, 1.
23. *Philadelphia Inquirer*, September 16, 1964, 41.
24. George Kiseda, "Phillies 'Shoot' Holes in Pressure Theory," *Philadelphia Bulletin*, September 17, 1964, 37.
25. Red Smith, "Phils Reminded of Those 1934 Giants," *Philadelphia Inquirer*, September 18, 1964, 48.
26. *Philadelphia Bulletin*, September 18, 1964, 33.
27. Francis J. Burke, "Town Goes Wild as Phils Near Pennant; Innkeepers, Bars Ready for Series Crowds," *Philadelphia Bulletin*, September 20, 1964, 1.
28. James Smart, "Go, Phillies! Bucky's Arm is Waiting," *Philadelphia Bulletin*, September 20, 1964, 4.
29. Dennis M. Higgins, "Tate and 2000 Greet Phillies After 3–2 Win Over Dodgers," *Philadelphia Inquirer*, September 21, 1964, 1.
30. Bill Malone, Daily News, "Dashing Phillies Leave Fans Miffed," *Philadelphia Daily News*, September 21, 1964, 3.
31. "Phils, Orchestra Home in Triumph: League Leaders Are Greeted by 2,000 Fans," *Philadelphia Bulletin*, September 21, 1964, 3.

Dick Allen's Second Act

Mitchell Nathanson

It is hard to imagine a more polarizing figure in Philadelphia sports history than Dick Allen. Countless gallons of ink have been spilled in furtherance of trying to capture and explain Allen's stormy relationship with the Phillies and the city of Philadelphia during his 1963–69 tenure with the club. Much less focus has been given, however, to his mid-Seventies return to Philadelphia amid circumstances that were seemingly far different from those in which he left it. Despite these purportedly changed circumstances, Allen departed Philadelphia in 1976 much as he had in 1969—amid controversy and bad blood on both sides of the equation. This article focuses on Allen's return to the Phillies and his abbreviated tenure with a club that was building toward greatness. Whether Allen ultimately contributed toward, or detracted from, that greatness remains, like so much else regarding Dick Allen and the Phillies, subject to debate.

The story begins on September 14, 1974, the date Allen announced his abrupt retirement from the Chicago White Sox despite the fact that at the time he was not only leading the American League in home runs (a title he'd retain at year's end despite missing the final two weeks of the season), but a key element in Chicago's divisional championship aspirations (they eventually finished the season nine games behind Oakland in the AL West). In typical Allen fashion, his retirement was awash in contradictions: he arrived at the ballpark apparently prepared to play, suited up, took batting practice, and then announced his retirement. As for whether Allen's by then well-chronicled difficulties with management were to blame, he claimed otherwise, having told his teammates just prior to his official announcement to the media that he'd "never been happier anywhere than here."[1] By most accounts, Allen's statement was sincere—the White Sox appeared to have been an ideal place for him, with his easygoing manager, Chuck Tanner, giving him the room he needed to blossom at last. And blossom he did, winning the 1972 AL MVP award and developing, before a hairline fracture of his left leg in June 1973 sidelined him, into one of the best all-around players in the game. Fully recovered from that injury in 1974 and, at 31, in the prime of his career, Allen picked up where he left off—he was hitting .301 with 88 RBIs to go along with his league leading 32 home runs at the time of his unexpected announcement. However, his body had been breaking down in other respects—a nagging shoulder injury hounded him all season and by September, the pain was radiating down his back.[2] Within weeks of his retirement, however, Allen had modified his stance with regard to his future in baseball, claiming that he was "gonna play somewhere next year—even if it's Jenkintown."[3] This was all some in the Phillies organization as well as the Philadelphia sports media needed to hear. With Allen looking for a place to play, many Philadelphians began to ask the question few would have dared to ask only a few years earlier: "Why not here?"

The question made sense in many ways. The 1974 Phillies bore little resemblance to the squad, either on the field or in the front office, which Allen had departed amid so much rancor only five years earlier. Having abandoned crumbling Connie Mack Stadium as well as the racially divided North Philly neighborhood that seemed to provide a microcosm of everything wrong with both the city and the club, for the clean, spacious Vet (located, not by accident, in a South Philly warehouse district that was largely liberated from the city's grid and all of the squabbles that were perceived to have emanated from it) in 1971, the Phillies were, in many ways, starting fresh despite their deep roots within the city.[4] Parking was plentiful, the team was young and exciting, led by rising stars such as Greg Luzinski, Mike Schmidt, Larry Bowa, and Dave Cash, and management was likewise young and enthusiastic, with Ruly Carpenter having taken over the reins from his father Bob, whose relationship with Allen during his initial tenure with the club was complicated to say the least. Along with general manager Paul Owens and manager Danny Ozark, the new Phillies bore little if any resemblance to the old ones in so many ways. If they could fix all that had been so wrong with the franchise for so many years, why could they not repair their relationship with Allen as well?

Beyond the redemptive aspect of Allen's return, his presence in the club's lineup seemed to make sense in more practical ways. In 1974 the organization's surplus of young talent finally began to mature and the Phils, cellar-dwellers for so long, managed to tickle the pennant-chase fancy of the Philadelphia sporting public for the first few months of the season until Luzinski was lost to a severe leg injury in June. Adding Allen's bat to the lineup would provide insurance for 1975 should the team suffer another major injury. In addition, it would give the '75 Phillies lineup the presence of both the 1974 American as well as National League home run champs (Schmidt won the NL title with 36). Add in the "Yes We Can" enthusiasm of second baseman Dave Cash, the fielding and fire of Larry Bowa, the steady hand of catcher Bob Boone, and the mastery of pitcher Steve Carlton, and the Phillies would no doubt be in the postseason conversation all year long. First, however, Allen had to be convinced to put aside his reservations and agree to suit up once again for the club he once so despised that he signaled his displeasure through messages such as "Boo" and "Oct. 2" (the last day of the 1969 season and, he hoped, his final day as a Phillie) scratched in the dirt for all to see.[5] That he would be willing to play, as he said, in Jenkintown for the 1975 season did not necessarily mean that he would just as willingly play a few miles away in South Philly for the Phils.

Initially, the leading proponent for Allen's return was Phillies' broadcaster Richie Ashburn, who repeatedly lobbied for the Phils to re-sign him in his *Evening Bulletin* columns.[6] Eventually Ashburn caught the ear of the front office who thought enough of the idea to organize a clandestine visit (to circumvent tampering charges) to Allen on his Bucks County farm to gauge his interest and to encourage him to consider the possibility.[7] Specifically, Ashburn, Schmidt, and Cash made the "secret" trek in February 1975, and were outed in the media almost immediately. By that time, Allen's rights had been purchased by the Braves who were unsure what to do with him after he announced that he'd never play in Atlanta.[8] Despite Allen's protestations, given that he was the property of the Braves, the Phillies' secret mission quickly erupted into controversy, compelling the club to respond to the Braves' tampering allegations. Nevertheless, Dave Cash, who by that point had become the team's de facto leader, came away from the meeting impressed with Allen and, despite Allen's departure from Chicago and his refusal to play for Atlanta, convinced that Allen would

Dick Allen, one of the most polarizing figures in Philadelphia baseball history.

NATIONAL BASEBALL HALL OF FAME LIBRARY, COOPERSTOWN, NY

not disrupt the young team's cohesive chemistry.[9] However, Cash seemed to be one of the dwindling few in baseball who still believed in Allen.

As spring training began and Allen remained on his farm, his list of potential suitors grew shorter and shorter. The Cardinals, for whom Allen played after his trade from Philadelphia, passed, with third baseman Joe Torre stating that he believed that the Cardinals' reluctance to sign Allen had much to do with ownership's belief that he would disrupt the team over the long haul.[10] In New York, Mets manager Yogi Berra tamped down speculation immediately, announcing that he wanted no part of Allen even if the Mets could obtain him without surrendering any players.[11]

Only in Philadelphia was the prevailing mood different. First baseman Willie Montanez, who would be displaced should Allen sign, stated that he'd gladly move to the outfield for Allen;[12] Schmidt announced that he did not see how Allen could do anything other than help the team win the NL East in 1975 and could not imagine a scenario where he would be disruptive; other players echoed similar sentiments.[13] While Luzinski remained, at least outwardly, hesitant, his voice was in the clear minority.[14]

Regardless, with spring training winding down and the Allen issue no closer to resolution, the Phillies "officially" ended their pursuit when they announced that they were unable to work out a deal with Atlanta to obtain his rights. Conspicuously silent was manager Danny Ozark, who was said to be pleased with the end of the courtship. No doubt aware of the perception of Allen's effect on previous managers in Philadelphia, Ozark was relieved his fate would not sink into the abyss some allege swallowed Gene Mauch and Bob Skinner. *Inquirer* columnist Frank Dolson wrote, in an article headlined "That Was a Smile on Ozark's Face," that now he would finally have a realistic shot at completing the new two-year extension he signed in 1974.[15]

When the Phillies withdrew their courtship, however Allen stoked the cooling embers, announcing to those members of the media who had followed him to one of his favorite haunts, Keystone Race Track, that he was "available and I want to play baseball."[16] He stated he was in "great shape" and "could be available to play in five days to a week." Finally, in April, the Phillies forced the Braves' hand when they put in a claim for Allen when Atlanta placed him on waivers. The Braves withdrew his name from the waiver wire and negotiated with the Phillies for his rights. On May 7, the Phillies announced that they had signed Allen to a contract. Right away, Cash exhorted Philadelphia fans to "give him a chance" when he arrived in uniform.[17] Very quickly, it was clear that the overwhelming majority of them were willing to do that and more. He was greeted by cheering fans while warming up before his first game and then, during the pregame introductions, received a standing ovation as soon as he was introduced. The cheers continued as PA announcer Dan Baker tried in vain to resume announcing the Phillies starters that evening. Eventually he gave up.[18] After the game Allen was beaming, stating that the cheers had affected him in a profound way: "You don't know what it means to me," he said. "It's a different situation altogether."[19] He said that he believed that, this time around, baseball in Philadelphia would be nothing but fun for him. This would turn out to be an overly-optimistic prediction.

The long layoff and the lack of spring training affected Allen more than he anticipated. By July he was hitting only .233 with only four home runs in 50 games. Hopes that he would eventually round into form were dashed by July when his average slipped into the .220s and he managed only one home run in the month. Defensively, age and injuries appeared to be catching up with him at last as he lacked the range and finesse of Montanez; the entire infield struggled due to Allen's inability to dig balls out of the dirt. Larry Bowa was the most directly affected by Allen's strug-

gles and, true to form, the one who protested most loudly as well, although even he tried to keep his public statements in check. When asked in early September why he had already amassed 22 errors—twice as many as in each of his five previous seasons in the majors—Bowa replied, "I'm not going to sound off. Knowledgeable people know what's going on."[20]

By season's end, Allen was hitting .233 with all of twelve home runs and 62 RBIs. Moreover, in just 416 official at-bats, he struck out 109 times. These were obviously not the numbers the Phillies had envisioned the previous winter when organizing their covert rendezvous at Allen's farm. Regardless, the team as a whole did improve markedly from 1974, finishing second, 6.5 games behind the Pirates, completing their first winning season in eight years. Besides, this time Allen's troubles appeared to be solely of the on-field variety. With a full spring training to help him prepare for 1976, the Phillies hoped that Allen would return to form. Therefore, they re-signed him for the '76 season, setting aside their doubts that perhaps he was finished as a ballplayer.[21] Although the '76 Phils would indeed succeed on the field as management hoped, they nevertheless endured a difficult season off it, with Allen at the center of much of the controversy that erupted as the team headed towards its first postseason berth in over a quarter-century.

Despite having the benefit of a full spring training, Allen's 1976 season began much the way his previous season ended. After only ten games, Ozark had come to the conclusion that the prospect of Allen at first on a daily basis was too much for the team to bear; he replaced him the next day with the defensively solid Tommy Hutton and thereafter Allen's playing time began to wane. A few days later, after sitting yet again, Allen refused Ozark's instruction to pinch hit in the ninth inning of a tight game against the Braves, forcing Ozark to scramble and call on Jerry Martin instead. After the game it became clear that Allen's troubles had migrated from the field to the clubhouse. Ozark attempted to deflect the brewing storm by telling the media that Allen was "unable to play."[22] When reporters continued to press the issue Ozark attempted to clear the room. When that failed, he threatened to punch a reporter who questioned Ozark's right to take such action. The exasperated Ozark then exited his office, slamming the door behind him and kicking the wall and waste paper basket on his way out. A few minutes later, Ruly Carpenter exchanged words with the same writer who had questioned Ozark earlier and then issued a more general epithet to the entire assembled press corps as he entered his elevator.[23]

Thereafter, Allen settled uneasily into a platoon with Bobby Tolan at first base with the organization and fan base waiting for his stroke to return. Although he did hit better for a while (even flirting with the .300 mark for a portion of the season) it was clear that he was no longer the hitter he had been just a couple of years earlier. When he was dropped to seventh in the batting order (at the time, he was hitting .250 with a lone double constituting his only extra-base hit of the season) he expressed his frustration with how he was being handled: "If I'm going to slow 'em up that much I'd rather not be in there at all," he said.[24] Regardless, he received strong support all season. When he hit two home runs in a June rout of the Cardinals, he received a game-stopping ovation from the Veterans Stadium faithful. Afterwards he revealed just how much the ovation meant to him by stating that fan support in Philadelphia meant more to him than anywhere else "because of what went on before."[25] Still, his feelings for the Philadelphia fans would not be enough to stave off another confrontation between Allen and the Phillies front office.

This one began innocuously enough. On July 25 Allen was injured in a collision on the basepaths with Pirate pitcher John Candelaria. The next night he asked out of the lineup by telephoning Ozark and complaining of dizziness.[26] Thereafter the seeds for the inevitable clash were sown. The following day he neither phoned anyone nor arrived at the stadium. The day after that he arrived, remained for three innings and then left mid-game without informing anyone of his departure. The following day he neither phoned nor showed up for the game. Finally Ozark had no choice but to call a team meeting to discuss Allen's repeated absences. At that meeting, Ozark classified Allen as being AWOL and then called a press conference to announce that Allen would be fined for his repeated unexcused absences. However, in a reversal reminiscent of Allen's first stay in Philadelphia, Ozark subsequently rescinded the fine when Allen showed up unexpectedly in New York. At that time, Ozark shifted gears by announcing that Allen was injured and would be placed on the disabled list despite the fact that he had yet to be examined by a physician.

His DL stint was scheduled to end on August 10; on that date he called the team and insisted that he was still hurt, indicating, according to *Inquirer* columnist Bruce Keidan, that he had finally seen a doctor the day before—the first time he had seen one since his collision with Candelaria. This resulted in several additional weeks on the sidelines when Allen insisted that he was unable to play. Finally, on September 3, six weeks after

the collision with Candelaria, Allen pronounced himself ready for action. When pressed into service, however, he struggled, going 3-for-40 during one September stretch. With the Phillies suddenly in the midst of a pennant race (having lost much of their once seemingly insurmountable lead and now struggling to stay ahead of the surging Pirates), and with Luzinski's now chronically sore left knee bothering him again, Allen was unable to stanch the bleeding.

The locker room was devolving as well. In August Allen stated that he believed that Ozark's outfield platoon was racially motivated. He questioned why black players, including Ollie Brown and Bobby Tolan, were not playing as often as their white counterparts, suggesting that the Phillies were "working a quota system."[27] By the time the Phillies finally righted themselves and clinched the Eastern Division, they were clearly and openly separated along racial lines—the communal spirit of Cash's "Yes We Can" mantra having been replaced with spite and suspicion. As the team celebrated its divisional title in the cramped clubhouse of Montreal's Jarry Park, Allen initially refused to join in, preferring to remain, alone, on the frigid bench.[28] When he finally entered the clubhouse, the club's racial division was presented for all to see: Allen, Cash, Maddox, and Mike Schmidt (whom Allen had taken under his wing) removed themselves from the rest of the club and celebrated in private, in a clubhouse broom closet.[29] "The Broom Closet Incident," as it came to be known, would haunt the team throughout its abbreviated postseason run.

When the team boarded the plane from Montreal to St. Louis, Allen was nowhere to be found. Later, he announced that he would not participate in the postseason unless Tony Taylor—who had all but officially retired during the season, having only 26 plate appearances all year and by then serving as a de facto bench coach—was activated for postseason play.[30] Although this ultimatum appeared to many to have come out of the blue, in fact Allen confided to a member of the black press back in July that he would demand as much if the team qualified for postseason play: "I remember when I was playing with the Phillies before and having a fantastic season. It was Tony who made it possible He always encouraged me and suggested things that would help me....If we get to the playoffs and I know we will...I think it's only right that a guy like Tony that gave so much should be there."[31] Now, determined to ensure that the club properly acknowledge Taylor's contributions to the organization over the course of his career, the postseason roster issue quickly progressed to a stalemate between the club and Allen. Hoping to head off a steamrolling player insurrection, Ozark then publicly granted Allen permission to go home rather than participate in the St. Louis series, even though Allen was already home.[32] Ozark then called another team meeting wherein he asserted that nobody was going to dictate the club's playoff roster to him. At this point, whispers of a postseason player boycott grew loud enough for the media to hear.

With the team headed for its first postseason series since 1950, the team was now openly feuding. Several black players questioned Ozark's managerial moves, echoing Allen in wondering why the white Jerry Martin rather than the black Ollie Brown played in the second game of the doubleheader in Montreal, after the Phils had clinched the division in game one. They were unsatisfied with Ozark's reply that Brown's recent struggles had put him on the bench.[33] White players voiced their anger and frustration with Allen and his decision to go home rather than accompany the team to St. Louis.[34] The Broom Closet Incident was rehashed, with Tug McGraw stating in a team meeting that "some of us white guys" were wondering "where all the black guys were."[35] As things continued to spin out of control, Garry Maddox responded to McGraw's comment by taking offense to what he thought McGraw's statement implied: "Either we had great unity on this team all year or it's been a great acting job by the players keeping their feelings inside…Now when all the racial stuff starts coming out, when guys start to say how they actually feel, then you know how it is…I signed a five-year contract with this team. I hope I didn't make a mistake."[36] Captaining the divided crew, Ozark was nevertheless adrift. He had considered quitting earlier in the season, during Allen's initial absence from the club, but decided to hold on due to the Phils' overwhelming divisional lead.[37] Now, with the playoffs at hand, he had no choice: he had to somehow steer the ship regardless of the infighting.

On the eve of game one of the League Championship Series against Cincinnati's Big Red Machine, the club was finally able to coax Allen back by promising that Taylor would be in uniform for the postseason, albeit as a coach and not as a player. Although Allen had previously insisted that Taylor be activated for the postseason, this time he stated that all he really wanted was for Taylor to be in uniform in some capacity and that he was happy with the brokered deal.[38] With that, it seemed as if the Phillies could finally focus their attention solely on the Reds. Very quickly, however, they became sidetracked yet again.

During the series, Allen, still smarting from the cavalcade of incidents over the past couple of months,

refused to participate in the team's pregame batting practice (Allen, not unlike some other top players of his era such as Ernie Banks and Willie Mays, considered batting practice to be an unnecessary ritual and often skipped it. But as with all things Allen, when he skipped it, more was made of the occasion).[39] Two of his broom closet brethren, Cash and Schmidt, then attempted to deflect attention from what they thought would be perceived by the media as yet another example of Allen's defiance by refusing to take infield practice before each of the three games of the series.[40] Not surprisingly, amid the heightened tension surrounding the club, the Phils were swept in the series and the once-hopeful 1976 season came to a sudden and disappointing end. Thereafter, Allen was informed that he would not be re-signed for the 1977 season and his second act drew to a close.

In assessing Allen's mid-Seventies return to the Phillies, there are, like so many things associated with Allen, contradictions and opposing points of view. On the one hand, the team as a whole did indeed improve during each of his two seasons with the club—he joined a club coming off a third place, sub-.500 finish in 1974 and left one which won 101 games and the National League's Eastern Division, reaching the postseason for the first time in over a quarter-century. On the other hand, disharmony and dissension trailed him throughout his return to Philadelphia as he was a key figure in the clubhouse issues that dogged the 1976 club which perhaps could have achieved even more than it did had it been free from such distractions and been able to focus more intently on the game on the field, particularly during the postseason. However, it is fair to ask if Allen was the cause of the dissension that enveloped the '76 club or merely responsible for bringing to the fore what was already there. Just as the 2008 election of Barack Obama failed to make the United States a "post-racial" society overnight, it seems difficult to fathom that the historically racially-troubled Phillies transformed as dramatically as touted in the short time between Allen's departure in 1969 and his return in 1975. Perhaps they had further to go in the department of race relations than many realized and it took Allen to bring that reality to the surface.

And then there was his impact on the young slugger Mike Schmidt. Allen took Schmidt under his wing in 1975 and Schmidt has frequently mentioned the pivotal role Allen played in his development. Schmidt followed Allen in many ways and to many places, including that Montreal broom closet. Whether Allen was ultimately a positive or negative force in Schmidt's career is a topic that has been debated for decades: did he help Schmidt develop into the Hall of Fame slugger he ultimately became? Or was he at least partly to blame for Schmidt's career-long inability to become the cohesive team leader fans and the club wished him to be? Most likely, the answer lies somewhere between these two poles. Bill James once described Allen as someone who "did more to keep his teams from winning than anybody else who ever played major league baseball."[41] On the surface, Allen's actions down the stretch in 1976 might appear to at least suggest as much. But beneath it, when focusing on actions that hindered the club's potential, one wonders if anything Allen might have done in '76 could match the organization's long-standing reluctance to embrace and encourage the development of black ballplayers in Philadelphia in the decades leading up to that season. Viewed through this lens, perhaps the succession of events that transpired during the club's '76 stretch run caused the organization to finally confront a demon it mistakenly thought it had slayed merely through its relocation to the Vet and the transition in ownership from father to son. As such, perhaps it was Dick Allen, more than any other factor, who finally compelled the organization to modernize its approach to black athletes at last. Perhaps. One thing is certain, however: when it comes to analyzing Dick Allen's second act in Philadelphia, so much depends upon where one sat while taking in the performance. ∎

Notes

1. "Tearful Dick Allen Announces Retirement," *Philadelphia Inquirer*, September 15, 1974.
2. Craig Wright, "Another View of Dick Allen," *The Baseball Research Journal*, 2, 10 (1995).
3. Bruce Keidan, "Dick Allen Back in Phils Uniform?" *Philadelphia Inquirer*, November 13, 1974.
4. For an in-depth analysis of the relationship between the Phillies and the city of Philadelphia, see Mitchell Nathanson, *The Fall of the 1977 Phillies: How A Baseball Team's Collapse Sank a City's Spirit*, (Jefferson, N.C.: McFarland & Co., 2008).
5. William C. Kashatus, *September Swoon: Richie Allen, the '64 Phillies, and Racial Integration* (University Park, PA: Penn State Press, 2004), 198.
6. See Frank Dolson, "Richie Allen: Phillies Could Go To Top—Or To Pieces—With Him," *Philadelphia Inquirer*, March 2, 1975. In the article, Dolson quotes Greg Luzinski as saying, "I think Richie Ashburn's the guy who's really making the push as far as whether Richie Allen comes here. His articles and his persuasion have maybe prompted the Phillies to do a little something."
7. Allen Lewis, "Phils Secretly Trying to Lure Dick Allen Off the Farm," *Philadelphia Inquirer*, February 4, 1975.
8. "Richie Allen Wants to Play This Year, But Not With Braves," *Atlanta Daily World*, March 28, 1975.
9. Bill Lyon, "Phils Believe They Can Win It All...With Dick Allen," *Philadelphia Inquirer*, February 11, 1975.
10. Frank Dolson, "Mets Tune Out Richie Allen, Fear Lack of Harmony," *Philadelphia Inquirer*, March 4, 1975.
11. Ibid.
12. Allen Lewis, "Montanez Ready to Vacate First for Allen," *Philadelphia Inquirer*, March 3, 1975.
13. Dolson, "Richie Allen: Phils Could Go to Top."
14. Ibid.
15. Frank Dolson, "That Was a Smile On Ozark's Face..." *Philadelphia Inquirer*, March 14, 1975.
16. Russ Harris, "Allen Set to Play But 'Won't Beg,'" *Philadelphia Inquirer*, March 26, 1975.
17. Frank Dolson, "Phils New Slogan: Give Him a Chance," *Philadelphia Inquirer*, May 8, 1975.
18. Frank Dolson, "The Boos Turn to Cheers for Richie Allen," *Philadelphia Inquirer*, May 15, 1975.
19. Ibid.
20. Ralph Bernstein, "Bowa: Stiff Arm, Failure to Adjust to Allen Blamed for Errors of His Ways," *Philadelphia Inquirer*, September 5, 1975.
21. Allen Lewis, "Allen's Future? 'I Gotta Play,'" *Philadelphia Inquirer*, September 13, 1975.
22. Frank Dolson, "Ozark's Composure Shatters Noisily..." *Philadelphia Inquirer*, April 26, 1976.
23. Ibid.
24. Allen Lewis, "Allen's Pride is Hurt: Bats 7th," *Philadelphia Inquirer*, May 19, 1976.
25. Allen Lewis, "Allen Clouts 2: Phils Win 12–4," *Philadelphia Inquirer*, June 26, 1976.
26. The events surrounding Allen during July and early August, 1976 are summarized in Bruce Keidan, "Today's the BIG Day that Allen Comes Back," *Philadelphia Inquirer*, August 10, 1976.
27. Dick Allen and Tim Whitaker, *Crash: The Life and Times of Dick Allen* (New York, NY: Ticknor & Fields, 1989), 163.
28. Bruce Keidan, "Allen Declines to Join in Phils' Fun," *Philadelphia Inquirer*, September 27, 1976.
29. See William C. Kashatus, "Dick Allen, The Phillies, and Racism," *NINE: A Journal of Baseball History and Culture*, 9, no. 2 (Spring 2001) 184; Tony Kornheiser, "Body and Soul," *Inside Sports*, Vol.1, October, 1979, 24, 30.
30. Keidan, "Allen Declines to Join in Phils' Fun."
31. John Rhodes, "Dick Allen Sees Future on West Coast," *Philadelphia Tribune*, October 9, 1976, 17. Rhodes wrote that he had not earlier published Allen's remarks because Allen "warned this reporter to keep what he was going to say under his hat because of damage that might occur with management and fellow teammates."
32. Bruce Keidan, "Phils are Resting Uneasily as Ozark Hides Hurt and Anger," *Philadelphia Inquirer*, September 30, 1976.
33. Bruce Keidan, "Phils Get Warning, Then Win," *Philadelphia Inquirer*, September 30, 1976.
34. Frank Dolson, "Phillies Bewildered in a Tower of Babel," *Philadelphia Inquirer*, October 1, 1976.
35. Ibid.
36. Ibid.
37. Keidan, "Phils are Resting Uneasily."
38. Bruce Keidan, "Allen to Play, Taylor to Coach: Owner Settles Dispute," *Philadelphia Inquirer*, October 1, 1976.
39. See Jerome Holtzman, "Why Allen, McLain and Conigliaro Really Were Traded," *SPORT*, Vol. 51, February, 1971, 38, 86.
40. Bruce Keidan, "'They Grew Up in a Few Days,' Ozark Declares," *Philadelphia Inquirer*, October 14, 1976.
41. Bill James, *The Politics of Glory: How Baseball's Hall of Fame Really Works* (New York, NY: Macmillan, 1994), 322–25.

Fan Perspectives on Race and Baseball in the City of Brotherly Love

Jen McGovern

The history of baseball in America has always been closely tied to the history of race in America. The progression of baseball from an exclusionary sport to a beacon for integration and eventually to a global game has paralleled our country's movement from slavery to the civil rights movement to modern day multiculturalism. While the changes have taken place nationwide, they have played out differently in cities and regions across the country. In each city, the story of race and baseball is enmeshed with the city's history and culture as well as with the actions of professional organizations and the attitudes of the fans. In Philadelphia, historic hostilities to integration blemished the city's reputation of racial acceptance. Current Phillies fans have gradually embraced diversity but some still sense lingering racial tensions.

Cities are important for the ways in which their local contexts influence ideas about race and ethnicity, but also for their function in building community and "place bonding." Sports teams produce strong positive identifications with cities or regions, produce a communal spirit, and unite the city as whole.[1]

For if residents invest themselves in favor of their local athletic teams, it is partly because those teams are exponents of a community to which they feel themselves somehow bound and in whose destiny they find themselves in some way implicated. The connection, however, is by no means a simple one. A local team is not only an expression of the moral integrity of a community; it is also a means by which that community becomes conscious of itself and achieves its concrete representation. Therefore, an athletic team must be something more than just an assemblage of skilled performers whose activities conform to physiological or psychological necessity. It is in fact, and above all, the representative of something beyond itself.[2]

Because baseball teams invariably come to represent their cities, the meanings and ideas about race and ethnicity that are generated on the baseball field are important elements of the local context and the way the local context is projected outward toward others. This article examines this process in Philadelphia by briefly reviewing the city's history of racial acceptance and by illustrating current fan attitudes on the subject.

Philadelphia has been a home to professional baseball teams for over a century, but currently hosts only Major League Baseball's Phillies.[3] The Phillies were infamously involved with integration in the early years. Early in Jackie Robinson's rookie season, Manager Ben Chapman and several Phillies players notoriously harassed Robinson with racial taunts and remarks. Later that season, Phillies' general manager Herb Pennock tried to dissuade Branch Rickey from bringing Robinson to Philadelphia. Rickey did not relent and Jackie traveled with the team, which had booked several rooms at Philadelphia's Benjamin Franklin hotel. When the team arrived, they were turned away by the hotel manager who told them not to come back "while you have any nigras with you!"[4]

The Phillies were slow to integrate despite pressure from the black press, leaders of the black community, and the local NAACP. Phillies' owner Bob Carpenter said, "I'm not opposed to Negro players. But I'm not going to hire a player of any color or nationality just to have him on the team."[5] The Phillies finally integrated their major league roster in 1957—ten years after the Dodgers broke the modern day color barrier—leaving the American League's Detroit Tigers and Boston Red Sox as the only teams with all-white rosters.[6,7] Once integrated, the Phils continued to struggle with racial issues. The organization didn't end segregation in spring training facilities until 1962. In addition, they didn't feature any star black players until Dick Allen's rookie campaign in 1964. Until then, while most major league teams were hiring prominent black players with big drawing power, such as Robinson, Willie Mays, and Hank Aaron, the Phillies only employed some marginal black and Latino players.[8]

It wasn't only the organization that had a negative image when it came to racial issues; Philadelphia fans

116

COURTESY OF THE PHILADELPHIA PHILLIES

Phillies general manager Ruben Amaro Jr. is one of the most prominent Hispanic figures in big league front offices.

were perceived to be a hostile bunch.[9] Roy Campanella, who was born and raised in the Philadelphia area, disliked playing in Shibe Park because he felt that the white fans "spewed racial hate."[10] Philly fans seemed to take things to the next level with Dick Allen who wore a helmet in the field to withstand the objects that were thrown at him during games.[11] Allen was known to speak his mind, to act out, and to complain about the adverse treatment. The white media described him as arrogant, militant, malcontented, and radical but rarely acknowledged the racism that Allen faced and described. The black media portrayed him as misunderstood. Kuklick wrote that "in Philadelphia's racially charged atmosphere, Allen's own situation was inevitably distorted, not only by the press but also by the city's baseball fans."[12]

As the civil rights movement swept across the country, some white fans still harbored prejudice against blacks, but the organization tried to move forward. General Manager John Quinn, hired in 1959, began to increase the amount of black talent in the organization through free agency and trades. In 1958, the organization had only three black players in its minor league system, but by 1961, that number increased to 34 and continued to rise through the mid-Sixties.[13] Even with these efforts, the Phillies had few black players and even fewer black stars throughout the 1970s and 1980s—a time when black players thrived in the big leagues. The 1993 National League Champions were one of the few teams in MLB with an all-white starting lineup, though they did feature several black platoon players and role players.[14] In *Great White High Hopes*, sports scholar Benjamin Phillips describes how the '93 team was symbolized by a "rugged, white masculinity emblematic of working

class males." Phillips shows that when speaking about the team, both the fans and the media most often spoke about qualities like teamwork, work ethic, hustle, scrappiness, and grit, qualities which are commonly associated with white athletes. He argues that fans celebrated the whiteness of the team by emphasizing these character traits over the athleticism and physicality of the players.[15]

Today the Philadelphia Phillies, like most major league teams, have a diverse roster. Of the 49 players who appeared for the 2012 Phillies, 69 percent of the players had a white European background. This is slightly higher than the league average of 61 percent.[16] The Phillies had five African American players, two of whom played prominent roles on their five consecutive division championship teams. Jimmy Rollins and Ryan Howard each have three All-Star games and an MVP award to their credit. The Phillies have recently strengthened their presence in Latin America and their 2012 roster listed eight Latino players from four countries: Cuba, Dominican Republic, Panama, and Venezuela.[17] One Hawaiian player and one player of mixed Chinese/European ancestry also appeared for the Phils in 2012.

The current roster demonstrates that the Phillies have moved away from racially intolerant attitudes and towards embracing diversity. A great deal of research exists on how this transition has happened with major organizations such as the Phillies and the MLB; however, far less research exists on current fan attitudes towards these issues.[18,19] Their viewpoints are important because fan actions and behaviors have always been intertwined with attitudes about race and ethnicity in Philadelphia, as illustrated by Dick Allen's career. It isn't only negative attitudes about race that are important. Bruce Kuklick notes that "white rooters seemed to come to the stadium to witness in Allen's behavior the attraction and the revulsion of this time of shifting race relations. The park was the place where many white people expressed puzzlement, rage, along with a modicum of grudging respect."[20] Matthew Jacobsen, in his essay, "Richie Allen, Whitey's Ways, and Me: A Political Education in the 1960s," probably spoke for many when he cited Allen's career as the issue that inspired him to learn about race and politics.[21]

Most of what researchers know about race has come through historical records and media analysis. Very few researchers have conversed with fans to ask them how they think about and understand race and ethnicity.[22] In the spring and summer of 2011, I conducted focus group interviews with baseball fans. The interviews, part of a larger project, generated great conversations about baseball in Philadelphia, including some about race and ethnicity in today's game and in the Philadelphia area. From these interviews, I was able to gain a sense of how fans think and feel about this issue. The ideas and opinions expressed in these conversations were informed by the history of the organization, the city, and the personal lives of each participant.

Over the course of four months, I conducted eight focus group interviews with fans from across the Philadelphia region that I recruited through online advertisements, social networks, and email lists.[23] In the focus group interviews, I placed various pictures of the Phillies on the table to spark discussion. I asked the respondents many questions about baseball and about Philadelphia; one subject that we discussed was race. I report the findings below including some thoughts and quotes from our conversations, using pseudonyms for all fans. My intention is not to amass data capable of addressing the level of racial equality in baseball today but to report on how at least some Philadelphia fans view and understand the issue. Overall, the fans I spoke to perceived race and ethnicity as issues that should not matter when it came to baseball, but had a range of opinions as to whether and how much race and ethnicity still do matter in today's game.[24]

Many of the older fans in my focus groups were able to articulate feelings about baseball and racial progress. Nick, a white fan, recalled some of his early memories of the Phillies as he "grew up in [Philadelphia's] very racist Kensington" neighborhood and began to root for the "mostly white" Phillies in the 1960s and 1970s. He vividly recalled the racial overtones associated with Dick Allen's career and the Phillies' poor reputation with racial issues. Nick remembered that his dad often commented on the team's lack of black players. For Nick, the Phillies only really achieved progress when they "got Hispanic players and more African Americans. That's when the team started taking off." He pointed to Gary Maddox, Manny Trillo, and Bake McBride as three minority players whom he admired while growing up.

Other fans noticed these changes as well. Dave, another white fan, found it a shame that in Philadelphia "there was a long period of time where ownership made a conscious effort to try to discriminate against certain racial types of ballplayers" but felt that "there's not nearly the sort of bias about baseball that there was in the sixties and all through the seventies... I think that's sorta [sic] gone away now because…it's a different world." The changes did not just occur within the Phillies organization, but in the media as well.

White fan Andrew stated that the "newspaper used to talk about people of a racial overtone as dark-skinned or dusky, or some other adjective that they used to attach to them. You don't see that anymore." In another group, Lisa, also white, commented that the Philadelphia media brought up race frequently when they covered education and other social issues, but not when they discussed sports.

The changes have made a difference to many, including some Latino fans that I interviewed. Long-time fan Mateo recalled a time when the "Phillies weren't that friendly to Latinos" and expressed how changes in the organization's position have made rooting for the local team more enjoyable to him (though he admitted that winning didn't hurt). The other participants in this group echoed Mateo's sentiments by recognizing differences in the mainstream English language media. "I remember when I started living in Philadelphia," said Ramona, "I used to watch the game and get infuriated because the name Guzmán, for example. They [the media] would say GUZman. Now, they say Guz-MAN, and you know that they make an effort to pronounce it correctly, and that for me has been a sign of improvement. They pronounce Ruiz's name correctly, Polanco's name correctly, and Valdez's name correctly, whereas before there was no effort put in." Hank, an African American fan, probably best expressed the change when he exclaimed, "Here in Philly we have broke that barrier and said to hell with that. You don't have to be just white. You don't have to be almost black. You don't have to be this or that. You can be anything."

These changes have an impact on all fans, who valued diversity on the field as symbolic of what we hope to achieve in our communities and our relationships. When talking about the facets of the game that were most important, Paul used a photo of three players celebrating at home plate to bring up the topic of team chemistry. He also pointed out that "two of these guys are Hispanic, Ibanez and Ruiz, and then you got Ross Gload who is Caucasian, so it really does reach across all races." To Paul, who is white, baseball has taught him not just about teamwork, but that good teamwork spans racial differences. Lenny, an African American fan, also commented on how he enjoyed seeing "a group of diverse guys from diverse backgrounds and countries and languages have a really nice collective vibe." Numerous other fans spoke of how they enjoyed seeing players from different ethnic groups and appreciated learning about those players' cultures and histories. Fans learned about teamwork from the players but they also learned about it from the leadership.

Hank noted that Ruben Amaro Jr. "is the first Latino that's general manager for us and he's making all the right moves. He got Lee, he got Halladay. I mean this guy is doing yeoman's work and he's a Spanish guy." Hank admitted that in admiring the Hispanic American's work, he gained more respect for Latinos working in baseball leadership.

Fans commented on the fact that while this rich cultural learning can take place in many sports, baseball is "probably the most racially mixed now that I think about it. I mean think about the Eagles and the Sixers and the Phillies. You have more of a mixture on the Phillies than you do on the other teams." In a separate focus group, Nam, who is black, added that "thanks to Asia and Latin America, [baseball] is the one sport where you can really find equality."

Our discussions were not limited to the diverse pool of competitors. A number of focus group respondents also talked about how baseball functioned as a way to bring the city's residents together, regardless of racial or ethnic divisions. White Philadelphian Tammy stated that "when the Phillies win, the whole city is in a good mood." In another group, Dave waxed triumphantly that baseball was the greatest sport because when the "team is going good, you got the whole city—even strangers talk to each other. People hold the door for you at Wawa [convenience store]." The other fans in Dave's group were of various races and ethnicities. This diverse group noted how they could talk about the Phillies with strangers in restaurants, on the subway, and in other public places in the city. The respondents felt that baseball united them with other city residents, rather than divided them. A third group, composed of multicultural fans, felt similarly. Rafael, who identified as Latino, mentioned that this "spirit of Philadelphia" carried over to the players, proudly claiming that it was one of the incentives that caused Cliff Lee to spurn millions from the Yankees.

It is clear that the focus group respondents witnessed positive racial change within the Phillies organization. These changes are important because they serve as symbolic representations of racial equality, both on and off the field. Despite the many positive messages that the game can teach about diversity, fans realized that the game "still has a long way to go" in order to reach true racial equality. They mentioned language barriers, changing demographics, lack of minority representation in key leadership positions, and the lack of minority fans. They also discussed potential biases within the media and within the fans themselves.

As the game has brought in a more diverse player pool, the number of players speaking different languages has increased. While some saw baseball players bonding across differences, others noticed how they could also be separated by cultural barriers such as language. At a Reading Phillies game, white fan Tommy was watching warm-ups and noticed that "all the American players, white and black, were all together and all of the Latino players kind of separated themselves together." Tommy also observed that Asian players with translators have a far different experience from Latino players who have to rely on teammates for communication assistance. Like Tommy, other fans discussed how language might actually prevent the type of teamwork-spanning difference that Paul described earlier. They even noted how it could be a barrier to promotion for some players. Many thought Carlos Ruiz was a great leader but worried that his struggles with English would prevent him from becoming a coach or a manager someday. Others agreed that while there were many talented, knowledgeable Hispanic players, they probably "could not get into the booth with an accent."

In addition to language differences, numerous fan groups discussed the decline of African American ballplayers. Multiple fans were concerned with this issue and believed that MLB should continue programs such as Reviving Baseball in the Inner Cities (RBI) in order to ensure that the game remains a diverse representation of our country. Other fans noticed the corresponding rise in Latino players. Hank sees the impact of Hispanic players on the city. He observed that if you "go to certain [Latino] neighborhoods in North Philly, Latinos have little league for the teams. And those kids can play!"

Despite the changing player demographics, fans largely agreed that opportunity to make the big league hinged more on a player's ability than his race. They did, however, observe a lack of minority players in key leadership positions on the field. Academic sport researchers refer to this phenomenon as "stacking."[25] In a group of black fans, Hank joked that if you had "a white guy, a Latino guy, and a black guy—tell me who plays second base? The white guy!" In a group of white fans, Paul turned to the group and asked, "Off the top of your head, can you think of any African American starting pitchers other than CC Sabathia?" In nearly all of the groups, fans commented on the abundance of white pitchers and the dearth of minority pitchers. In doing so, they were calling attention to the fact that while baseball has made many advances towards racial equality, there were still some signs that all groups did not have equal opportunities. These fans felt that baseball was truly at its best when the best athletes were given a shot to be the best at any position. Paul lamented having to imagine a baseball world without the likes of Sabathia, Dave Stewart, and Bob Gibson.

While some fans talked about the composition of teams, others talked about the demographics of other baseball personnel. They noted that there were more minority managers and coaches than in the past but felt that baseball "still had a long way to go." Marcus, a Puerto Rican fan, felt as if organizations "were not interviewing Hispanic candidates for managing positions at the same rate that they do with whites." Data published by Richard Lapchick confirm that the number of minorities in high leadership positions has improved, but is still low when compared to whites.[26] The fans in other groups stressed that best baseball leaders were the ones who could gain respect of others—regardless of their race. Paul felt that policies encouraging organizations to hire more minorities were helpful because such policies "forced people [owners] to look in a different direction rather than going back to the same pool of candidates, many of whom stunk."

Just as some fans noticed that full racial equality had not been achieved on the field, another set of fans questioned the ability of baseball to bridge racial divides among fans in the stands. Dave noted that he rarely saw any black fans at Phillies games. Salina, a Latina fan, agreed and stated that she noticed "mostly white men" at Phillies games. She questioned the ability of the team to bring the city together if sports fans were racially polarized and if only certain social classes could afford to attend the games. Many agreed with Salina, showing that fans can have a range of opinions about how a sport can affect a community.

Fans also had differing opinions on how the media deal with race and ethnicity. As stated earlier, many noticed that the amount of racism in the media has decreased over time, though some claimed that was only because broadcasters needed to "be more careful" about what they say and how that say it. Lai, a Chinese immigrant, stated that while broadcasters may not make explicit references to race, he "feels from the tone that it is a little different" when the media discuss players of different races. He gave the example of media coverage of Barry Bonds versus that of Mark McGwire and said that he observed subtle differences in how the players were described and criticized that he attributed to race. In another group, Andrew, who earlier claimed that the media ceased to use overt discriminatory terms, said that he thought racism could still be "hidden in code words." Andrew felt that

COURTESY OF THE PHILADELPHIA PHILLIES

Ryan Howard is one of five African American players to appear on the Phillies roster in 2012.

"there was a little bit of a racist attitude from the sports writers who were reporting on some of the things that Jimmy Rollins did," such as being benched by his manager for failing to run hard to first on a weakly-hit ground ball. The other fans in this group unanimously agreed that Rollins was in the wrong and should have hustled but they were unsure as to whether or not a white player in a similar situation would have been treated differently than Rollins was.

Phillies fans had varying opinions on how the media treated African American players such as Rollins. They also had a number of opinions on how the fans themselves treated the same group of players. Dick Allen's case was illustrative of the negative reputation that Philadelphians had regarding African American players during the sixties. The world around baseball has changed drastically since that time, but the negative reputation has lingered. Several days after the Phillies were eliminated from the 2010 playoffs, Philadelphia sportswriter Marcus Hayes was conducting an online interactive chat with fans. During this conversation, Hayes noted how fans did not seem to be too upset with the numerous fielding miscues that Utley had made in the final playoff series while they harshly criticized Howard for striking out looking in the final at-bat. Hayes believed that the fans gave Utley this "free pass" because he was white.[27]

I asked the fans what they thought about Hayes's remarks and if they thought fans still treated black and white players differently. Most fans agreed that Howard was criticized more harshly than Utley, and many admitted to being some of the worst critics. A few fans thought that race played a role in this differ-

COURTESY OF THE PHILADELPHIA PHILLIES

Howard has three All-Star appearances and NL MVP award under his belt, but fans feel that there are still not enough non-white players in leadership positions in baseball.

ence—Tommy even confessed that he had "a friend who went on this tirade of racial slurs after that [incident]—like 'he's a big monkey' and 'blah, blah, blah.' And I was like 'Dude, calm down!'" Most other fans believed that criticisms of Howard were due to the fact that he was the highest paid player on the team who failed to come through with a clutch hit. Erica stated that "some fans came down harder on Howard for that [failure], and part of it, I think has to do with his race, and the other part of it has to do with the situation." In another group, Mike also contended that Howard's race may have been a partial factor but Mike's opinion was quickly overwhelmed by the other fans, who attributed the differences entirely to the situation.

While Hayes was only using Howard's performance in the playoffs as an example of a larger phenomenon, most fans could not separate their overall opinions about Howard and Utley from their opinions about that particular situation. None of the fans shifted the conversation to a discussion of other examples, perhaps from a less dramatic moment, that might illustrate the feelings of Philadelphia fans towards these two players. The groups focused so much on the situation that they ignored the second part of the question asking whether fans preferred white players over black players, until after they came to the conclusion that race didn't matter. At this point, they began to name other situations where race did not play a role rather than thinking about ones where it might. Because most fans believed that baseball players were judged only by their talent and not by their race, I concluded that it was easier for them to find examples of meritocracy rather than examples of racism. Based on my research I have come to believe that those fans who were personally disappointed by Howard's performance wanted to make it clear that their dissatisfaction was due to the strikeout so that their attitudes were not perceived by other fans as racism.

Baseball is an intricate game and this situation is no different. In this case, Howard's role on the team, the pressure of the situation, and his race are all plausible explanations for the criticism he received; but sorting through those layers of complexity to isolate the role of race can be very difficult. There was a time in American society where unequal treatment of racial groups was far less complex; white and dark-skinned players could not play in the same baseball leagues, dine at the same establishments, or ride together on public buses. Since Jackie Robinson's ground-breaking achievement and the successes of the civil rights movement, many racial barriers have fallen but not all racial issues have fallen away. American society and the game of baseball are both still dealing with the complexities of race and racism. So is Philadelphia.

In these interviews, Philadelphia fans demonstrated that the city is moving away from its sordid racial past. Many fans have adopted more open-minded attitudes and behaviors towards racial issues, though some racial tensions still remain. In the sixties, fans threw batteries at Dick Allen but now they cheer loudly for black players. Despite this change, some still believe that white players remain the true fan favorites of the city. Many minority respondents reported that they felt more welcome and respected as Phillies fans today than they did in the sixties, seventies, and eighties and others still feel out of place among a largely white fan base. Some fans value how diverse groups of players model the cooperation that we hope to achieve in our society while others are skeptical at the lack of diversity in leadership positions and unfair treatment in the media.

COURTESY OF THE PHILADELPHIA PHILLIES

Some fans felt that coverage of Jimmy Rollins displayed "a little bit of a racist attitude" by sports writers.

Struggles within the game of baseball have always symbolized larger struggles in our nation and in our cities. Over time, baseball has become multicultural and the US has transformed into a diverse nation, but full equality has still not arrived in either sphere. This trend is reflected in Philadelphia, where baseball fans show that the local game has made great strides but still faces persistent challenges to full racial equality. It is my hope that the game of baseball will continue to serve as a symbol of diversity but more importantly that this wonderful game will also forge ahead in the push for racial justice and equality. ■

Notes

1. John Bale, "The Place of 'Place' in Cultural Studies of Sports," *Progress in Human Geography 12*, no. 4 (December 1, 1988): 507–524.
2. Barry Schwartz and Stephen F. Barsky, "The Home Advantage," *Social Forces 55*, no. 3 (March 1977): 657.
3. In addition to the American League Philadelphia Athletics, the region also was home to many prominent professional and semi-professional Negro League organizations including the Philadelphia Pythians, Excelsiors, Giants, Stars, and the Hilldale baseball club. For more information on black baseball in Philadelphia, see Jerrold Casway, "Octavius Catto and the Pythians of Philadelphia," *Pennsylvania Legacies*, May 2007 and Robert Gregg; "Personal Cavalries: Sports in Philadelphia's African-American Communities, 1920–1960," *Ethnicity, Sport, Identity: Struggles for Status*, edited by Andrew Ritchie, 1st ed. Routledge, 2004, 88–115.
4. Harold Parrot. *The Lords of Baseball*. (Praeger 1976)
5. Bruce Kuklick, *To Every Thing a Season* (Princeton University Press, 1993), 148.
6. John Kennedy was the first African American to appear on the Phillies' major league roster.
7. Kuklick, *To Every Thing a Season*.
8. William C. Kashatus, *September Swoon: Richie Allen, the '64 Phillies, and Racial Integration* (Pennsylvania State Univ Pr, 2005).
9. The fans' poor reputation is not limited to racial issues. According to Kuklick, a gang of fans once mobbed Ty Cobb after an Athletics game at Shibe park and later disconnected the electric cable to the trolley that Cobb attempted to escape on. Additionally, the national media can't seem to forget that Eagles fans threw snowballs at Santa Claus.
10. Kashatus, *September Swoon*; Neil Lanctot, *Campy: The Two Lives of Roy Campanella*, 1st Simon & Schuster hardcover ed (New York: Simon & Schuster, 2011).
11. Kashatus, *September Swoon*.
12. Ibid., 158.
13. William C. Kashatus, "Dick Allen, the Phillies, and Racism," *NINE: A Journal of Baseball History and Culture 9*, no. 1 (2000): 151–191.
14. Benjamin Phillips, "Great White High Hopes: Race, Masculinity, and the 1993 Philadelphia Phillies," *NINE: A Journal of Baseball History and Culture 19*, no. 2 (2011): 61–76.
15. Ibid.
16. Richard E. Lapchick, "2012 Racial and Gender (sic) Report Card: Major League Baseball," 2012, http://web.bus.ucf.edu/documents/sport/2012-MLB-RGRC.pdf.
17. Paul Hagen, "Phillies Boost Their Latin Grade," *Philadelphia Daily News*, May 3, 2011.
18. Max Blue, *Philadelphia Baseball* (PublishAmerica, 2012); David M. Jordan, *Occasional Glory: The History of the Philadelphia Phillies* (McFarland & Company, 2003); Kashatus, *September Swoon*; Kuklick, *To Every Thing a Season*; Christopher Threston, *The Integration of Baseball in Philadelphia* (McFarland & Co Inc Pub, 2003).
19. Alan M Klein, *Growing the Game: The Globalization of Major League Baseball* (New Haven, CT: Yale University Press, 2006); Adrian Burgos, *Playing America's Game: Baseball, Latinos, and the Color Line* (Berkeley, CA: University of California Press, 2007); Rob Ruck, *Raceball: How the Major Leagues Colonized the Black and Latin Game*, First Edition (Beacon Press, 2011); William M. Simons, *The Cooperstown Symposium on Baseball and American Culture 2003* (Jefferson, NC: McFarland, 2003); Sumei Wang, "Taiwanese Baseball: A Story of Entangled Colonialism, Class, Ethnicity, and Nationalism," *Journal of Sport & Social Issues 33*, no. 4 (November 1, 2009): 355–372.
20. *To Every Thing a Season*, 163.
21. Matthew Frye Jacobson, "'Richie' Allen, Whitey's Ways, and Me: A Political Education in the 1960's," *In the Game: Race, Identity, and Sports in the Twentieth Century*, ed. Amy Bass (Palgrave Macmillan, 2005), 19–46.
22. One of the few published articles about fan opinions was published by Alan Klein, "Latinizing Fenway Park: A Cultural Critique of the Boston Red Sox, Their Fans, and the Media," *Sociology of Sport Journal 17*, no. 4 (2000): 403–422.
23. The recruitment method was not intended to yield a representative sample of Philadelphians, but to locate individuals who were willing to engage in conversation about baseball. The recruitment did result in a diverse subject pool. Twenty five percent of the participants were women and the remaining seventy five percent were men. Thirty-six respondents listed their racial or ethnic identification: White/Caucasian (14), Black/African American (8), Asian (8), Hispanic/Latino (4), Jewish (1), Afro-Latino (1).
24. Most of the opinions did not differ by racial group; however, I listed each participants self-identified racial or ethnic group to show how these opinions were shared by a diverse group of Philadelphians.
25. Eric Smith and Wilbert M. Leonard II, "Twenty-Five Years of Stacking Research in Major League Baseball: An Attempt at Explaining This Re-Occurring Phenomenon," *Sociological Focus 30*, no. 4 (1997): 321–331.
26. Lapchick, "2012 Racial and Gender (sic) Report Card: Major League Baseball."
27. "Phillies Chat with Marcus Hayes," *Philadelphia Daily News*, October 26, 2010," accessed November 21, 2010, www.philly.com/philly/blogs/phillies/Phillies_chat_with_Marcus_Hayes_102610.html.

Home Run Hitters

FROM THE UNIVERSITY OF NEBRASKA PRESS

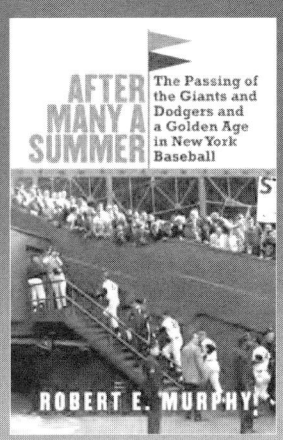
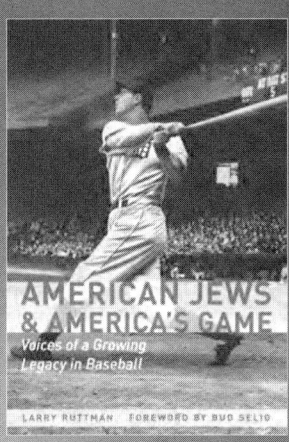
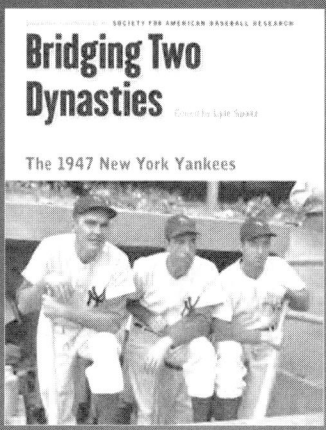

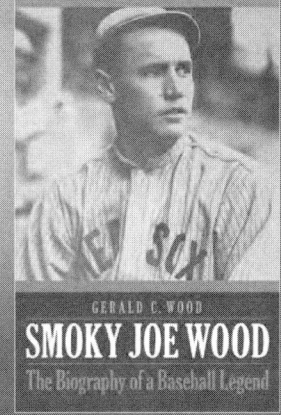

For more information about these books and to order, visit us online!

UNIVERSITY OF
NEBRASKA PRESS

NEBRASKAPRESS.UNL.EDU
800-848-6224 • publishers of Bison Books

SABR BioProject Books

In 2002, the Society for American Baseball Research launched an effort to write and publish biographies of every player, manager, and individual who has made a contribution to baseball. Over the past decade, the Bio-Project Committee has produced over 2,200 biographical articles. Many have been part of efforts to create theme- or team-oriented books, spearheaded by chapters or other committees of SABR.

THE YEAR OF BLUE SNOW:
THE 1964 PHILADELPHIA PHILLIES
    Catcher Gus Triandos dubbed the Philadelphia Phillies' 1964 season "the year of the blue snow," a rare thing that happens once in a great while. This book sheds light on lingering questions about the 1964 season—but any book about a team is really about the players. This work offers life stories of all the players and others (managers, coaches, owners, and broadcasters) associated with this star-crossed team, as well as essays of analysis and history.
Edited by Mel Marmer and Bill Nowlin
$19.95 paperback (ISBN 978-1-933599-51-9)
$9.99 ebook (ISBN 978-1-933599-52-6)
8.5"X11", 356 PAGES, over 70 photos

DETROIT TIGERS 1984:
WHAT A START! WHAT A FINISH!
The 1984 Detroit tigers roared out of the gate, winning their first nine games of the season and compiling an eye-popping 35-5 record after the campaign's first 40 games—still the best start ever for any team in major league history. This book brings together biographical profiles of every Tiger from that magical season, plus those of field management, top executives, the broadcasters—even venerable Tiger Stadium and the city itself.
Mark Pattison and David Raglin, editors
$19.95 paperback (ISBN 978-1-933599-44-1)
$9.99 ebook (ISBN 978-1-933599-45-8)
8.5"x11", 250 pages (Over 230,000 words!)

SWEET '60: THE 1960 PITTSBURGH PIRATES
A portrait of the 1960 team which pulled off one of the biggest upsets of the last 60 years. When Bill Mazeroski's home run left the park to win in Game Seven of the World Series, beating the New York Yankees, David had toppled Goliath. It was a blow that awakened a generation, one that millions of people saw on television, one of TV's first iconic World Series moments.
Edited by Clifton Blue Parker and Bill Nowlin
$19.95 paperback (ISBN 978-1-933599-48-9)
$9.99 ebook (ISBN 978-1-933599-49-6)
8.5"X11", 340 pages, 75 photos

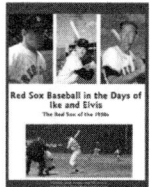

RED SOX BASEBALL IN THE DAYS OF IKE AND ELVIS: THE RED SOX OF THE 1950s
Although the Red Sox spent most of the 1950s far out of contention, the team was filled fascinating players that captured the heart of their fanbase. In *Red Sox Baseball*, members of SABR present 46 biographies on players such as Ted Williams and Pumpsie Green as well as season-by-season recaps.
Edited by Mark Armour and Bill Nowlin
$19.95 paperback (ISBN 978-1-933599-24-3)
$9.99 ebook (ISBN 978-1-933599-34-2)
8.5"X11", 372 PAGES, over 100 photos

The SABR Digital Library

The Society for American Baseball Research, the top baseball research organization in the world, disseminates some of the best in baseball history, analysis, and biography through our publishing programs. The SABR Digital Library contains a mix of books old and new, and focuses on a tandem program of paperback and ebook publication, making these materials widely available for both on digital devices and as traditional printed books.

MEMORIES OF A BALLPLAYER
by Bill Werber and C. Paul Rogers III
    Bill Werber's claim to fame is unique: he was the last living person to have a direct connection to the 1927 Yankees, "Murderers' Row," a team hailed by many as the best of all time. Rich in anecdotes and humor, Memories of a Ballplayer is a clear-eyed memoir of the world of big-league baseball in the 1930s.Werber played with or against some of the most productive hitters of all time, including Babe Ruth, Ted Williams, Lou Gehrig, and Joe DiMaggio.
$14.95 paperback (ISNB 978-0-910137-84-3)
$6.99 ebook (ISBN 978-1-933599-47-2)
250 PAGES, 6"X9"

BATTING **by F. C. Lane**
First published in 1925, *Batting* collects the wisdom and insights of over 250 hitters and baseball figures. Lane interviewed extensively and compiled tips and advice on everything from batting stances to beanballs. Legendary baseball figures such as Ty Cobb, Casey Stengel, Cy Young, Walter Johnson, Rogers Hornsby, and Babe Ruth reveal the secrets of such integral and interesting parts of the game as how to choose a bat, the ways to beat a slump, and how to outguess the pitcher.
$14.95 paperback (ISBN 978-0-910137-86-7)
$7.99 ebook (ISBN 978-1-933599-46-5)
240 PAGES, 5"X7"

NINETEENTH CENTURY STARS: 2012 EDITION
    First published in 1989, *Nineteenth Century Stars* was SABR's initial attempt to capture the stories of baseball players from before 1900. With a collection of 136 fascinating biographies, SABR has re-released *Nineteenth Century Stars* for 2012 with revised statistics and new form. The 2012 version also includes a preface by **John Thorn**.
Edited by Robert L. Tiemann and Mark Rucker
$19.95 paperback (ISBN 978-1-933599-28-1)
$9.99 ebook (ISBN 978-1-933599-29-8)
300 PAGES, 6"X9"

GREAT HITTING PITCHERS
    Published in 1979, *Great Hitting Pitchers* was one of SABR's early publications. Edited by SABR founder Bob Davids, the book compiles stories and records about pitchers excelling in the batter's box. Newly updated in 2012 by Mike Cook, *Great Hitting Pitchers* contain tables including data from 1979-2011, corrections to reflect recent records, and a new chapter on recent new members in the club of "great hitting pitchers" like Tom Glavine and Mike Hampton.
Edited by L. Robert Davids
$9.95 paperback (ISBN 978-1-933599-30-4)
$5.99 ebook (ISBN 978-1-933599-31-1)
102 PAGES, 5.5"x8.5"

SABR Members can purchase each book at a significant discount (often 50% off) and receive the ebook edtions free as a member benefit. Each book is available in a trade paperback edition as well as ebooks suitable for reading on a home computer or Nook, Kindle, or iPad/tablet.

Contributors

REBECCA T. ALPERT is Professor of Religion at Temple University. Her most recent publi-cation is *Out of Left Field: Jews and Black Baseball* (Oxford University Press, 2011). Her areas of special-ization are Contemporary American Religion, Religion and Sexuality, and Religion and Sport.

STEPHEN D. BOREN MD, FACEP is an emergency medicine physi-cian and Assistant Professor of Emergency Medicine at the University of Illinois College of Medicine and was stationed in the US army in Korea. In addition to multiple publications in the *Baseball Research Journal*, *The National Pastime*, and *Baseball Digest*, he has many medical publications.

PAUL BROWNE is Executive Director of the Carbondale Technology Transfer Center. He is a Carbondale City Councilman and Presi-dent of the Carbondale Community Development Corporation. He researches and writes about nineteenth century base ball. He is a relative of former New York Giants player Pete Gillespie. Fam-ily stories led him to SABR and to writing Pete's biography for the BioProject. In researching that article, he came across another nineteenth century major leaguer, Eddie Kennedy, and the New York Metropolitans.

DR. JERROLD CASWAY is the Dean of Social Sciences at Howard Community College in Columbia, Maryland. He is the author of *Ed Delahanty in the Emerald Age of Baseball* and has completed, *The 'Olde' Ball Game: The Culture and Ethnicity of Nineteenth-Century Baseball*. He has written many articles on the early game and has frequently spoken at the Hall of Fame's Nineteenth-Century Symposiums. He at work on a history of baseball in Philadelphia from 1832 to the building of Shibe Park.

ROB EDELMAN is the author of *Great Baseball Films* and a frequent contributor to *Base Ball: A Journal of the Early Game*. He is a Con-tributing Editor of *Leonard Maltin's Movie Guide* and is co-author of *Matthau: A Life* and *Meet the Mertzes*, a double biography of *I Love Lucy*'s Vivian Vance and celebrated baseball fan William Frawley. He teaches film history at the University at Albany—SUNY and is an interviewee on extras on the DVD of *The Natural*.

BROCK HELANDER is the author of *The Rock Who's Who* (1982), *The Rock Who's Who Second Edition* (1996), *The Rockin' '50s* (1998), and The *Rockin' '60s* (1999). Since joining SABR, he has been researching nineteenth century baseball, focusing on the history of baseball in cities that were represented in the major leagues exclusively in the nineteenth century.

RICHARD HERSHBERGER researches and writes about early baseball up to 1885. He has published in *Base Ball: A Journal of the Early Game*, as well as SABR publications, and has both pre-sented and served as a panelist at the Frederick Ivor-Campbell 19th Century Base Ball Conference. His particular interests are the organizational development of baseball, and early baseball in Philadelphia.

RICK HUHN is the author of *The Sizzler: George Sisler, Baseball's Forgotten Great*, as well as *Eddie Collins: A Baseball Biography*. His third book will be released by the University of Nebraska Press in 2014. It details the controversial 1910 batting race in which Ty Cobb and Larry Lajoie vied for a Chalmers automobile. Rick is an organizer and one of the coordinators for SABR's Hank Gowdy Columbus (Ohio) Chapter.

BILL JENKINSON is the author of *The Year Babe Ruth Hit 104 Home Runs*, and *Baseball's Ultimate Power: Ranking the All-Time Greatest Distance Home Run Hitters*. He has consulted to the Baseball Hall of Fame, Major League Baseball, The Babe Ruth Museum, and ESPN.

STEVEN A. KING is a physician specializing in pain management and a clinical professor at the New York University School of Medicine. The primary focus of his baseball research is New York City baseball at the beginning of the twentieth century. His most recent baseball publication was on the myth of the Amos Rusie-Christy Mathewson trade that appeared in the Fall 2012 issue of *Base Ball: A Journal of the Early Game*.

JEFFREY LAING is a retired English teacher who has published more than 150 articles on arts and culture, pedagogy, and sports. His baseball writing has appeared in *The National Pastime*, *Fan Magazine*, *Base Ball: A Journal of the Early Game*, and *Black Ball: A Negro Leagues Journal*.

JIM LEEKE is the creative director of Taillight Communications. He contributes to the SABR Baseball Biography Project and has written or edited several books on American and military history. His latest book is *Ballplayers in the Great War*. He is also the author/editor of several books on Civil War and naval history.

MORRIS LEVIN is a member of the Athletic Base Ball Club of Philadelphia, and of the Business Association of West Parkside, which stewards the Philadelphia Stars Negro League Memorial Park. Morris is the editor of the *Game Worn MLB Jersey Guide* (2012) by William F. Henderson, and was previously on staff at the Mitchell & Ness Nostalgia Co.

PETER MANCUSO is Chairman of SABR's Nineteenth Century Committee. A native of Staten Island, New York he is the former Assistant Director of Training for the NYPD. He is an owner and partner of Mancuso Show Management which organizes and presents quilting festivals, antiques shows, and antiquarian book fares.

JENNIFER MCGOVERN earned her PhD in sociology from Temple University. She presented and volunteered at past SABR confer-ences. She is primarily interested in sport and equality, sport fan narratives, and social issues within sports, though baseball is her favorite sport to study and to watch.

ANDREW MILNER is a freelance writer has written for the *SABR Review of Books*, *The Cooperstown Review* as well as *Base Ball: A Journal of the Early Game.* He has contributed to *American Sports: A History of Icons, Idols, and Ideas* (2013), *Sports in America from Colonial Times to the Twenty-First Century* (2011) and the *St James Encyclopedia of Popular Culture* (2000).

MITCHELL NATHANSON is a professor of legal writing at Villanova University School of Law. He authored "The Irrelevance of Baseball's Antitrust Exemption: A Historical Review" in 2006. His books *The Fall of the 1977 Phillies: How a Baseball Team's Collapse Sank a City's Spirit* was published in 2008 and *A People's History of Baseball* in 2012. His most recent article is "Who Exempted Baseball, Anyway: The Curious Development of the Antitrust Exemption That Never Was." He is at work on a biography of Dick Allen, to be published in 2015.

JOE NIESE is a librarian and member of the Society for American Baseball Research. He has written several articles on baseball's Deadball Era. His first book, *Burleigh Grimes: Baseball's Last Legal Spitballer* was published in spring, 2013 by McFarland Press.

BILL NOWLIN has written or edited four books on Ted Williams, and has another one on the drawing board. As a 12-year-old, he was inspired by Williams's 1957 season, when Ted hit .388— in the year he turned 39. Bill has been vice president of SABR since 2004.

RON SELTER is a retired economist, formerly with the Air Force Space Program. He is a member of the Ballparks, Minor League, Statistical, and Deadball Committees, and his area of expertise is twentieth-century major-league ballparks. Selter served as text editor for *Green Cathedrals* (2006 edition, SABR) and as a contributor to *Forbes Field* (2007). He is the author of *Ballparks of the Deadball Era* (2008).

JAMES D. SZALONTAI is the author of three books published by McFarland, including a history of the 1945 major league season, and *Small Ball in the Big Leagues: A History of Stealing, Bunting, Walking and Otherwise Scratching for Runs.* Two of his favorite subjects are World War II baseball and spring training.

SAM ZYGNER is chairperson for SABR's South Florida Chapter. His article, "Racing the Dawn," appeared in the *Baseball Research Journal* 2012 fall edition. He has written sports- and travel-related articles for *La Prensa de Miami* from 2001–2005, and is writing a book, *The Forgotten Marlins: A Tribute to the 1956–1960 Original Miami Marlins.*